WHOLE HEALTH HEALING

The Budget-Friendly
Natural Wellness Bible
for All Ages

Dr. Thomas J. Potisk

MAVEN
MARK
BOOKS

Published by
MavenMark Books, LLC
1288 Summit Ave. #107/115,
Oconomowoc, WI 53066
www.mavenmarkbooks.com

ISBN: 978-1-59598-069-4

Library of Congress Cataloging-In-Publication Data

    Potisk, Thomas J.
     Whole health healing : the budget-friendly bible of natural wellness
    for all ages / Thomas J. Potisk.
      p. : ill. ; cm.
    Includes bibliographical references and index.
    ISBN: 978-1-59598-069-4
    1. Health--Popular works. 2. Self-care, Health--Popular works. 3.
    Holistic medicine--Popular works. 4. Alternative medicine--Popular
    works. 5. Healing--Popular works. I. Title.

    RA776.95 .P68 2010
    613   2009937695

Photography by John Lathrop and the author.

Cover design and illustrations by Czysz Design.

Printed in the United States of America.

To my wife, Susan,
and my three children,
Andy, Emily, and Mike.

Acknowledgments

Special thanks to my office staff, my book coach/editor Kira Henschel, my colleague Dr. Jerry Zelm, and my many wonderful patients.

Thank you also to my graphic designer, Carolyn Czysz, model Shannon Carney, and photographer John Lathrop.

My gratitude to my family for their patience, understanding, and encouragement in writing this book.

Disclaimer

Table of Contents

Preface

Here's my outrage. Where's yours?
(Why I had to write this book)

I did not want to write a book. I did not want to be an author. But I had to. Let me tell you why.

For over twenty years now, I've been a very successful doctor. I own and operate one of the largest natural healthcare clinics in the state of Wisconsin, serving thousands of patients each month, from infants to senior citizens, with a wide variety of health problems. Each and every case is uniquely interesting, and working with all these people has really taught me a lot of practical lessons about health, lessons that are not always taught in any schools—not only about becoming healthy (healing), but also about staying healthy (prevention).

A calling to share this knowledge and experience, a sort of inner voice, has been nagging at me for years. I've suppressed it and swept it under the rug, using all kinds of excuses, like "no time," "don't want the hassle," "don't want the fame it might bring," and even "can't type well." I can best describe the calling to bring this book into the world as an intense bother, a never-ending and gradually intensifying urge that could no longer be ignored.

Since you are now holding this book in your hands, you might suspect that I just caved in and wrote. But what really inspired me and got me started was when I recognized and defined my life's purpose!

At some time in your life, you must have asked yourself the ageless question, "Why am I here?" Some people live their entire lives assuming they'll never really know. Some know the answer from their earliest days of consciousness. Some answer it simply by observing their current state of affairs and stating, "I'm here to be the best spouse to …," or "the best parent to …," or "the best employee of …" Perhaps those responses are sufficient to some, but to me, those are givens. I decided there had to be more, there had to be something deeper, something that would "rattle my soul" when I defined it.

Have you explored what your life's purpose may be?

In the hot summer of 2006, I crossed paths with two wonderful, insightful ladies who brought me closer to that "rattle": Sunni Boehme, a self-defined "joy manager," and Kira Henschel, a book coach. It all started when Sunni asked me the following profound question, explaining that the answer would satisfy my quest for purpose: "What do you want people to say about you at your funeral?" she asked.

"Why, do I look ill?" I replied.

"No," she laughed. "What do you want engraved on your tombstone?"

I immediately recognized the point she was making and without hesitating, answered: "Here lies the guy who improved the world by empowering people to make wiser healthcare choices."

Stating those words was the first time I was sure, without a doubt, of my purpose. The question was now *how*?

On a small scale, I had been empowering thousands of individuals one on one over the past two decades through my clinic. It was time to move on and reach out to the millions of people I never had the chance to meet in person, to help each and every one in some way. How better to do so than by sharing my knowledge and experiences in healthcare with a book and more.

With the assistance of Sunni and Kira, I envisioned a mass multi-media health information outlet that anyone could access easily. It would contain simple, commonsense, natural (when possible), and practical procedures for people of all ages to help themselves become and remain healthy.

Listen to what your mind is telling you and pray for more direction. Pay attention to it and follow your intuition. Much of that insight is about your life's purpose and it's important that you use and share it for the greater good of all.

I also decided that any information I shared must be "clean." By clean, I mean uninfluenced by commercial sponsorships from professional organizations, pharmaceutical or vitamin manufacturers, or other healthcare product distributors.

The book you hold in your hands is the beginning of this grand adventure. I present to you this book with great delight.

You will find it easy reading, to the point, and full of practical tools. You might already be aware of many of the things I will be talking about, such as exercise, good nutrition, and more, but perhaps you have forgotten the details or are hesitant to apply that knowledge.

If you find yourself skeptical or surprised as you read, then congratulations! Those emotions are some of the first steps toward learning and being enlightened. I can assure you that everything you will read comes from my heart, soul, training, and most of all, experience.

I'm well aware that there are doctors who have practiced longer than I have, or have more training or more letters after their names. Some have done a good job sharing their experience with the masses. But my sharing is different in a more practical, simplistic, really usable form. I've always had a knack for condensing and simplifying things. Best of all it's a practical, objective, and uninfluenced book, and that's very rare these days.

On some pages, I'll illustrate the text with stories from my practice, like this:

> All the information in this book is a compilation of my training and experience over the last 20-plus years. The actual words and sentences came to me, though, in a rather bizarre way. For years, this book was not so much on my mind, but rather, in my mind. I'd be doing some activity, not anything in particular, walking, working, even sleeping, and there it was, just as clearly as if someone were talking in my head. I tried ignoring it, and I worried because I'd heard that mentally ill people claim to hear voices.

Sunni, the self-described "joy manager" I mentioned above, really a life coach, taught me that those "voices" are usually a blessing of creativity, that I should embrace and recognize them, and use them for the greater good of all. So I started paying attention, first by writing the words and ideas down, then by dictating them into a tape recorder. Doing so gave me a deep feeling of relief. I found that what I was expressing was of profound content that people could use for their betterment, and that the words and information came more often and more easily if I was relaxed, not hungry, and well rested.

Being a Christian, I also came to recognize and realize that the inner voice, one's calling and purpose is really divinely inspired. I began praying more frequently and intensely for answers and directions from God and Jesus, my personal savior. What you are reading here is really from my ultimate guide: The Holy Spirit.

Laughter is the best medicine so occasionally I'll add some humor like this:

> I treated a sweet, elderly lady named Myrtle on several occasions. During one visit, she mentioned she had recently had cataract surgery.
>
> "Can you see better?" I asked.
>
> She looked up at me, smiled and said, "Well, I can see your gray hair now."
>
> (Don't worry. All names have been changed to protect the innocent.)

Here's My Outrage. Where's Yours?

I sincerely want this book to be positive in content, to inspire, motivate, and encourage you to make wiser healthcare choices. However, sometimes the words you read might come across as a bit negative, critical, and even accusatory at times. Some of the schemes, scams, and darn right dishonesty in the healthcare system do need to be exposed for your benefit. I apologize in advance if what's written here causes you to second-guess the healthcare provider you've trusted and counted on for so long.

For years, I've told my patients that my only concern, my only "agenda," is for them to get and stay well. I have the same intentions with this book.

If you're a doctor or healthcare provider of any kind and are reading this book, congratulations for at least opening it up! That alone shows that you want to improve your services. If some of what you see here makes you feel guilty about what you've been doing to people, that's another step in the right direction. If this information makes you fear for a patient's safety, you've got a lot to learn. I'll put the safety record of natural providers like me up against that of conventional medical providers any time.

> **First they ignore you, then they laugh at you, then they fight you, then you win.**
> —*Mahatma Gandhi*

I respect anybody's decision to disagree with these writings, but I do believe the recommendations presented here should at least be tried and will help most people. I can't promise to help everybody. If any doctor promises you a cure, don't just walk away, run! You see, the human body is far too complex for anyone to ever make a promise like that. Confidence is only good to a point.

I didn't write this book to gain friends; in fact, I expect to lose some when they come to realize what I stand for. I welcome critics and consider them blessings. Even the greatest healer ever known, Jesus, has his critics.

You won't see me quoting much research, even though I do keep up with what's going on in the healthcare field. I've learned to be very suspicious of much of the published information, mainly because it doesn't take long before the results of one study contradicts another. Much of the so-called science coming out these days has more to do with business and the marketing of products than with good health. I recognize science as being valuable but not when it belittles common sense.

For years I've tried, really tried hard, to open the lines of communication between mechanistic health professionals (mainly medical providers) and vitalistic health professionals (like myself who focus on the inborn healing ability of each person). I attempted this because increased cooperation between health providers would be more beneficial to patients.

On the rare occasion when I did manage to get some attention from other healthcare providers, they may have acted interested in what I was proposing; however, it soon became apparent that he or she wanted me to refer my patients for drugs and surgery, even if the patients did not need anything more than the care I was providing. For the record, I have never hesitated to refer patients for medical care when they really needed it.

Several examples of deft and clever attempts to win over my referrals include a pain management doctor who specialized with injections of drugs directly into the spine. He started dropping off basketball tickets and bottles of fine wine at my office. A radiology clinic brought golf balls and invited me to expensive dinners, urging me to send more patients to them for highly profitable MRIs (magnetic resonance imaging). I could go on and on.

Sadly, in over two decades of reaching out, I can't say I really connected with any medical providers. I can't help but chuckle when I hear the stargazers ask, "Is there any intelligent life out there?" I can relate.

The principles and practices of getting and staying healthier presented in this book are not all new or revolutionary. Many are basic concepts like making better food choices and getting more exercise that have remained unchanged over time, but have been too difficult or confusing. The new advancements in healthcare featured in the media like full body diagnostic scanning to detect early problems (expensive and rarely helpful) or the endless advertisements for new drugs (with lots of expensive side effects), are tending to drown out the basic commonsense principles and practices of getting and staying healthy. Bringing the basic, age-old principles back into common practice is my intention with this book, not to mention some new, fresh concepts, like the importance of balanced body structure, that are suppressed by the medical industry for lack of understanding or, worse yet, economic advantage.

So my outrage lies with the current healthcare system. I see through the untruths told about what health really is. I see through the over-promotion. I see through the reluctance to fully reveal the dangers and side effects in the new advances except in fine print. Don't misunderstand me; I realize that many modern healthcare procedures are lifesavers and miracles in and of themselves. But unless there is an emergency, or the simpler, more natural, commonsense approaches have failed, they should be delayed because of increased risk and expense.

> I actually started out studying to be a medical doctor. I was following the pre-med program at the University of Wisconsin. As I progressed, I became more and more disenchanted with the system as I observed the focus on profit, the arrogance, the ignorance and disrespect for other healthcare ideologies, and the general unhappiness of those I was learning from. One fall afternoon, early in my pre-medical studies, as I was studying organic chemistry at the kitchen table, I overheard a program about chiropractic featured on a popular documentary-type TV show, *60 Minutes.*

As it turned out, the show presented interviews of MDs (who I later found were misinformed) espousing the danger and lack of science behind chiropractic. But the program did provide a fairly accurate explanation of the chiropractic principle: how disturbed body structure (particularly misaligned spinal joints) affects health through disruption of the nervous system. That made more sense to me than anything I'd learned about medical care at school so far. The physicians were followed by interviews of several chiropractic patients who extolled the benefits they'd received.

The next day, I was in the college library, looking up chiropractic, trying to navigate through the mostly negative, critical books about chiropractic to find the truth. Within days, I made up my mind that chiropractic was the career I was looking for. My med school colleagues soon abandoned me, considering me a traitor. Off I went to four more years of chiropractic training at the renowned Palmer College of Chiropractic in Davenport, Iowa.

The Smoke and Mirrors of Drugs

Can you see through the smoke? Have you noticed the increasing number of advertisements for medications in the media? Have you looked at all that fine print at the end or back pages of magazine drug advertisements? Those are the potential side effects known about—so far! Worse yet, the investigative teams/ researchers who are supposed to determine and report the potential side effects are most likely employed by the manufacturers of the drug, creating a tremendous potential for dishonesty. Have you noticed attractive, sharply dressed young people frequenting your medical doctor's office? Many of them are drug salespeople, who come bearing gifts like free tickets to sporting events, seminars in exotic places, pens, stacks of sticky notes, and prescription pads with the drugs' names already on it, in hopes of influencing your doctor to prescribe their particular drugs.

> **If we don't hang together, we'll each hang separately.**
> —*Benjamin Franklin*

Have you noticed the numerous professionally produced news clips about the newest advances in medical care, whether it be a new surgical procedure, medication, or injection? Those are produced and distributed by public relation firms working for the medical societies and drug manufacturers!

Have you noticed the price of all that fluff? My neighbor told me his wife recently went through a procedure to take care of a lump in her breast. She's doing fine and certainly needed medical care, but when the bills were tallied, they amounted to a whopping $153,000.00! And how about the many people paying hundreds of dollars for medications each month. Don't worry, the new Medicare drug plan will cover it. Ha! We all pay for it in higher taxes!

If you're not as outraged by this as I am, I call on you to **become** outraged. I can't accomplish this plan to improve the world alone. I need your help!

> I propose that health be a priority and a personal responsibility. And I propose that health through natural methods, through common-sense principles and practices, be the main source of health and wellness for everyone.

I want you to go about your healthcare differently, more intelligently, and for the better. Don't abandon or completely alienate yourself from your old ways but build on them. Don't quit medical care cold turkey. Not all of what you are, or were, doing is bad. The information contained in this book is in no way a substitute for any other healthcare you may need. I'm not stating this as a cop-out the way many other health writers do, as they hope to avoid legal troubles. My point is that you may need help other than what I offer here; don't hesitate to seek it out. I'll help you with getting the best of both worlds (holistic/natural healing and medical) with the suggestions I give you in my favorite chapter, Chapter 7, "Talking to Your Doctor."

How is my own health, you might wonder? For years, my medical bills have been at or near zero. Ditto for my wife and three children. No, we don't always feel perfect. If you think we should or that you should, then you really need to read Chapter 1, "What is *Real* Health?", where I explain what health really is. If you want to know our secrets for doing so well, you'll learn it all in this book. We practice what I preach. Yes, we expect to die someday; but at least we'll die healthy!

True, the average person is living longer. But particularly for Americans, overall health is declining. People are fatter, lower in energy, less active, on more medications, and paying more for healthcare than ever before.

But I call for more than just your outrage! And I need more than just your help! I need you to join me! You can start by taking better care of yourself and your family by using the information I provide in this book. Then spread the word to your friends, neighbors, and co-workers.

Let's have a healthcare revolution and take control of our well-being. Let's get wild about our health!

Dr. Tom Potisk
Milwaukee, Wisconsin

Chapter 1
What Is *Real* Health?

A practical definition of health that can help YOU
(instead of helping your doctor become wealthy)

Ready for a shocker? The way you feel has very little to do with how healthy you are. That's right. Whether you feel good or not doesn't mean as much as you might think. Now notice I'm not saying it doesn't mean *anything*.

The problem lies in the fact that most people believe that the way they feel means *everything*. I call it "worldly healthcare," because it's what most of the world mistakenly follows, particularly people in the U.S. Symptom relief is what most of modern medicine focuses on (mainly by writing prescriptions for medications) and is one of the ways they shortchange people because, quite often, the true cause of the symptom is not fully addressed. Now before you accuse me of being a fanatic or worse, know that I realize some medications are necessary. But let me remind you that our healthcare system is broken as I detailed in the Preface, and the prevalence of symptom relief through medication is a big part of the problem.

This concept is so important it bears repeating: *The way you feel has little to do with how healthy you are.* Until you can comprehend this, until you can accept it, and embrace it, you're not truly enlightened and on your journey to better health. *There is much more to real health than what you have been led to believe.*

The assumed, incorrect definition of health as "an absence of symptoms" and its common misuse is responsible for millions of people being unhealthy and an equal number dying prematurely.

> The current healthcare system is severely flawed.
>
> Let's look at health from a new, better perspective.

So, if health is not defined by how good or how sick you feel, then what is it? Check *Webster's Dictionary*—you'll see that health is truly defined as a condition of wholeness to which all of the organs are functioning 100 percent of the time; and the World Health Organization says that health is a state of optimal mental, physical and social well-being and not merely the absence of disease and infirmities. I'll go a step further and state that spiritual well-being needs to be added.

Now if you were to ask me, "Dr. Tom, having total mental, physical, and social well-being makes me feel good, right?" I would answer, "Not necessarily." And if you would ask me,

The art of medicine consists in amusing the patient while nature truly cures the disease.
—Voltaire

"Not having total mental, physical, and social well-being makes me feel bad, right?" I would again answer, "Not necessarily."

Here's an example. If you accidentally ate some food that was spoiled, you might very well get some unpleasant symptoms like headache, vomiting, and/or diarrhea. Suffice it to say, you feel awful. But these terrible feelings are simply the result of your body doing exactly what it should: expelling the toxins you swallowed as quickly as possible. In this case, you could be healthy, but feel awful.

Here's another example, quite a common one, in fact. John or Mary was a picture of health, was never sick, didn't smoke or drink, but dropped over suddenly from a heart attack. In this case, the person was unhealthy but felt good until it was too late. (Nearly every case of heart attack involves a long buildup of unhealthy heart tissue.)

Gary, a husky man of 58, recently retired, occasionally came into my clinic seeking help for sports injuries acquired during his frequent hunting and fishing excursions. As he described where he felt bad, where he had a muscle ache or sore back, he would always end his sentence with, "Other than that, my health is good!" Although I helped him with his backaches, he rejected my explanations of what real health is, not to mention my suggestions of how he could prevent further health problems.

One day, his wife called my office. She said Gary had died that morning from a massive heart attack simply upon rising from a chair. On top of that, she said he had had a thorough medical physical just days before. That's a nice, quick way to go but I

> can't help wonder if Gary would have enjoyed his
> retirement longer had he been wiser about his
> healthcare choices.

There are numerous examples of how you can feel lousy but be healthy, and vice versa. Cancer, for example, starts with the mutation of one cell and can commonly progress with no symptoms until it's at an advanced stage. Some cancer is only found by accident, like when a doctor spots it during a routine X-ray. Here again, the patient was unhealthy all the time their cancer was progressing, but likely thought they were healthy because they felt no symptoms. In my own practice, as another example, I've seen many cases of arthritis on X-rays of my patients, yet upon questioning, they had no idea it was there. Having no apparent symptoms led them to believe they were healthy.

Another common example of how the presence or absence of symptoms does not define true health is fever. Rarely does your body ever raise its core temperature (fever) other than as a self-helping reaction to fighting a foreign invader like a bacteria or virus. Fever makes us feel awful, but in reality, our bodies are doing exactly what they should (real health), using our own natural healing ability. True, some fevers are a problem that need professional help, but in most cases, it's best left alone and best to remember that healthy bodies use fever as a valuable tool to fight infection.

The vast majority of healthcare providers are getting wealthy through "sickness care" or "symptom relief" rather than true "healthcare." Nearly the entire modern healthcare marketplace—

hospitals, clinics, drug manufacturers, vitamin manufacturers, doctors, and so on—are banking on you to come running for help when you're desperate and don't feel good. Some will clean up even more when you feel good but don't do anything to maintain real health, because soon you'll not only come running, you'll come running with an emergency like a heart attack or other silently accumulating problem. That is, if the undertaker doesn't clean up first! Do you see the ridiculous cycle or trap it's become? Some would say the current system has you "coming and going."

This book, and your thorough understanding of what true health really is, will empower you to make better decisions not only when you are truly sick, but also concerning real practical prevention.

> Have you ever noticed that the names of most prescription medications either start with or contain an unusually high number of letters from the end of the alphabet; for example: Valium®, Vytoxin®, Nexium®, Viagra®? Is it a coincidence? Not hardly!
>
> You see, the medical/pharmaceutical industry is big business, we're talking trillions of dollars. They do their homework, and they learned through market research that the public is more impressed with and will pay more for drugs that are named this way. Here are some more examples: Xanax®, Celebrex®, Vytorin®, Zoloft®, Prozac®, Paxil®, Vicodin®, Vioxx®, or Zantac®. They're brilliant! Have they got you sold?

"Sickness" Insurance

Health insurance is a misnomer when you consider that it really doesn't cover the true definition of health. They will provide payment for exams, X-rays, therapies, and surgeries for illnesses, accidents, and injuries (sickness care); but any costs associated with exercise, exercise equipment, vitamins, mineral supplements, eating healthier, guidance on lifestyle modifications, or periodic chiropractic preventive care (real healthcare) are rarely covered by health insurance policies. Sure, some health insurance companies now encourage smoking cessation classes, offer discounts at health clubs, and require regular wellness checkups. Those are all steps in the right direction, but still rare.

Nevertheless, "sickness insurance" would be a more accurate name for the coverage. Practically every week the newspaper features an article about the skyrocketing increases of health insurance premiums, and there is no end in sight. The current system is doomed to fail because of the flawed understanding of what health really is and the weak encouragement of prevention and personal responsibility. The larger the mess gets, the harder it will fall. It's already slowly imploding now.

Evidence of this is seen in the growing numbers of uninsured people, the swelling incidence of obesity, and the public's increasing unhappiness with the service they are getting in the healthcare marketplace. Health insurance has become big business and they want maximum profits.

No, I don't think a government-run health insurance overhaul is the answer, either. That will be at most a temporary patch. The ultimate answer is in having wiser consumers and more personal responsibility. I want you to be a responsible, wiser consumer of healthcare; for most, all it takes is better under-standing and some lifestyle changes.

> Some make a good argument for a national health-care system. But I'm quite sure that would be a short-term fix and become a long-term nightmare. Case in point; I've been blessed to travel to several countries like England, Mexico, France, Belize, and Canada. They all have government run universal health coverage. As I've been driven through their cities by taxi, I've noticed numerous private doctors' offices.
>
> When I ask the cab drivers if anybody can go there, the consistent reply I get is, "Yes, anybody can go to those independent doctors, but we must pay out of pocket for that good care. If we want to see the government doctors, we go to the public clinic, take our chances, and, most times, wait a long time."

Money Well Spent

The idea of spending money to maintain your well-being is the same principle involved in maintaining your home, car, or any-thing you own. You are responsible for spending a little regularly to avoid bigger expenses later. As an analogy consider this: if you avoided some car maintenance like oil changes, you'd be able to keep driving your car for quite a while, saving a few bucks. Even-tually, though, you'll face an engine rebuild that costs hundreds, if not thousands, of dollars.

A (50-something) lady named Julie periodically sought my help for her fibromyalgia and chronic fatigue. She responded well, understanding the principles by which I practice, and was enlightened about what true health means, but she acted on very few of my lifestyle recommendations like exercises, nutritional supplements, detoxification, and massage.

I was confused by her lack of action. While she sought relief from the pain and lack of energy, she seemed to be focused only on what her health insurance would or would not cover, even though she and her husband drove new cars, owned a nice house, traveled frequently, and appeared to be well off. On one visit to my office, she told me a recent flare-up of her illness was due to stress, worry, and general unhappiness. Since she never seemed to follow much of my advice, I suggested she see a colleague whom I thought might be able to help her symptoms.

She responded with, "I know, I know, there are lots of things that could help me, but I just can't bring myself to spend the money!"

I truly believe some people have gotten conditioned or brainwashed into believing that if their health insurance doesn't cover certain procedures, they can't or shouldn't have them. I know some truly can't afford what they need, but I see many people who convince themselves that they *won't* afford it. What are your priorities when it comes to your own and your family's well-being?

You will have to spend some money and time to obtain and maintain true health, but it's money well spent. It's an investment. What good is a fat savings account if you're not able to be active and enjoy it? Investing in yourself is the best investment you can make. Be wary of financial advisors who don't have that outlook. Your wellness must come first.

Let's keep our private health insurance, modifying it, or at least not expecting it to cover much more than our crisis needs and emergencies. We'll beat the system at its own game by investing in ourselves, taking responsibility for improving and maintaining our well-being (real health), and keeping control of what's best for us.

A prevailing myth is that people get sick because of bad luck, bad germs, or bad genes. I say that the leading cause of death is really suicide by lifestyle choices. You don't have to be a part of the insanity of how most of the world sees health: waiting until you have symptoms and then covering them with higher risk and more expensive prescription medicines.

That's what I earlier referred to as "worldly healthcare." There is a better way: focus on your physical, mental, and spiritual well-being. Details about how to prevent illness and maintain health are provided in later chapters, but I'll cut to the chase and tell you that it's really about the choices you make. For example, are you going to spend hundreds or maybe even thousands of dollars for a big-screen TV with monthly cable charges, or will you commit that time and money to improve the well-being of your family? I'm not saying you shouldn't have luxuries like that big TV, but I am saying you ought first be spending money for better, fresher food (organic), regular holistic preventive treat-

Expect criticism because we seem different to those who don't yet have the enlightenment about health that we do. They'll accuse us of being fanatics or belonging to a cult simply because we take better care of ourselves through things like better eating, exercise, and structural balance. But don't mock others who are still trapped by the old system. Help them to gently see the truth about their choices. Sometimes all you can do is plant seeds.

ment (massage, chiropractic, nutritional supplements), physical recreation (bicycling, hiking, skiing, swimming), and exposing yourself and your family to positive, uplifting, and inspiring information and education (reading, lectures, classes, better quality schools). Simply having the ability to make these choices is a blessing in itself. Don't throw that away.

Be prepared for ridicule from adversaries if you choose to put into practice your new-found enlightenment about true health and that it really involves taking responsibility for your own well-being. Most of the world is on the other side of the fence. Their focus is on taking the short road to instant gratification with things like materialism, accumulating debt, and covering symptoms with medication. Einstein said, "Great spirits have always encountered resistance from mediocre minds."

Also be aware that the providers of that old, insane system of what they call healthcare are also well entrenched, partly because that's where the big bucks are. The medical industry is very profit driven, and it won't budge easily. Bartholomew Joshua Palmer, the developer of the chiropractic profession said, "The path of least resistance makes rivers and men crooked."

If the better way fails you, you can always cross back over to the other side for traditional medical help. Traditional medical care works wonderfully in crisis situations, like heart attacks, stroke, broken bones, open wounds, and so on. Seek that help immediately when needed, but do so cautiously and with an escape plan.

> Karrie, a patient of mine, told me she was worried about her 81-year-old mother who had been suffering with a respiratory infection for several weeks. Her mother refused to visit any doctors due to pure stubbornness. I volunteered to call her mother and urge her to get some medical care, warning her of the risk of pneumonia and other respiratory illnesses.
>
> Karrie's mother cussed and swore and promptly hung up on me. Karrie later told me that her mother soon did go to the medical clinic and got the help she needed. Soon after, her mother became my patient, thanked me and utilized the preventive care I offer. I shared with her much of what you read in this book.

If you're hesitant at this point to accept this more logical way of looking at health, that's okay. This is a big change for most people and it takes time. Many people get confused because the media (where most people get their health information) is slanted toward their advertisers, favoring the popular "worldly healthcare" system. Also, it's easy to focus on the exceptions rather than the rules. For example, we all know or have heard of somebody who lived into their 80s, 90s, or beyond, smoking,

Let's be wise to the current "sickness-care" system,
use it when necessary, but focus our efforts on true health,
our physical, mental, and social well-being.

drinking alcohol, eating poorly, breaking all the rules for true well-being. That does happen but it's far from common. And consider how much more fulfilling, rewarding, and productive a life like that could have been, had they followed at least some well-being concepts. Quality of life is overlooked for length of life. Consider this half-truth: you'll see frequent reports about how the average longevity is increasing year after year. It's true but they fail to mention that true health, as defined by well-being, is decreasing. Also, they don't mention that the life expectancy in the U.S. still lags far behind many other countries, even though we have the easiest access to all the modern "health" technologies.

Share your knowledge and experience because you care. It's awfully hard for others to chastise you if you're sincere. At the very least, try asking, "Have you considered some natural approaches?" or "Can I suggest a book called …?" (Hint, hint). If you at least make a suggestion, then you have fulfilled your responsibility. The guilt of not doing so is worse than the rejection or ridicule you may encounter.

Lifestyle Changes

So for now, relax and take a quick survey of your own well-being, and enjoy reading all of this book. Physical well-being involves eating properly, exercising regularly, and maintaining structural balance. Mental well-being involves feeding your mind with positive material, learning new things, and helping others. Spiritual well-being involves learning more about yourself, where you came from, your purpose, and where you're going. Which of these areas do you think you need to work on? For most of us, the answer is "all of them." Don't be overwhelmed. Pick one that really strikes a chord with you and focus on just that. You'll find details on each of these items in this book.

A man and his wife were sitting in recliners, watching television and drinking beer.

The man turned to his wife and said, "Honey, I want you to know that I don't ever want to be left in a vegetative state, dependent on some machine, and given fluids."

So his wife got up, unplugged the TV, and threw away all of his beer!

Well-being Checklist:

- ❑ Daily exercise
- ❑ Eating several portions of fresh vegetables and fruit daily
- ❑ Prayer
- ❑ Learning something new
- ❑ Minimizing alcohol
- ❑ Complete relaxation
- ❑ Several glasses of pure water daily
- ❑ Stretching and balancing body structure
- ❑ Good postural habits
- ❑ Generosity
- ❑ Reading positive, uplifting material

I'm always amazed at how much healthier people can become by making even one change. Weight management, for example, when practiced as a long-term lifestyle change, can produce astounding benefits. Chapter 4, "Enjoying Eating," shows you how to accomplish it. Chapter 6, "Help For Your Ailments," contains numerous examples of practical applications to deal with common health problems. It's also important to focus your efforts on prevention after gaining control of your illness. You'll find that practical plan in Chapter 8, "Strategies for Prevention of Illness."

Relax and enjoy learning about this new way of enhancing the quality of your life. We're talking about lifestyle changes, so that will take some time and patience.

But first, can you accept these new ideas? What wake-up call do you need—cancer, a heart attack? By then, it may be too late!

Throughout my career, I've helped a lot of people with their back pains. My success rate is very high, in the 90 percent range. One challenging case was an overweight young man named Ernie. His back pain responded well to my treatment, but he'd feel better for only a few days, then the pain would return. This went on for weeks. He was getting angry with me for the repetitiveness of treatment, and I was getting angry with him because we both knew his weight was the holdup and he wasn't following any of my weight-loss recommendations.

After one of the treatment sessions, we both blew up, flying off the handle with our words. I said, "You're not getting better because you're fat! Your poor little backbones can't hold all that weight!" Ernie turned red in the face and stormed out of the office. I never thought I'd see him again. It shook me up also, but I had to give him a wake-up call.

One year later, a young, trim gentleman stopped in the office. I noticed tears in his eyes. He said, "Do you recognize me? I'm the guy you scolded for being too fat. No one ever made that so clear to me before and it hurt my feelings, but it made me start eating smarter and exercising. The back pain that bothered me for years finally is gone thanks to your treatment and wake-up call. I just wanted to stop in and thank you."

Symptom Covering

Be wary of symptom covering. This is the mainstay of current worldly healthcare. You go to the doctor with a symptom, you walk out with something to cover it up. I don't blame you for wanting relief, especially in the most extreme situations. But consider that the symptom is a signal that your well-being is weak in some area. Simply covering it is temporary and may result in something worse down the line.

Returning to our car analogy: If your oil pressure warning light turns red on your car's dashboard, would you cover the light and keep driving, or would you stop as soon as possible and check the oil level? If you had to proceed driving your car with the red oil warning light on, you would do so cautiously, knowing that you must address the cause of the warning soon, before more serious, more expensive damage occurs. If you have to cover up one of your body's symptoms, proceed in this same cautious fashion and with a plan to soon seek the source of the symptom.

Consider also that covering symptoms might suppress your body's inherent ability to heal. For example, in the earlier example where someone had food poisoning, taking medication to ease those symptoms might very likely prolong that illness, because the body produces those uncomfortable symptoms to eliminate the toxins. Minimizing or eliminating the symptoms would allow the toxins to remain.

When you have a cold or flu, the fever, tiredness, aches, and weakness are symptoms your body uses to force you to lie down and rest. If you can't rest, then at least reduce your work load or activity level. The fever is your body's inherent knowledge to alter your temperature to create an undesirable environment for the bug that caught you. The nasal discharge or frequent bowel movements are a similar story. Does it make sense to cover or eliminate all these? Of course not. Your body is doing exactly what it needs to. Leave it alone if at all possible. Perhaps help yourself by drinking extra water, soaking in a hot bath, and setting up a vaporizer in your sleeping quarters.

Help your body; don't fight the symptoms.

Focus on strengthening your body's natural defenses and resistance. The result will be faster recovery and stronger immunity to prevent a recurrence. A good adage to remember when you get a flu or cold is that "you don't really catch germs; they catch you when your resistance is down." So focus on increasing your resistance. Strengthen your immunity with things like more rest, a chiropractic adjustment, more fluids, nutritional support like Vitamin C, and so on. If you absolutely have to take a pill or potion to have relief, then do so as minimally as possible, and try the natural approaches as presented in Chapter 6, "Help for Your Ailments." Save the medications as a last resort.

An elderly lady named Carol, a patient of mine for many years, came into my office for treatment of her neck problems. She had tears in her eyes because her son, James, had recently died from addiction to prescription pain killers. I remembered James; he had been a patient of mine a few years before, appeared to be a trim, fit young man, but was non-compliant, meaning he didn't follow my directions for easing his knee pains. James chose the worldly path, the path of least resistance, and decided it was easier to get a pain medication pre-scription instead of the natural help I had to offer like chiropractic treatment and some rehabilitative exercises.

Over the years since James was in my office, I'd heard from his mom, Carol, about how he'd been struggling with an addiction to those pain meds. I tried to suggest some help such as a thor-ough internal cleansing that might help him, but all Carol said at the time was, "We'll see." I believe Carol's lack of assertiveness here contributed to her son's demise. Sometimes we all need to be more outspoken.

If you currently have no symptoms, congratulations! But you've got a real challenge. Can you accept that you may still be in great danger? The "worldly way" would be to tell yourself that "all is fine." Those are famous last words. I can assure you there is trouble brewing if you're not focusing on maintaining your physical, mental, and spiritual well-being. Go ahead, take a chance at doing nothing.

When you're feeling great, let that also be a calling to actively pursue and main-tain your wellness, keeping it a priority.

That's how we'll laugh at and beat the current racket.

Make your well-being a way of life!

Accepting and living your life in accor-dance with the true definition of health is more respectful of your creator. If you tell me that you don't believe in a creator, I'll slam dunk that argument by pointing out that human physiology is highly organized, and there is no organization without higher intelligence. Abandoning or ignoring the body's innate healing ability is a total disrespect for the intelligence of the creator.

As a Christian, I'm amazed how many fellow Christians and others who believe in creation by a higher power, claim to be wise to the ways of the world, but then never question the "worldly ways" of healthcare. I teasingly call them "healthcare heathens." Not all invasive procedures, such as surgeries and medications, are bad. Certainly, many are gifts from God, even miracles at times, and many doctors, clinics, and hospitals are excellent, but let's not get the priorities mixed up. The body's inherent, God-given healing ability needs to be respected and given priority, instead of circumvented.

A Vitalistic Person:

- Believes in a vital force that exists outside and animates the body.
- Believes a human is made up of more than just chemical elements and compounds.
- Believes a human's organization and animation comes from a "Creator."
- Has more respect for the spirit/soul.
- Has more respect for common sense/principles and intuition.
- Has less respect for scientific research.
- Questions conclusions based on partial facts.
- Focuses more on the spiritual.

- Believes a human is more than a machine.
- Believes the whole is greater than the sum of its parts.
- Focuses on removing interference to allow "real health."

A Mechanistic Person:

- Believes a human is made up of just chemical elements and compounds.
- Believes a human's organization and animation comes from "self."
- Questions the existence of the spirit/soul.
- Has less respect for common sense/principles and intuition.
- Relies mainly on scientific research.
- Makes conclusions based on partial facts.
- Focuses less on the spiritual.
- Believes a human is more of a machine.
- Believes a human is equal to the sum of its parts.
- Focuses on adding to (medications) and/or removing (surgery) to allow relief of symptoms.

The care and advice that doctors like myself offer can be termed "vitalistic," meaning alive with a vital, spiritual, internal guiding force. We say all true healing comes from within, and that there is more to a person than just the sum of his or her parts.

True or Real Health:

- Focuses on principles.
- Emphasizes optimal function.
- Takes an inside-out approach (improves oneself).
- Seeks underlying source of symptoms.
- Practices prevention by action to improve oneself.
- Accepts that some symptoms are actually good.
- Uses a proactive approach.

Apparent Health:

- Focuses on research studies.
- Emphasizes absence of symptoms.
- Has an outside-in approach (through medication/surgery).
- Covers symptoms.
- Attempts prevention through periodic testing.
- Practices a "waiting-for-a-breakdown" approach.

Recently in my local newspaper was a front-page article about a group of high school students. They were caught skipping school and getting high on cold medicine. As a result, some needed emergency medical assistance. I bet they hadn't been taught much about respect for their bodies or health. Instead, they were most likely influenced by what they observed their parents doing or what they saw on TV. When Mom and Dad don't feel good, they reach for medicine to feel better, just like on TV. When teenagers are feeling a little down, heartbroken, or are low on

All OTC drugs also interact with prescription medications, so always consult with a physician if you are using these. Check for the following ingredients on any OTC drug.

HEARTBURN DRUGS: ANTACIDS

Examples: Aluminum-magnesium, magnesium, calcium carbonate, sodium bicarbonate

Some side effects: Thirst, stomach cramps, whitish discoloration of stools, constipation, diarrhea, headache, fatigue, difficulty urinating, mood swings, muscle weakness or pain, swelling of feet or ankles. Can also mask stomach ulcers and stomach cancer. Excessive calcium carbonate intake can cause kidney stones.

HEARTBURN DRUGS: ACID BLOCKERS

Examples: Cimetidine, famotidine, nizatidine, ranitidine

Some side effects: Abdominal pain, constipation, diarrhea, headache, joint pain, dizziness, drowsiness, confusion, insomnia, hallucinations; impotence and enlarged breasts in men. Prolonged use can also mask stomach ulcers and stomach cancer.

PAIN RELIEVERS

Examples: Aspirin, ibuprofin, naproxen, acetaminophen

Some side effects: Heartburn or indigestion, stomach cramps, nausea, decreased clotting; bloody or tarry stools, with prolonged use, rebound headaches, anemia, kidney or liver damage.

ORAL DECONGESTANTS

Examples: Pseudoephedrine

Some side effects: Restlessness, nervousness, insomnia, headache, sweating, difficult or painful urination, nausea, shortness of breath.

TOPICAL DECONGESTANTS

Examples: Oxymetazoline, phenylephrine

Some side effects: Burning, dryness, stinging inside nose, nasal discharge, sneezing, headache, irregular heartbeat, blurred vision, dizziness, drowsiness, insomnia.

self-esteem, what do you think they'll reach for when they've grown up in an environment that lacks respect for the well-being of the body?

Wouldn't the respect I propose be one of the answers to the recreational drug problem? Do you see how important the focus on true health needs to be and how it could influence future generations like your own children and grandchildren? Do you see why I had to do something about it? Why I call for a revolution in the introduction of this book? Will you help?

The Bible says, *Do you not know that your body is a temple of the Holy Spirit, who is in you, whom you have received from God? Therefore honor God with your body* (1 Corinthians 6:19).

We can really improve the whole world by improving how we go about our health. Young people are watching and learning from us. Treat your body as if it's a temple housing your spirit. We are responsible for setting a good example. Think of the consequences our actions are having on generations to come.

Make your health a priority.
Be passionate, be "wild" about your health and well-being!
Don't just focus on symptoms, focus on wellness.
Utilize invasive procedures only when absolutely necessary.
Learn and use natural methods, like those I cover in this book.
Respect your body's inborn ability to get and stay healthy.

The World's Greatest Tragedy

Some say hundreds of thousands have died. Others say it was millions. No one will ever know for sure, although the death toll is certainly much higher than that of all the wars combined through history. Nonetheless, the numbers are still growing each day. Yes, this battle is still going on, even as we speak. Will you or a member of your family be the next victim? It's a real possibility.

The battle I refer to is between healthcare philosophies: mechanistic/allopathic/medical versus vitalistic/holistic/chiropractic/clinical nutrition/acupuncture and massage, and the deaths inadvertently induced by a physician or surgeon, treatment, or procedure shown opposite. The differences between these approaches are presented above on pages 19 and 20. If you rely solely on the advice of one or the other type of practitioner, you can be caught in the middle, possibly becoming collateral damage. There can be no ultimate winner. Only mutual cooperation can end the battle, because both sides hold benefits for the public. The vitalistic/holistic side openly and voluntarily comes to the bargaining table regularly, almost pleading to be heard. The mechanistic/allopathic side is already holding most of the territory, most of the inhabitants, and most of the assets. The vitalistic side holds on with higher safety, patient satisfaction, and patient approval.

Deaths occur when patients don't get the best choice of treatment. Due to the lack of cooperation, patients are at risk because of the high incidence of medication side effects or complications of surgery. Fatalities due to complications are called *iatrogenic deaths* and their total dwarfs those of all the war deaths combined. As the table and graph on page 25 indicate, some scholars believe that these iatrogenic deaths are the leading cause

Yearly Deaths Inadvertently Induced by a Physician or Surgeon, by Medical Treatment, or by Diagnostic Procedures in the United States since Approximately 1985			
Condition	Deaths/Year	Cost/Year	Author
Adverse Drug Reactions	106,000	$12 billion	Lazarou, Suh
Medical Error	98,000	$2 billion	IOM
Bedsores	115,000	$55 billion	Xakellis, Barczak
Infection	88,000	$5 billion	Weinstein, MMWR
Malnutrition	108,800	--------	Nurses Coalition
Outpatient Procedures	199,000	$77 billion	Starfield, Weingart
Unnecessary Procedures	37,136	$122 billion	HCUP
Surgery-Related	32,000	$9 billion	AHRQ
TOTAL	**783,936/Year**	**$282 billion/Year**	
We could have an even higher death rate by using Dr. Lucien Leape's 1997 medical and drug error rate of 3 million. Multiplied by the fatality rate of 14 percent (that Leape used in 1994, we arrive at an annual death put this number in place of Lazarou's 106,000 drug errors and the Institute of Medicine's (IOM) 98,000 medical errors, we could add another 216,000 deaths making a total of 999,936 deaths annually.			
ADR/med error	420,000/Year	$200 billion/Year	Leape 1997
Estimated medically induced deaths: TOTAL	**999,936/Year**		

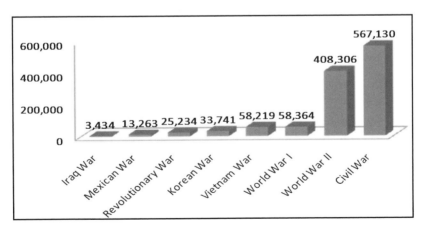

U.S. deaths from medical care complications (last 20 years)—estimated 20 million vs. U.S. deaths from all wars (last 200 years)—estimated 1.2 million.

of death. I truly believe many could be prevented had they gotten holistic care. Many patients may never have known that there were other options to surgery and drugs. Similarly, patients are at risk when they have conditions too complicated and too serious to be dealt with adequately through holistic methods.

This turf battle dilemma leaves patients caught in the middle, forcing some to choose and rally on one side or the other. The better choice is to utilize the benefits of each, but deciding when to use one or the other isn't easy at times. It's perfectly clear to me and will be to you as you read this book that generally, in non-emergency situations, it is better to choose the less invasive, more natural, holistic treatment, and relying on the allopathic side for a backup or at least some relief until the body has time to do its healing.

Currently, this protocol is reversed but slowly changing. There is a slow increase in cooperation among the philosophies. Some allopaths, however, are beginning to embrace some utiliza-

At a healthcare convention, a medical doctor and a chiropractor who reluctantly knew of each other coincidentally walked into a restroom. They stepped up to urinals, unzipped, shook it out, and began relieving themselves, coldly staring straight ahead.

The chiropractor finished first and bounced it back in, zipped up, and headed for the door. The medical doctor shouted, "Hey there, in medical school they taught us to wash our hands after urinating!"

The chiropractor shouted back, "In chiropractic school, they taught us not to pee on our hands!"

tion of holistic care, but instead of referring cases to properly trained, qualified, and licensed practitioners, they attempt performing natural treatments with little or no experience.

Economics is a major factor at work on both sides, the holistic side not wanting to lose what little market share it has and the allopathic side not wanting to give up any piece of the pie.

One would expect that malpractice lawsuits or licensing boards would settle this matter, driving each side to do what's best for the consumer, the patient. To some extent, those controls do work, but the vast majority of the malpractice lawsuits are initiated by patients suing medical personnel and institutions for mistakes and complications, and the vast majority of disciplinary actions from the licensing boards are found to be on the medical side and the abuse therein. This further reinforces my notion that the protocol for healthcare is reversed, as evidenced by the fact that lawsuits against holistic providers are rare due mainly to the safer, less invasive treatment.

Let's all demand the cooperation needed for our well-being. Insist that your doctor communicate with all your other healthcare providers.

In my eyes, altruistic cooperation between the holistic side and the allopathic side is the only solution. Unfortunately, it won't come easily and the media, government agencies, and corporate world seem biased toward the old allopathic order. Market forces are ultimately in control as patients vote with their feet. What I mean here is that a shift will occur in healthcare as patients become wiser with their choices. I'm happy to be a part of that with this book.

I've personally sought medical services a few times. On one occasion, I was experiencing some questionable mild chest pain so I quickly and rightfully went to a medical doctor to get checked out. The testing showed nothing wrong, thank goodness. The doctor suggested it was probably stress related and musculoskeletal in nature. But then the doctor asked me a most disturbing question: "Would you like some medication?" I was stunned! He had told me there was nothing seriously wrong! I was of the impression that prescription medications were to be given only upon the clearest of needs, and that only the doctor was to make the decision. Was it that easy to get pills? If I wanted them I could have them. Being too shocked to ask why or what kind, I said no and left. Now that years have gone by, I realize he likely meant well and offered what he could. I'm glad I had the common sense to decline his offer and look elsewhere for the relief I needed.

Congratulations!

You are now a graduate and have a new understanding of what health really is. Your former belief that how you feel determines your health, that you have no control of your well-being, and that you need medication to feel good was a trap set up by those who could profit from you. Your mission now, should you choose to accept it, is to start taking more responsibility to improve and maintain your physical, mental, and spiritual well-being. The next chapters will guide you in making better choices on exercise, eating, talking to your doctor, aging, and even your children's health. Failure to take a responsible, proactive approach to your health will cause you to self-destruct in . . .

Chapter 2

Exercises that Really Work— and Those to Avoid

If it isn't fun, it won't get done

Throughout my 20-plus years of practice, I've had many patients ask me, "What exercises can or should I do?" Often I've wanted to ask them, "Are you sure you're really going to do them?" I'd learned from experience that few people keep up an exercise routine. Health clubs don't like to let it be known, but about 85 percent of those who join aren't seen much after the first few weeks. That's right! Most people endure for only a few weeks!

I don't want to discourage you from exercising. The point I'm making is that there has to be a better way, and I'm happy to say that there is. Regular exercise, several times per week, is necessary to wellness. If it's going to be a regular part of our lifestyles, though, it needs to be fun and

Most people view exercise in a negative way and therefore may start, but don't keep it up. Let's have a fresh, new, effective idea about exercise.

something we enjoy doing. I'll go a step farther and say it also needs to be varied. By varied, I mean several different kinds, because boredom is the primary reason people give up exercising regularly. Of course, there are exceptions. If you have a regular, singular routine and have the wherewithal to keep it going, by all means proceed. For the rest of us, me included, fun and variety are the solution.

I'm always amazed at the positive response people have to what little exercise they do manage to accomplish. There is always noticeable benefit. Isn't that great news? Your efforts, however limited they might be, won't be in vain. Even the simplest movements bring progress. Remember, though, exercise has to be kept up or the progress is just as easily lost.

There are a number of things to consider when you start an exercise program: safety, time, expense, fear, pain, and what benefit you're aiming for. The benefits may include: strengthening, aerobic conditioning, posture improvement, or just wellness maintenance.

Guess what? I'd be willing to bet that simply reading the above paragraph gave you feelings of "Oh, no. Too complicated. I don't know if I want to start…!" and more. And I agree with you—the whole concept of deciding, finding, planning, and committing to an exercise program is way too difficult for most of us. It really would be best to leave all those details up to a professional, perhaps at a health club, to lay it all out for you and serve as a guide. If that's what will work for you, then go for it; those pros do excellent work. But if you're like most of us, those considerations of cost, time, and inconvenience make letting someone else make our decisions for us in that fashion a poor, short-term choice.

Read the message to the right. Doesn't that sound and feel better? Yes, that can be done. Yes, the benefits are there. Yes, this is the long-term answer. Later in this chapter, I'll show you some specific exercises that I know will help most people. But there's much more to it than just that. For example, as is true with weight management, your physical activity aimed at overall better health needs to be lifelong. Stop and focus now on what physical activities you really enjoy doing. Options might include walking/hiking, swimming, tennis, golf, gardening, bicycling, dancing, bowling, and so on. There are many options.

Let's combine all the benefits of strengthening, aerobic conditioning, posture improvement, and wellness maintenance into fun, physical activities that can be continued for your entire life!

Due to the boredom factor I mentioned earlier, you'll need to pick out several or be prepared to try new ones. Variety is very important for most people to maintain lifelong physical activity.

Also, know your limitations. You may need to focus on some specific movements to recover from any particular conditions or injuries you may have. For example, if you have bad knees, then walking or hiking is probably not a great choice. Swimming would be better suited to a person with bad knees. Something like tennis or golf would not be a good choice for those with shoulder limitations, whereas walking or hiking would be.

Our human nature leads most of us to listen intently every time a new exercise gadget comes on the market. It's as if we all have this deep, hidden desire to find some magic machine out there, not yet discovered, that will easily solve the exercise dilemma. Many of the machines on the market are quite interesting and may produce some good benefits. You'll notice the advertisers always have beautiful models with well-sculpted bodies and gorgeous hair demonstrating these get-fit-quick devices. That's part of the marketing. But look in most basements, attics, or rummage sales and you'll see lots of these products in barely used condition. My patients frequently show me advertisements and ask, "Do you think this might help me?" I'd often answer, "Yes, if you will really use it and keep it up. Do you have any other exercise equipment that you're not using?" Most would quickly get the point.

If you were to ask me which exercise choice is the best, I'd answer swimming. Being in the water reduces the gravitational burden on your joints and the multiple muscles being used to propel yourself can't be beat. Don't panic! By "swimming," I don't mean that you have to swim 50 laps at breakneck speed. Instead, several deliberate laps with alternating strokes will go a long way. You will even see benefits with hanging onto the side of the pool and kicking your feet. Or better yet, how about moving to some music in the water? Water aerobics are phenomenal!

Be creative. Search for combinations of activities to save time and money.

From my observations, golf and bowling as exercise choices, although having plenty of benefits, are probably the least effective. But remember, having a variety to circumvent the boredom is key. Think lifelong!

If you really want to have the upper hand with regard to lifestyle, consider ways you can combine regular physical activity with saving money and/or time. Can you walk or bike to work, school, or the market? Or can you teach a class in dancing or water aerobics? Can you combine your golf or tennis games with schmoozing or making connections for business? I've heard so many excuses for not biking or walking to work, like "I don't want to come to work sweaty." But who's talking about doing it with such intensity that you'll sweat? Why can't it be a leisurely ride, and why couldn't you bring another pair of work/school clothes to change into upon arriving. Better yet, why couldn't you wash up briefly in the restroom if you do get sweaty?

Forget about torturous, sweaty activity unless you really want it. Minimal activity is adequate. What's important is that you keep it going for a lifetime.

Here's another one: "I don't play golf/tennis well enough to play with business contacts." You're kidding yourself if you think they are expert players. Besides, it might be better for your business relationship if they win anyway!

One of the worst excuses of all: "I'd get too tired by the time I'm done." If you're that tired when you're done with any physical activity, you've done it too intensely. Most people will get energized from mild to moderate physical activity.

The bottom line? You can just as easily find reasons to do exercise. It's really an attitude. I challenge you to get wild and try something new!

Please notice that I haven't mentioned anything about the need to be counting your heartbeats or any other technical calculation. If you personally feel a need for that, fine. Anything complicated or involving self-torture really is not necessary and will discourage most people from moving or exercising. Even minimal physical activity has noticeable benefit.

> Stop thinking about getting started and just get moving. Simply walk if you have no other choices. Make a promise to yourself to keep it up. If you do have to stop for some reason, it's never too late to restart.

The important point is that it needs to be lifelong. Who wouldn't want to have fun, physical activity their entire lives, especially when you realize its importance, and that it's easier than you thought.

Relaxation and Breathing

I must draw your attention for a moment to relaxation and breathing. "That's a given," you might say. Or, "it comes automatically." But I've found that these two important aspects of real health and wellness are easily forgotten.

For example, most people breathe very shallowly, never fully inflating and deflating their lungs. Take a really deep breath right now. Notice the difference, the exhilaration? Feel the almost deliberate change in your focus from being on the world around you, to being more on just you. It might even make you cough or feel dizzy if you've been neglecting real breathing. Add to this real wellness experience by taking time regularly to disconnect, that is, taking time to just be. That might happen through meditation, prayer, or simply sitting in a quiet place. Minimally, I believe one needs to meditate or sit quietly daily for at least thirty minutes.

Two Simple Relaxation Exercises

Have you ever been completely relaxed? I mean *completely*. Our fast-paced American culture seems to discourage this, and at times even labels it "odd" or "lazy." Here are two exercises to attain complete relaxation. Make sure you do these in private, because they run so counter to "the norm" that others might panic and call for help.

First, a **mental relaxation exercise**: Sit comfortably and pick an object in front of you to focus on. It might be a picture, a tree, a distant landscape, or even a flower. Stare at it for at least five minutes. Yes, it's OK to blink your eyes. The goal here is to notice details you would normally not see. You'll be amazed at the distractions that will pop into your mind. The five minutes will seem like an eternity. Getting more focused results in relaxation.

Progress on focusing your mind will come slowly, but you'll be amazed at how little focus you really have—and then how much you can improve. Even more importantly, you'll discover how energized and enlivened you can become. You'll also be better able to deal with stressful situations.

Next, a **physical relaxation exercise**: Lie down in a comfortable, quiet place. Close your eyes and start taking slightly deeper, deliberate breaths. With each exhalation, focus on one part of your body—your right leg, for example—and relax any tension you might feel there. Take about ten deep breaths for each body part before moving your mind's focus to another. You'll be astounded at the amount of tension you've been holding all this time. As you relax, your body will seem to sink deeper, get looser, and feel lighter. Don't be surprised if your heart rate decreases significantly, any musculoskeletal pain fades, and you gain an immense feeling of calm. Be sure to spend some of the time to release your scalp, your face, and your abdomen.

In reality, these two things—deep breathing and thoroughly relaxing, are exercises. I've heard people say that they discovered what true relaxation feels like for the first time after doing these exercises. The best part is that after doing these exercises a few times, your body and mind can recall the relaxed feeling quickly, even in the face of stressful times. That's quite important and helpful to your well-being, don't you think?

Do you see the misconceptions about exercise that exist? It's been easier than you thought all along. The perceived difficulty keeps most people from attempting exercise and even more from continuing. It's never too late to start, but the longer you delay, the harder it might be to get going.

Delaying also applies to what time of day you do your physical activity. I've observed that if physical activity is not made a priority, such as doing it early in the day, it likely won't get done. At the latest, plan on doing something during your lunch hour. Even if you've only got one-half hour, you should easily be able to eat something light in 10 or 15 minutes and then spend the remaining time taking a walk. Yes, even that little bit of physical movement will do you good.

Stop contemplating how difficult it has to be! Remember, the simpler, the better. Ultimately, strive to get your physical activity in the morning. It's a wonderful start to a productive day.

Stretching

In addition to regularly engaging in some form of physical activity, you'll need to maintain flexibility by stretching. Through the process of trial and error mixed with observation, I devised a quick, safe, and thorough stretching routine, one that I do myself several times weekly, as well as before any potentially trauma-inducing activities, sports, or exercises. It takes between 5 and 10 minutes.

These stretching maneuvers need to be a regular part of everybody's hygiene, just like bathing, teeth brushing, and so on.

First of all, wear some loose-fitting clothing or do these stretches in your underwear. I suggest they be done first thing in the morning. If you can't perform some of the maneuvers, perhaps due to a physical disability or restriction, modify them as necessary. Do all of these slowly, deliberately, and gently. Breathe normally; don't hold your breath. If you find yourself straining, hurting or grunting, then back off—you're doing the movements too aggressively.

Most of the benefit will come from holding each position for at least 15 seconds. You'll find yourself becoming more flexible as you do these consistently at least three days per week. Don't be discouraged if you start out feeling so stiff, maybe inflexible—depending on how little you've moved or stretched for the past several weeks, that you can only partly complete each maneuver. You may also be a little sore the next day after starting the process. You may hear or feel some cracking or popping noises during the movements. These are normal.

I've taught the following stretching routine to many patients. Some start out so inflexible they can barely get up and down off the floor. Some people have to start off on their beds, although it's best to do these stretches on a firm, flat, carpeted surface or mat. Many want to give up after the first or second try because they think it's too hard. Those who persevere make amazing progress over time by just going through the motions, barely pushing themselves a little each time.

> All told, these stretches take between 5 and 10 minutes. How much simpler can it be? That's about the same time it takes to brew a pot of coffee or boil a pot of water. Put the TV on or some music if you need some entertainment during the maneuvers. What's your excuse? Ok, on the floor! Now!

I recommend that everyone do these stretching maneuvers, not only before any physical activity for prevention of injuries, but for general health maintenance. It will also benefit your posture. Many fitness centers, recreational programs, and health clubs offer flexibility classes. Enjoy them if you wish, but my routine involves no cost, can be done in the privacy of your home, and when it's convenient for you. Put on some music. Oh, and did I mention that this stretching routine greatly benefits your posture, circulation, and the alignment of your bones and joints? In Chapter 5, "Structure-Based Healthcare," you'll learn how important posture is for your health.

STRETCHES

1. Start by kneeling down, and then curl yourself forward, into a ball, bringing your head as close as possible to your knees. The tops of your feet should be flat against the floor. Your arms should be loosely to your sides on the floor. Hold for 15 seconds.

2. Next, raise your upper body to an upright position, sitting on your heels, with your toes on the floor. Raise your arms up, reaching as high as possible with your fingers. Hold for 15 seconds.

3. Next, while still sitting on your heels, drop your left arm to your side and slowly rest your palm on the floor. This will arch your torso to the left. Let your right arm lean over to your left while over your head.

4. Slowly straighten, bringing both arms directly overhead. Now repeat the last maneuver, this time tilting your body to the right, placing your right palm on the floor, and letting your left arm lean over to your right while over your head. Hold for 15 seconds.

5. Now slowly straighten, bringing both arms to your sides. Then lean forward, placing both palms on the floor in front of you. Slowly walk your hands forward, keeping your knees on the floor, until you can gently arch your body by bringing your abdomen towards the floor, while slowly lifting your chin towards the ceiling. Hold for 15 seconds.

6. Next, slowly position yourself on your back, legs straight and arms straight above your head. Reach with both hands, making yourself as long as possible. Hold for 15 seconds.

7. Then flex one knee and grab it with your hands, drawing it as close as possible to your chest. Hold for 15 seconds then repeat with the other knee.

8. Next, grabbing both your knees, slowly draw them both toward your chest while slowly raising your chin towards your knees. Hold for 15 seconds.

9. Next, remaining on your back, cross your right ankle over your left knee. Slowly drop your right knee toward the floor. Your legs should be in a figure-4 position. Hold for 15 seconds, and then reverse legs and repeat.

10. Now return to a straight lying position, this time with your hands to your sides. Slowly raise one leg and cross it over the other keeping both straight, making as wide an angle as possible between them. Hold for 15 seconds and repeat on the other side.

11. Next, slowly rise and position yourself on your hands and knees. Slowly tuck your chin to your chest while arching your mid-back toward the ceiling. Hold for 15 seconds.

12. Next, while still on your hands and knees, slowly raise your chin up while arching your back toward the floor. Hold for 15 seconds.

13. Then, while still on your hands and knees, with your back and head in a neutral position, slowly walk one hand over the other, bending your torso to the right as far as possible, also turning your head to the right, looking as far back as possible. Hold for 15 seconds, and then repeat on the other side.

14. Next, while still on your hands and knees, in a neutral position, raise yourself to only your hands and feet, slowly walking your hands back as close as possible toward your feet, while keeping your legs as straight as possible. Hold for 15 seconds.

A man named Dan, only 27 years old, who had suffered through three back surgeries with limited progress, nearly cried when he tried these and came to realize just how tight his body had become. I challenged him to keep at it, telling him that it may take months to regain at least some of the mobility he needed to function somewhat normally again.

When I saw him years later, golfing, he thanked me. He also said his next challenge is to get over the anger he feels because no one before me ever took the time to show him what he could do to help himself!

Exercises to Avoid

There certainly are exercises and physical activities that can be harmful. In Chapter 5, "Structure-Based Healthcare," you'll learn how important it is to avoid or at least minimize all forms of trauma and stress on your body's framework. For now, make note of the high-risk activities I point out in this chapter. With regard to the fun, regular, physical activities that are an essential part of achieving well-being, all have some level of

Don't let irrational fear stop you from seeking well-being from exercise.

risk, but when done properly, gently, and with good equipment, the risks are minimal. In most cases, the benefits outweigh the hazards. For example, bicycling requires good brakes, adequately inflated tires, bright clothing, and an awareness of your surroundings (cars, pedestrians, curbs, signs, and so on). And don't forget the helmet. Our current culture is producing wonderful off-road bike trails in most communities; seek those out. Most are even paved. There is also an increasing number of bike-only lanes on many city streets. Don't let the rare accidents featured in the media discourage you from bike riding.

Activities like skiing, rollerblading, or any of the faster-moving sports carry slightly higher risks, but still, when done properly (i.e., wearing a helmet and protective pads on your knees, elbows, and wrists for rollerblading), the risks are not high enough to justify avoidance. In most cases, unless you're a professional athlete, you're not in a race; so move slowly, gently, leisurely, and rhythmically. The benefits come from the consistency of doing these activities, not from the intensity. Striving for intensity raises the risks.

Higher-contact sports like football, rugby, and martial arts have even higher risks. However, when done properly and not overly aggressively, the benefits outweigh the risks. I wouldn't discourage a relatively fit and able person from doing them.

Golf, unless it involves aggressive winding and twisting of the spine as a pro would, rarely seems to cause damage, even for those with mild to moderate bad backs. Needless to say, walking the course, rather than riding the cart, carries with it far more health benefits, but put your golf bag on wheels.

Jogging is an activity that can have significant risk. The repetitive jarring to one's frame (feet, ankles, knees, and spine) is damaging to many who jog. The negative effects are slow, gradual, and accumulative. The benefits to the cardiovascular system are superior, but other, less traumatic and intense activities are adequate. If a person is determined to jog or run regularly, I advise that some preventative measures be taken. I'd suggest thorough stretching beforehand, quality running shoes with custom-made orthotics (supportive inserts), and supplemental nutrition for joint support. These precautions will minimize the traumatic effects.

Jogger's/Runner's Injury Prevention Plan
- ☑ **Thorough stretching**
- ☑ **Quality running shoes**
- ☑ **Custom made orthotics/inserts**
- ☑ **Joint support nutrition**

Many people find it surprising that yoga routines can be harmful. In my practice, I've observed many yoga-related injuries, most due to over-aggressive instructors. These observations are partly responsible for my devising the simpler stretching routine outlined above. But overall, yoga stretches are good.

I'm always disappointed when I hear someone say, "My days of physical activities are over." No matter your situation, there is always something that you can do. If you've had an injury during recreational activity that has left you fearful, you must overcome that irrational thought pattern and get moving again. For example, maybe you need to avoid one or more of the particular movements that may have hurt you in the past, but what about all the other choices? In all my years, I have yet to see someone who should not do any physical activity. If your healthcare provider told you to be inactive, find a new one!

AVOID:

Standard Exercises

There are several specific, "therapeutic"-type exercises that I've observed consistently hurting people. The military-type sit-up for example, done for abdominal strengthening, traumatizes the lower back and neck. These are commonly performed lying on the back, hands behind head, knees bent or legs straight, the sit-up performed by raising the upper torso. I believe this exercise should be avoided.

There are better, safer, equally effective movements. My favorite is to assume the same position, but to keep the head back on the floor, raise the legs so the heels are approximately an inch off the floor and then glide the heels toward the buttocks as the legs are bending, then extend the

The military sit-up traumatizes lower back and neck. This exercise should be avoided.

legs straight. This maneuver strengthens both the upper and lower abdominals without traumatizing the neck or lower back. The arms can be either flat to the sides or behind the head, with the head kept back. Repeat the movement until a slight discomfort or fatigue is noticed in the abdominal area. Rest for about a minute, then repeat again. Usually three sets are adequate.

CORRECT:

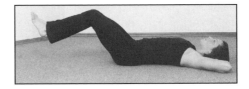

Correct posture for strengthening abdominals

There are also many devices advertised for abdominal strengthening. Most work quite well but are not necessary. They commonly end up collecting dust.

Extension exercises against resistance has an unreasonably high risk. These are usually done sitting with a pad behind the upper back. A person leans back against resistance and repeats the movement. Many people do this hoping to strengthen their backs. I've seen this contribute to a lot of back injuries. If you must do this exercise, then keep the resistance to a minimum.

Back rotation exercises against resistance are best avoided. These are also done sitting with the hands/arms on handles or

Back rotation and extension exercises against resistance are best avoided.

arms/hands in a praying position and pads next to the forearms. The person then rotates (turns) the upper torso against resistance both right and left. Many people do this maneuver hoping to tighten their love handles. Unfortunately, the spine and discs don't like that movement when under resistance.

Neck rolling is best avoided all together. This is done mistakenly in hopes of stretching or loosening the neck joints and muscles. A person essentially draws a circle with the nose

Incorrect! Neck rolling should be avoided all together.

while moving the neck, combining all the lanes of motion the neck can make. Due to the complex nature of the many joints in the neck, this motion causes an unnatural grinding, ultimately producing premature wearing of the joint surfaces.

Below, you can see the six planes of movement for the neck. A preferred alternative for stretching the neck is to separate each motion, doing each deliberately.

Correct neck exercises, done deliberately and carefully

1) Forward bending (flexion)   2) Backward bending (extension)

3) Right tilting   4) Left tilting

5) Right turning   6) Left turning

Personality Counts

There are many different personality types I have encountered in my practice. One in particular I label the "executive/manager" type. Many actually were executives or managers, but really, they could be in any occupation. The characteristic that stood out in this group was that they tended to be very independent and self-directing. I'm not being critical; in fact, I realize that the world desperately needs these leader types. I suspect I'm a bit this way. Their gift of needing to be in control often interferes with their needed treatment. They usually want to find some way they can get better themselves or at least be able to claim some level of credit for their recovery. They felt intimidated if I plainly gave them orders of what to do or what not to do. Instead I learned to present them with options and let them choose, dropping some strong hints about what would be best. That way, they attained a level of control over their treatment. I never minded it and most of my patients loved it.

Does your personality contribute to your health problems? If so, it's kind of like doing a harmful exercise. You need to accept your personality, and then modify it in the direction you choose.

> True health is multi-faceted, meaning it involves a combination or balance of physical, mental, and spiritual well-being. Some people fall into the trap of focusing on just one facet. Harold, for example, a 70-year-old patient of mine, focused intensely on the physical aspect, specifically exercise.
>
> He'd tell me, "Circulation is everything, you know. That's why I exercise."

He'd complain about his legs hurting and his hips being uneven, but never accepted the true cause of his ailments—spinal misalignment—even when I would show him on the X-ray. He ignored my advice that he needed chiropractic treatment, going away disappointed that I didn't agree with him, that there must be some secret exercise he could do to make it all better.

Children

I am particularly concerned about the lack of physical fitness seen in children and young adults. In the United States, childhood obesity rates are alarming. I can't believe our government isn't promoting fitness more adamantly, for more fitness would shave billions of dollars off the nation's healthcare expenses.

> Be your kid's parent, before being his or her friend.
> —*Dorothy Stiemke*

Children need to start experiencing fun, physical activities as young as possible, both at school and at home, several times per week. They need to be guided because they are more vulnerable to injury as their bodies are developing. I recommend avoiding body-building-type exercises such as free weights or resistance exercises unless supervised by professional fitness personnel. But lots of general physical activities are essential. I have more to say about children's health in Chapter 10, "Raising Healthier Children."

> Take exercise seriously and make it a priority. Think of it more like regular, fun, safe physical activity. It does not have to be a burden. Parents need to set a good example for their children.

I've taken this issue very seriously with my own three children. Of course, they want to watch television and play all the electronic games as much as other kids. We do have those things in our house; the difference is that I require them to complete some exercise before using the electronics to compensate for the physical inactivity. My younger kids (7 and 9) must complete 20 pushups, 20 sit-ups (the safe kind), 20 squat thrusts, and 50 jumping jacks. My twelve-year-old son must complete twice that. They don't particularly like this, but I see them doing those activities now without my even asking. Physical activity has become expected and routine. They notice the difference between themselves and other, less active kids. You ought to see how solid, yet trim, my kids are!

Faster, faster!!! The Potisk kids: Andy (12), Emily (9) and Mike (7)

Strengthening

If you need to do specific, strengthening-type exercises, it's a sign you're lacking a variety of and participation in regular, fun, physical activity. The exception would be if you need to recover from some type of injury or are body building. The following maneuvers will assist you in strengthening and stabilizing commonly weak or injured areas. But remember, your goal first needs to be long-term health and maintenance with fun, regular physical activity.

Knees

Wear a boot or a strap-on ankle weight between 1 to 5 pounds as tolerable. Lie face down, starting with your legs straight, slowly bend your knee, lifting your ankle toward your buttock, and then let it back down. Repeat this until you feel muscle fatigue.

Second, while sitting, use your hands to hold up one leg under the thigh, slowly straighten your leg, and then let it back down again. Repeat until you feel fatigue. Always work both knees equally, whether simultaneously or individually.

 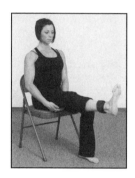

Shoulders

Stand perpendicular to a wall, with one shoulder about a foot away from the wall. Place your fingers of that side on the wall and slowly walk them up as high as tolerable, ultimately reaching directly above your head, as high as possible. It's okay to assist with the other hand. Repeat this with both shoulders. When you can fully raise your arm to its highest possible point, repeat with small amounts of weight, starting with one pound in each hand and working up to five pounds. Always work both shoulders evenly.

Ankles

Starting with a bare foot, from a sitting position on a chair, slowly rotate your foot as if drawing a circle with your big toe, your heel resting on the floor. Rotate your foot both clockwise and counterclockwise until feeling fatigue. When you're able to rotate twelve times, then begin adding progressively heavier foot wear, first a shoe and then a boot. Always work both ankles equally whether simultaneously or individually.

  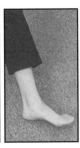 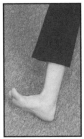 

Hands / Fingers

Place a medium thickness rubber band over the first knuckle of each digit including your thumb. Slowly expand your fingers and thumb, creating as large a circle as possible with the rubber band. Repeat until fatigue, always working both hands equally.

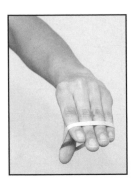 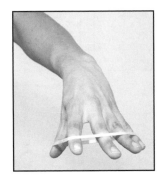

Wrists

Make a loose fist and slowly rotate your hand, making as large a circle as possible, both clockwise and counterclockwise until fatigue. When you can rotate at least twelve times, progressively add small amounts of weight beginning with one pound and gradually to five.

Neck

In a standing or sitting position, with your head in a neutral position, place your right palm on the right side of your head, pressing one into another, maintaining neutral head position. Only light pressure is needed holding progressively as tolerable to a count of twelve. Repeat in forward, backward, right and left planes of movement, using one or both hands.

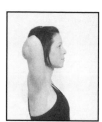 

Back

Starting with both hands and knees on the floor, slowly raise an opposite arm and leg up as high as possible, maintaining balance. Hold progressively for up to 30 seconds then repeating on the opposite sides.

Understand that all of these exercise maneuvers must be done cautiously and deliberately. Be aware of your limitations and expect to progress slowly. You may likely encounter some soreness or stiffness when starting any exercise routine. Remember, for true long-term wellness, you need to get regular, fun physical activity. If you can keep up the above routine several times per week, then congratulations, but I would highly recommend having a variety of activities to nix the boredom that discourages most people.

Chapter 3
Enjoying Eating
And doing it in ways that are good for you!

New Medicine, Silver Bullet!
Available for Weight Loss!

There they go again! The pharmaceutical industry, together with its scientists and researchers, have redefined, converted, and translated another human dilemma into something they can make a pill for. I'd bet many of you will fall head-over-heels for this one: they're now calling being overweight or fat "metabolic syndrome." That's right, according to them, your overweight or out-of-condition situation isn't so much due to your lack of activity or poor eating habits. Instead, you've got a disease and you need a pill. The drug manufacturers are lining up at the Food and Drug Administration and U.S. Patent Office to see who's going to be able to make the billions on this.

Yes, the drugs will produce weight loss, but a lot of side effects as well, like depression and leaky, runny stools. You'll be thinner but more unhappy. I repeat, many of you will fall for this, unable to resist the clever marketing, which I'm sure will highlight and portray thin, good-looking, happy people. Make some more room on your kitchen counter or wherever you keep your other prescriptions. Best of luck and may God help you. Now for the rest of you with some level of common sense, enlightenment, and minimal self control, I propose a better, safer, more sensible solution in this chapter.

Let's live instead of diet, but within reason. When it comes to eating, some self-control and better choices will go a long way toward getting and staying healthier. Making some good lifestyle changes will produce lifelong weight management.

It seems like every week there's a new weight loss plan on the market. I'd estimate less than one percent of those participating in weight-loss programs really benefit long term from any of them. Let's look at some more simple and effective ways of respecting one of God's most wonderful creations—your body.

I'm not about to tell you to turn vegetarian, eat all organic foods, throw out all the goodies in your cupboard, or even avoid all fast food joints, so relax and learn. Remember, just as in the other chapters on health and exercise, you'll find that I'm a realist. My goal is to teach you how to make healthier choices. I trust your intelligence when you're given the correct information. I'm not even into counting calories. It makes much more sense to me that if you're hungry you should eat, and when you're not hungry, you should not eat. It's what and how you eat that makes a difference.

I've watched thousands of my patients attempt diets. Some do lose weight on some of the many diets out there, only to gain it back. The answer lies in making the conscious decision that you will make healthier choices in how and what you eat for the rest of your life. I assure you that it can be enjoyable.

In many other countries, the lack of obesity is obvious. Some will argue that it's genetic, but studies have been done showing that's not often the case.

> **Trust yourself. You know more than you think you do.**
> —*Dr. Benjamin Spock*

For example, when foreigners come to the U.S., they almost all have substantial weight gain when they start eating like the rest of us. Also, as other countries become more "Americanized," such as more fast food establishments, and more processed, preserved foods in their supermarkets, the people rapidly develop more of the typical American physique: too large. We need to observe and learn from the foreign places with trim people. Aside from some areas of extreme poverty, these

LONGEVITY IN SELECT COUNTRIES	
Longevity (in years)	
Canada:	80.3
Japan:	81.4
France:	79.9
Australia:	80.6
Italy:	79.9
England:	78.7
United States:	78.0
Source: World Health Organization	

people are well nourished and content, so their thinness is not usually due to lack of food. Also, their general health and longevity has been shown to be well above our average in many countries.

It's a real blessing to have all of our huge grocery stores. I wouldn't want to live anywhere but in the U.S. However, the abundance here—without self-control—can hurt us. We've got easier access to food in the U.S. than almost anywhere else in the world, but it's not as fresh. We pay the price with harm to our health.

> In my world travels, I always intently watch how and what the locals are eating. In many places, Europe for example, it's obvious that meals are much more of a social experience than our "eating for necessity" culture. Europeans eat a lot more slowly, not only chewing slower but spending more time at the table. Where our typical supper may average 20 to 30 minutes, theirs seems to last twice that long or more. Go to a restaurant in Europe, and typically the table is yours for the evening.
>
> Although their grocery stores or markets are tiny compared to ours, on average, the food is fresher and of greater variety. In many cases, people go to the market every day, rather than building up vast stores in their freezers and refrigerators.
>
> When I ate like the locals in most countries I've visited, I usually felt full with less food and had more energy when following their example.

I'm not about to propose that we abandon all of our American ways of eating, but I've observed that by adding a few fresher servings per week, people can benefit immensely. That means filling your cart with a few more items from the produce department versus the frozen and canned varieties. Some nutrition gurus recommend eating "live" food. Eating this fresher produce with less cooking is what they mean. The smaller the interval between when something is picked to the time it goes into your mouth has benefits for you. Some nutritional experts say there is a "vital force" in these live foods that will add to your vitality. Scientists scoff at this because they haven't yet found a reliable, sound way to measure such a vital force, but that doesn't mean it isn't there.

Convenience often hampers benefit.

The less vegetables and fruits are cooked, the better. However, you need to make sure that your produce has been cleaned and washed thoroughly. Raw is better than steamed, which is better than boiled, which is better than fried. Do you cringe at the thought of raw vegetables? Some people seem to have an aversion for them. Sadly, they have lost or maybe have never

A man walks into the doctor's office. He has a cucumber up his nose, a carrot in his left ear, and a banana in his right ear.

"What's the matter with me?" he asks the doctor.

The doctor replies, "You're not eating properly!"

taken the time to recognize the unique flavor, even sweetness of each vegetable. If this sounds like you, you're really missing out on the important health benefit of eating fresh produce.

Have you ever really tasted things, or have you just been taking them for granted? Try this simple experiment to retrain your taste buds. Purchase some frozen carrots and some fresh carrots, tasting them side by side whether raw or steamed. Go a step further and compare the "corporate grown" carrots in your supermarket's produce section to some carrots purchased from your local farmer's market.

You can take another step up and compare some organically grown varieties from a natural food store or the market. When you carefully and slowly chew the carrot, notice the superior taste of the better product—you're closer to what eating really needs to be. The very best would be to try some fruits or veggies you've grown yourself, using mulch or manure as fertilizer, eaten directly after you picked and washed them. This applies to any food item. I can guarantee you there is a substantial difference. You'll forever crave the better choice.

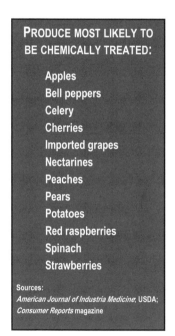

PRODUCE MOST LIKELY TO BE CHEMICALLY TREATED:

Apples
Bell peppers
Celery
Cherries
Imported grapes
Nectarines
Peaches
Pears
Potatoes
Red raspberries
Spinach
Strawberries

Sources:
American Journal of Industria Medicine, USDA; *Consumer Reports* magazine

Get it now? Herein lie four of the answers to healthier eating and realistic weight management: fresher food, grown organically, with less cooking, eaten more slowly. Now don't get scared off by thinking this is an all-or-nothing concept. Even a little healthier eating will do wonders for your well-being. Can you think of some simple alterations in your grocery purchases that could be improved on? At least consider substituting the "most chemically treated foods" with organic varieties. Okay, I bet some of you are thinking I'm a fanatic for organic food and vegetables. Let me state again that I'm a realist. I've observed that few people can eat perfectly all the time; I can't either. But look around at all the obesity, illness, and medication usage. Something has to change. My message here is that substantial benefit to your health can be had by making a few simple changes:

> **Slow down your eating. Take the time to savor the flavor of even the simplest foods. Rediscover this overlooked pleasure. Seek fresher foods.**

1. Eating more slowly and taking your time at meals

2. Seeking and eating fresher foods, at least a bit more than you have been

3. Eating smaller, more frequent meals

4. Never eat anything in the three hours prior to sleeping

With regard to eating smaller, more frequent meals, I want you to kind of "graze" through your day versus eating three larger meals. Nibble on small quantities of quality foods through your day. About five to eight small, healthy meals per day is about right. An example would be:

- Hard boiled egg and half an orange at 7 a.m.

- A handful of almonds and a carrot at 9:30 a.m.

- A bowl of soup and a slice of whole-grain bread with real butter at 12 noon

- A can of tuna and a green pepper at 2 p.m.

- 4 whole-wheat crackers and slice of cheese at 4 p.m.

- A large, fresh salad with grilled chicken and fruit smoothie at 6 p.m.

If your sweet tooth comes calling, it's OK to have a handful of raisins or two to three dates or figs. Are you a "choco-holic"? Consider carob as a great alternative.

Such grazing is much better for balanced blood sugar, energy levels, and digestion. It also results in lower calorie intake, less hunger, fewer cravings, and a smaller you!

The satisfaction gained from consciously doing these four simple things will result in fewer calories being eaten. Don't forget about the higher "vital force" you'll be taking in as well. If you can't take these better choices all the time, at least strive to do so once in a while. Eating fresher foods might cost a bit more in time and money, but it's another example of how investing in yourself is the best investment you can make. When viewed from the benefits of better health and well-being, I'm not so sure that choosing fresh, live foods really even costs more, because the savings in your healthcare expenses and your increased energy and productivity will offset any higher costs.

Also, ingesting items with higher vitamin and mineral content results in less food cravings. The higher the quality means the lower the quantity of food in-take, which translates into fewer calories. This quality is found in fresher, organically grown foods.

Fresh Foods / Gardening

I must encourage you to grow at least a little produce yourself. I've had a modest garden for years and have never considered it to be work. The joy of being outdoors, getting some physical activity, and the anticipation and excitement of watching something sprout and grow, far exceeds any burden involved with gardening. When I do encounter some people who complain, saying "Gardening is too hard," or "It's cheaper to go out and buy the stuff," or "I haven't a clue how to garden," I conclude that they take it too seriously and are misinformed.

I'm always amazed and sometimes envious of what can grow in containers like pots or even hanging baskets. What a great option for those who have limited space, live in apartments or condos, or don't want to get their hands or shoes soiled. You can even get wild and grow a tomato plant upside down from a hanging basket. Your neighbors will be impressed!

Minimally, you'll benefit by growing your own vegetables even if you dig up a 2-foot-by-2-foot patch of soil, scatter a $1.79 package of lettuce seeds and water it twice a week. Is that so hard? Yes, there will be some weeds, but big deal. Yanking those out is a good way to vent your frustrations! And don't expect everything to grow perfectly all the time; they won't, even for the best gardeners. Like anything else, you'll get better at it year after year.

Push yourself a little further and start composting. This means you'll be turning your food scraps into organic matter for your soil's benefit. It's as easy as keeping one of your gallon-sized plastic ice cream containers and filling it with food scraps like fruit peelings, egg shells, vegetable waste, and other leftovers. Leave out animal products like meat and cheese, for those will decompose differently and could smell. When the bucket's full, pour it out on a pile tucked away in a somewhat out-of-the-way place in your yard, or garden, turning the pile over with a shovel every few months. Add the fully decayed matter to your soil for the best tasting, most nutrient rich vegetables you can get. Don't hesitate to add your grass clippings, leaves, and pulled weeds (minus weed seeds) to your compost pile.

"Supermarkets are like mausoleums; the dead food lies in state. Once heat and pasteurization takes place, the enzymes are dead and the molecular structure of the food itself changes, making it hard to assimilate (absorb) even the few remaining nutrients."
—*from* The Gerson Miracle *by Stephen Kroschel*

Don't be afraid to try growing some fruit. They are easier than vegetables because most fruit plants are perennials, meaning they'll produce year after year. Don't let me hear any excuses about the burden of spraying to keep insects and diseases in check. For years, I've enjoyed growing apples, peaches, pears, raspberries, grapes, strawberries, and blackberries, without spraying anything.

Stop judging the produce you buy strictly by appearance. With at least some of your produce, tolerate some flaws, and question how it was grown or grow it yourself.

My secret weapon is tolerance. Yes, I tolerate the insects, birds, and diseases that devour some of my produce, and leave much of it spotted. We still end up with plenty. Many years, I have some to give away. My family and I don't mind eating around a few blemishes. The uneatable stuff goes in the mulch pile, which goes back under the plant or tree, and the cycle continues.

I've always felt that the quest for beautiful, spotless, well-formed fruits and vegetables is done at too great a price to our health and environment. That corporate-grown food has less taste, has been genetically modified, has a lower nutritional value, has less vital force, probably has residues of insecticides, herbicides, and artificial fertilizers and likely has been force-ripened. Yet, unfortunately, most people are looking for "the pretty ones" in fruits and vegetables.

The principle involved with having a healthy garden is similar to that of having a healthy body. Both we and plants don't necessarily catch diseases; they catch us when our resistance is low. An easily forgotten key to health for both plants and animals like us is strong resistance. Good quality soil, adequate water, and sunlight produce plants that are less susceptible to illness and insects. That principle should sound familiar to you from the previous chapters on real health and will guide you in making better choices for your own health.

In my travels to other countries, in addition to observing healthier eating habits, I've also noticed the prevalence of vegetable gardens. What little vacant space people have is usually planted with something they can eat. True, they do so mainly out of economic necessity, but having these gardens benefits their health in so many ways. Contrast that with our increasing reliance on convenient, corporate-grown food. When I've treated patients during my voluntary mission trips overseas, their healing ability seems superior to what I've observed here. I attribute this to their better eating habits, consumption of fresher foods, and increased activity levels. The percentage of dramatic recoveries was always higher and people often required less treatment.

If growing some of your own produce is completely out of the question, consider a membership in a local organic food co-op. For a fee, a local farmer will share fresh produce with you and the other members. You'll get a large basket or box each week. In most cases it will come with information on how to process it and cook it. You'll find a link to finding a local food co-op on our website, www.WholeHealthHealing.com.

I'd love to tell you never to eat at fast-food establishments, but I'd be wasting my breath. The convenience is just too tempting. I must admit I partake of them myself on occasion, especially with the pressures from my three young children. Consider, however, that there are some choices there that are better than others. Seek a fast food place with a salad bar or at least salad offerings. Some have baked potato options instead of French fries. Some offer grilled meats versus fried and coated. The best option in beverages is plain water. Don't be fooled by the fruit juices; most contain abundant sugar or worse. And I'm pleased to see some of these fast food places offering fruit options— take advantage of it.

> I once rented a video, a documentary about a guy who became very sick from frequenting one of the popular fast-food establishments. It's called *Supersize Me* and I'd highly recommend it. Watching with my wife and children, I hoped it would discourage their cravings for those empty calories.
>
> It worked for a while, but fast-food marketing is too overwhelming. I'm glad many of those places offer some better options like salad and fruit because we still go there on rare occasions. We minimize our visits to such places; but I frequently have to remind my family, "Remember when we saw...?"

The only franchised fast-food establishment I can wholeheartedly recommend is Subway®. My family and I frequent it and enjoy the numerous choices (Subway even offer wraps and sub sandwiches in a bowl without bread), the variety of fresh vegetables you can add to your sandwich (cucumbers, spinach, tomatoes, onions, peppers, and so on), as well as the great prices.

In that same vein, the only franchise restaurant I sincerely recommend is Noodles®. They have wonderful, healthy courses with an abundance of vegetables, high in fiber, low in fat, and very tasty… again, at great prices.

Moderation

I'm a true believer that you can eat just about anything you want, and most items won't hurt you, but I must include the adage, "Everything in moderation."

Just what is moderation? It really depends on what particular item you're asking about. "Moderation" will differ somewhat among individuals. The best-case scenario would be not to take in anything that's harmful to you. I realize, though, that some indulgence is generally unavoidable, and even the topic of what's harmful and what's not is very debatable. I certainly feel confident, though, in offering the following advice on what I would consider to be reasonable and moderate as far as indulging in the not-so-good-for-you stuff (assuming a single serving size and an average-sized person): no more than 3 soft drinks per week, 3 alcoholic beverages per week, one dessert item per day, 2 pats of butter per day, one fried food item per day, and 2 animal protein sources (meat, poultry, fish, eggs) per day.

Some other better choices to make include:

- baked or boiled versus fried foods,
- whole grain breads and pastries versus white,
- honey and other natural sweeteners versus white sugar, and lastly,
- snacks like fruit or nuts instead of candy and pastries.

I've got no problem with splurging on some of the lesser-quality food choices on occasion. It's inevitable, but let's not make a habit of it. When possible, compensate a poor food choice by adding something high in fiber to neutralize its ill effects and moving it through your system faster. For example, insist on fresh fruit and whole grain toast with fried eggs and bacon. Or how about a side salad with that cheeseburger? If you're having fried chicken, add a baked potato. Better yet, a sweet potato.

> I can't help but continue sharing more of my observations about food in foreign places. It's easy to observe how cultural traditions shape health. For example, look at the typical American breakfast and you'll usually see a lot of sugary, greasy things like bacon, sausage, fried eggs, pancakes, cereals, or doughnuts. Look at the typical foreign breakfast and you'll see fresh fruits, cheese, yogurt, nuts, grains, and vegetables. Yes, even vegetables for breakfast. In Poland, I was served fresh radishes; in Israel, fresh tomatoes; and in Italy, fresh cucumbers. All were accompanied by a good protein source like eggs. In France, I was served salad with an omelet. Who made up the unhealthy traditions of the American eating habits like the prevalence of fried, greasy, sugary, and oversized portions? And why do we continue to follow them?

Dependence on carbonated soft drinks is a real problem for many. Some people are truly addicted to these. The poor quality carbohydrates, artificial flavors and colors, and maybe even caffeine are real health robbers. The carbonation is equally bad because it leaches minerals from your body. Some people rationalize their use by picking ones with low calorie artificial sweeteners, but these beverages are still a problem, some say more so due to the potential long term negative health effects of these chemical compounds. Nothing beats clean, plain water. If you crave more flavor, consider water with a slice of lemon or lime. Most restaurants would be happy to accommodate that request.

Always leave the table a little hungry.
—*Arnold Schwartzenegger*

Be wary of emotional eating. An example would be nibbling because you're anxious, nervous, or worried. First of all, learn to recognize this habit, and then substitute the eating with a less harmful activity. Some good emotional satisfiers are talking, reading, exercising, and planning.

Another emotional eating scenario would be being afraid to say "no" when food is offered at social events. Here you must stand your ground and take control. Anyone offended by your polite refusal is not worth socializing with. My favorite polite refusal is, "Thank you, it looks good, but no. I'm feeling full and I'm following a health program." What a great way to start a conversation and share your enlightenment about real health!

Lastly, some people eat or don't eat to deliberately hurt themselves. Don't hesitate to seek professional counseling on these issues.

Your intake of restaurant food is something to monitor closely. There are exceptions but most commercially prepared food is set before you with one goal in mind: to make you want to eat more and come back again. Unfortunately, to please your palate, they'll go to any means possible. That means that those sweet vegetables and savory meats you're so impressed with probably have had sugar added during the cooking process, and possibly more things like MSG (monosodium glutamate), an artificial flavor enhancer. And that irresistible salad dressing probably has unhealthy oils in it.

To increase your perceived value of the meal, the common procedure is to provide huge portions, and they keep getting bigger. Those child-sized meals you see at fast food shops were the standard adult size offered in the 1970s! To some extent, we can't blame the restaurants for being progressive businesses, but be aware that your well-being is among the least of their concerns.

Don't stop going to restaurants; simply make wiser choices when possible. For example, you don't have to choose the large size if there is an option, and when you've been provided a huge portion, take some of it home. Sometimes one of those platefuls provides two, or even three, meals. It can be awfully hard to stop eating half way through a plate of

> **Be aware of traps that contribute to overeating and being unhealthy .**

food, so ask for the doggie bag right away, getting the other half of the food out of the way, eliminating the temptation. If you're with another person, consider splitting an order. So what if the restaurant charges a few bucks for the extra plate, you still come out way ahead. When you're first given the menu, scan it first for the healthiest choices and then make your compromises from that high point. Learn to quickly spot the baked and broiled choices, the salads, soups, and darker, whole grain breads. Always ask for your salad dressing on the side, and remember you don't have to use it all!

Cleansing

Have you ever considered thoroughly cleansing yourself on the inside? It's a great way to get back in control, especially if you've been misbehaving with food.

Internal cleansing, also known as "detoxing," can be done in several ways. The benefits can include more energy, stronger immunity, improved concentration, and even reduced arthritic pains. Even though I eat quite healthfully, I still do an internal cleansing at least once yearly as a preventive measure.

A mild, simple internal cleansing would be starting your day drinking a warm cup of water, adding a teaspoon of lemon juice. "How often?" you might ask. Drinking the lemon juice/warm water mixture for two weeks will usually produce noticeable differences, like less abdominal bloating and more energy. If you want to get serious about keeping your internal digestive tract cleansed, make drinking warm lemon water in the morning a daily habit for the rest of your life.

> Cleanse yourself internally on a regular basis.

Another, somewhat more thorough, internal cleanse would be through fasting. What would happen if you just stopped eating for a short time? I've done it several times and find a lot of benefit and minimal discomfort. I'd recommend no less than one day and no more than three. The hunger pangs quickly leave after skipping the first meal or two.

Always, always drink abundant water during any cleanse: at least one cup of water every two hours. Some people report short-term headaches or abdominal discomfort as their bodies eliminate accumulated toxins. These are harmless and quite common when cleansing. If you're on medications or have a high-risk health condition like diabetes, consult your doctor first before any fasting, detox, or internal cleansing. Don't expect understanding or acceptance about cleansing from your medical professional, as such concepts are completely foreign to most of them; but do demand cooperation. Chapter 7, "Talking To Your Doctor," will help you communicate your needs.

Going a step further for a more thorough cleanse, there are many advertisements for cleansing products that involve making teas or using powders and capsules. In my office, I've consistently recommended two products: Ultraclear® powder from Nutrition Dynamics and ChiroKlenz® Tea. Both are available on our website, www.wholehealth-healing.com.

Over the years, I've observed that many people with addictions to prescription medications, recreational drugs, smoking, and alcohol never truly recover unless they follow a thorough internal cleansing. This is an often overlooked step. Toxic substances are often trapped and hidden in fat cells, the liver, the digestive tract, and other body tissues. A properly trained holistic professional can guide those in need of a thorough cleansing.

Are you one who feels good, eats well, and has good body composition? Do you think there's no need to do an internal cleanse? Think again! Everybody has some level of toxic accumulation. Some of it comes from the pollution in the environment around us. I do an internal cleansing at least once a year as a health maintenance / prevention measure. You should, too, regardless of your lack of symptoms.

FOODS TO INCLUDE AND EXCLUDE FOR INFLAMMATION CONTROL

	Foods to Include	Foods to Exclude
Fruits	Unsweetened fresh, frozen, water-packed or canned; unsweetened fruit juices except orange	Oranges
Vegetables	All fresh, raw, steamed, sautéed, juiced or roasted vegetables	Corn, creamed vegetables
Starch (non-gluten) / Bread / Cereal	Brown rice, oats, millet, quinoa, amaranth, teff, tapioca, buckwheat, and produces made from these and rice, potato flour, or arrowroot	Wheat, corn, barley, spelt, karnut, rye (be sure to check all packaged and processed food labels for these grains)
Legumes	All beans (except soy), peas, lentils	Soybeans, tofu, tempeh, soy milk, other soy foods
Nuts and Seeds	Almonds, cashews, walnuts; sesame (tahini), sunflower, pumpkin seeds; and butters made from these	Peanuts, peanut butter
Meat, Fish and Eggs	All canned or fresh fish, chicken, turkey, wild game, lamb	Beef, pork, cold cuts, frankfurters, sausage, canned meats, eggs, shellfish
Dairy Products & Milk Substitutes	Milk substitutes, such as rice milk, almond milk, oat milk, coconut milk, other nut milks	Cream, yogurt, butter, ice cream, frozen yogurt, non-dairy creamers, margarine
Fats	Cold-expeller-pressed olive, flaxseed, canola, safflower, sunflower, sesame, walnut, pumpkin, almond	Shortening, processed (hydrogenated) oils, mayonnaise, spreads
Beverages	Filtered or distilled water, herbal tea, seltzer, or mineral water	Soda pop or soft drinks, alcoholic beverages, coffee, tea, other caffeinated beverages
Spices and Condiments	All spices unless excluded, e.g., cinnamon, cumin, dill, garlic, ginger, carob, oregano, parsley, rosemary, tarragon, thyme, turmeric, vinegar	Chocolate, ketchup, mustard, pickle relish, chutney, soy sauce, barbecue sauce (be sure to read condiment labels carefully)
Sweeteners	Brown rice syrup, fruit sweetener, blackstrap molasses, stevia, agave	White or brown refined sugar, honey, maple syrup, corn syrup, high-fructose corn syrup; desserts made with these sweeteners; candy; all artificial sweeteners

Many of my patients have gone through colonoscopy procedures. I've frequently heard many report that they benefited from the bowel-cleansing procedure required before the test. For example, these people frequently experience a lessening of musculoskeletal pains, and get a burst of energy. They soon lose the benefits if they return to their old habits. This is a good example of how everyone can benefit from internal cleansing.

Food Recommendations

I'd highly recommend some helpful, inexpensive additions to the typical American diet like olive oil, roasted nuts (especially almonds and walnuts), oily fish (especially tuna, trout, salmon, and sardines), and flax. These are high in Omega 3 and other natural, anti-inflammatory compounds. You'll sometimes see or hear them referred to as "essential oils." Many common health conditions, such as arthritis and cardiovascular disease, are inflammatory. These are on the rise and may be at least partially due to worsening eating habits and lack of essential oils. For even more anti-inflammatory strategy, use real butter (although sparingly), eat eggs at least three times weekly, eat oatmeal twice weekly, and minimize white sugar and white flour products. See the chart on the previous page for details on foods to include or exclude for inflammation control.

Learn also that there are "good" carbohydrates and "bad" ones. They are rated by something called their "glycemic index." Their rating on the index (see table on following page) indicates the level of difficulty the body has in utilizing the energy in the food. Seek to choose carbohydrates that have a low glycemic index, as these foods are converted to energy more easily and are used more beneficially by our bodies (see table on page 82).

THE GLYCEMIC INDEX OF SOME COMMON FOODS

Food	Glycemic Index (relative to glucose)	Glycemic Load	Food	Glycemic Index (relative to glucose)	Glycemic Load
Glucose, 2.5 tsp.	100	10	White rice, 1/2 c	43	15
Potato, Russet, baked, 3/4 c	85	26	Banana, under-ripe	42	11
White bread, 1 slice	70	10	Apple, 1 whole	40	6
Sucrose, 1.5 tsp	68	7	Sweet corn, 1/2 c	40	13
Rye bread (light), 1 slice	65	10	Yam, 3/4 c	37	13
100% whole grain bread, 1 slice	62	9	Brown rice, 1/2 c	33	11
Sweet potato, 3/4 c	61	17	Milk, skim, 8 oz.	32	4
Potato, new, boiled, 3/4 c	57	12	Cracked wheat, 1/2 c	32	8
Pita bread (white), 1/2 of 6.5-inch pita	57	10	Meal replacement bars / shakes	31	6
Corn flakes, 1/2 c	53	14	Milk, whole, 8 oz.	27	3
Banana, ripe	51	13	Pearl barley, 1/2 cup	25	8
Orange juice, 8 oz.	50	13	Lentils, 1/2 c	21	3
Oatmeal, 1/2 c	50	8	Kidney beans, 1/2 c	21	7
Green peas, frozen, 1/2 c	48	3	Fructose, 2.5 tsp.	19	2
Spaghetti, 1.25 c	44	20	Soybeans, 1/2 c	12	1

Let medicine be your food and
food be your medicine.
—*Hippocrates*

Vitamins and Mineral Supplements

Do I recommend vitamin and mineral supplements? Absolutely! But beware that, due to lack of regulation, there are a lot of poor quality products out there. Make sure the brand you choose to utilize is listed on the GMP (Good Manufacturing Practices) list, available on-line at www.naturalproductsassoc.org. GMP certification means the supplements are of superior quality (pharmaceutical grade) and independently assayed (this means they are tested by independent reliable labs to ensure that what's on the label matches what's in the bottle). For specific needs, please refer to the Vitamins and Minerals List in the Resource section at the back of this book.

Do you have any fears of taking vitamin/mineral supplements? The recent Annual Report of the American Association of Poison Control Centers stated: **"No Deaths from Vitamin/Mineral Supplements."** *I suspect the drug manufacturers are envious!*

There are numerous methods available to specifically determine just what vitamins or mineral supplements a person needs. These include hair analysis, blood analysis, muscle reflex testing, and saliva analysis.

In reality, if a person eats perfectly, then there is no need for any supplementation. As discussed throughout this chapter, however, perfect eating is difficult in today's culture and society. If you can eat a well-balanced diet of fresh, nutrient-rich organic food on a regular basis, keep it up! Most of us will manage to at least modify our eating with the earlier suggestions and therefore will need supplements.

Through my training and certification as a nutritional counselor, and from monitoring thousands of patients over the past two-plus decades, I've concluded that the best analysis for nutritional supplement needs is using a symptom survey. This is a questionnaire completed by a patient. Each answer has a score, which is then tabulated and graphed. The graph then indicates which body systems—cardiovascular, nervous, immune, for example—are weak. Supplements are then recommended accordingly. This is the least expensive, most accurate analysis to determine just what to take for what symptoms. You can find a symptom survey on our website at ww.wholehealthhealing.com.

If a person has no symptoms and is looking for prevention, I recommend following as many of the eating modifications found in this chapter as possible, and taking both an organic, high-quality multivitamin/mineral supplement, and a high-quality Omega 3/6 complex daily. Recommended brands are available on my website.

An excellent, easy, reasonably priced way to add more trace minerals to your diet is to replace regular table salt with sea salt. Trace minerals are tiny amounts of minerals that your body needs like selenium, chromium, and manganese. These are difficult to obtain in the typical American diet. Utilizing sea salt is an excellent way to get them. It can be found in any heath food store or organic grocery section. Sea salt has a slight bitter taste but after using it a few days, you'll never know the difference. Don't even bother telling your family you made the switch; they probably won't notice the taste difference.

I hear people say they've tried everything to lose weight but either get nowhere or quickly reach a plateau. Most of them simply need to get back to the basics as described in this chapter. Being overweight or underweight is better evaluated in terms of body composition, in other words, what is your body fat percentage. This is best measured with an impedance analyzer, which is a device that sends a small electric current through your body and registers the resistance of that signal. The National Institutes of Health indicates that a healthy fat percentage for females is 20 to 25 percent and for males is 10 to 15 percent.

Consider also the possibility of one or more hidden food allergies as a source of weight issues. You can read more about hidden food allergies in Chapter 6, "Help for Your Ailments."

If you eat out more than two meals per week, buy strictly packaged, commercially grown food, never grow anything yourself, use sugar substitutes, drink soft drinks or juices more than once per day, drink more than one serving of alcohol per day, don't have several servings of vegetables per day, use white flour or sugar in your cooking, and aren't consistently active—don't even talk to me about your weight problem.

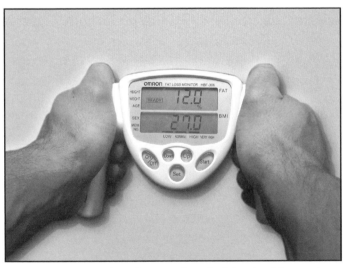

Impedance analyzer to determine fat percentage

Make your eating habits a deliberate process of carefully selecting the best quality, with lots of variety, eaten slowly, and enjoyed thoroughly! *Bon appetit!*

Weight Loss and Eating Tips

- Eat smaller quantities and more often
- Eat fresher foods
- Eat organic grown varieties
- Eat slower
- Don't drink more than a few sips while eating
- Start a garden
- Eat more variety
- Add more fresh herbs and spices

Please also refer to "Herbs: Benefits and Potential Problems" in the Resource section at the back of this book.

My Favorite Recipes

Broccoli and Walnut Stir-Fry

2 tablespoons sesame oil

½ cup walnut pieces or halves

4 cups broccoli florets

1-2 tablespoon(s) soy sauce

1 dried hot chili pepper (optional)

In a large skillet heat sesame oil over high heat. When hot, add walnut pieces and sauté for one minute. Add broccoli florets and cook over medium heat about 4 minutes, tossing frequently. Add soy sauce and cook another 30 seconds, stirring. To make it more spicy, add the hot chili pepper before the walnuts.

Pear/Gorgonzola Cheese Salad

Carefully remove cores from 2 very ripe, juicy pears. Carefully cut them into ½-inch cubes, leaving skin on. Cut approximately 1 cup of ½-inch cubes of Gorgonzola cheese. Combine cubed pears and cheese with fresh salad greens in a medium-sized salad bowl. Sprinkle with a dash of freshly ground pepper. Toss carefully and serve. Needs no other dressing!

Asparagus on the Grill

Obtain the freshest possible, full-length asparagus spears. Lightly brush or toss in extra virgin olive oil. Sprinkle lightly with coarse sea salt. Carefully place asparagus spears on very hot grill. Turn spears frequently to char, but avoid burning. Total cooking time on grill 2 to 4 minutes.

Sweet Potato "French Fries"

Gently wash whole, medium-sized sweet potatoes. Cut ½ inch off both ends. Quarter and then slice sweet potatoes into wedges approximately ⅛ to ¼ inch thick. Brush or toss lightly in extra virgin olive oil. Sprinkle lightly with coarse sea salt. Place wedges on non-stick cookie sheet. Bake until golden brown at 425°F, approximately 15 minutes.

Tomato-Feta Breakfast Burritos

1 cup halved grape tomatoes
1 cup diced or crumbled Feta cheese
½ cup chopped onion
4 eggs
¼ teaspoon sea salt
⅛ teaspoon ground pepper

Scramble the eggs with salt, pepper, and onion. Turn off heat and carefully toss eggs, adding the tomatoes and Feta cheese. Chunks of Feta cheese should remain whole but well-mixed in eggs. In a separate skillet, warm corn or flower tortilla shells slightly on both sides. Place 3 tablespoons of egg/tomato/Feta mix on tortilla shell and carefully fold and roll to form a burrito. Serve with fresh-cut fruit bowl.

Heavenly Healthy Toast

Spread almond butter on slice of whole-wheat toast. Sprinkle lightly with either wheat germ or ground flax. Cover with 4 to 6 banana slices. Drizzle with slight amount of honey.

Stir-Fried Beef With Vegetables Over Noodles

Heat water to a boil and cook whole-wheat pasta with a pinch of sea salt. Strain and set on side. Slice sirloin steak into very thin strips (about one-eighth-inch thick) and stir fry in a skillet with 1 tablespoon olive oil, 1 teaspoon diced garlic, and a pinch of sea salt and pepper. Remove from pan when cooked and set on side.

Add sliced fresh vegetables to pan with additional tablespoon olive oil and stir fry until cooked yet firm. I suggest using zucchini, summer squash, onions, green, red, or yellow peppers, carrots, and cherry tomatoes (added last). Return meat to the pan and toss lightly with the vegetables while slowly adding Italian dressing to desired taste.

Serve over hot pasta. Dress with grated Parmesan cheese.

Healing Salad

1 head of any organically grown, dark green lettuce

1 cup unsalted, shelled walnuts

¼ cup slivered, unsalted almonds

4 tablespoons ground flax seeds

8 tablespoons extra virgin, cold-pressed olive oil

1 teaspoon sea salt

½ teaspoon pepper

1 lemon to be squeezed or 4 tablespoons lemon juice

1 cup cooked or canned kidney beans

1 cup halved organic grape tomatoes

Chop lettuce after washing and place in large bowl. Add all other ingredients except ground flax. Toss thoroughly. Divide into four servings. Sprinkle 1 tablespoon of flax seeds on each serving. Needs no other dressing.

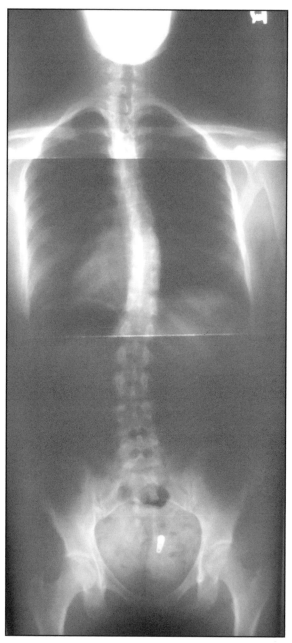

The full-spine X-ray. A foolproof posture evaluation. Notice the unlevel hips, uncentered head, and curved spine of this 32-year-old male.

Chapter 4
Your Posture

How to check it, improve it,
and how it influences your health

Stand up straight!

Sit up! Don't slouch!

Shoulders back!

Suck in your gut!

Do you feel guilty when you read those words? Not happy with your posture? You're not alone. Most people are as sensitive about their posture as any other physical attribute. The next time somebody's pleasant appearance catches your eye, take a closer look at his or her posture. You'll notice that part of the appeal is likely that the person's head is more directly above the torso, the back is relatively flat, the shoulders are level with each other, and the most forward part of the person's front side are the toes, not the belt buckle.

A balanced and erect physical stature makes up as much a part of beauty as hair, eyes, build, and skin tone. Also, I've observed it being a vital, but often forgotten, component of real health and wellness. And the improper way beds and chairs are made, there's a lot working against our efforts.

Posture is an important component of health and wellness. Bad posture can be improved.

In the first few years of my practice, I had time to offer classes on a variety of topics such as headaches, exercise, weight loss, sports injuries, and so on. I'd talk for about an hour, explaining the details of the topic and demonstrating some self-help methods. Out of all the topics, I consistently found that posture was the most popular, attracting the most interest.

Back in Chapter 1, "What is *Real* Health?," we discussed what real health really is. One important real health concept is that it has little to do with how you feel.

It's a similar story with posture. You can't look completely great and have bad posture; it has to be part of the total package. Can you feel good and have bad posture? Yes, but the bad posture is a sign of trouble to come because your posture is a symptom indicator of structural imbalance, and you'll know how very important structural balance is when you read Chapter 5, "Structure-Based Healthcare."

Getting worried? Let me put you at ease by telling you that there are some excellent and not-too-difficult things you can do to improve your posture. The even better news is that by doing something about it, you'll usually benefit by having fewer pains, more energy, more confidence, and some research indicates, you may likely live longer as a result.

My first piece of advice to you is this: don't wait. The older you get, the more difficult it becomes to change your posture and the more limited the changes become. More good news here though. In my practice, treating thousands of patients, I've yet to see anyone who can't get some improvement in his or her posture, even those many patients I've seen in their 80s, 90s, and beyond. Some improvements are dramatic, some are minuscule, but improvements can always be made. And even the little improvements prove vital.

I know, I know, some of you might say, "This is the way I was born." Or, "This is the way God made me." Or "It's genetic." Or "Nobody's perfect." To some extent they are correct. But don't use those as excuses to do nothing. All cases of deformities from birth and genetics have been accelerated and aggravated by accumulated stress, injuries, and postural habits. They can all be improved.

Here's how to check yourself. Find a wall or door and turn your back to it. In a relaxed state, slowly walk backward with baby steps until you just start to feel a part of you touch. In the **ideal situation**, the back of your head, the middle of your back, your butt, and your heels should all touch simultaneously. In very overweight

Ideal posture

people, the butt may very likely protrude enough to nullify this general self-evaluation. In those cases, the back of the head, middle back, and heels should be equidistant from the wall or door when the butt touches.

As you stand in this position, reach behind with your hand. You should be able to slide your hand behind your lower back just above your beltline. You should also be able to slide your hand behind your neck.

The most common disruptions seen in this test are primarily head-forward posture (back of head does not touch) and secondarily, sway back (upper back and heels touch but not butt, or there might be too much room when you slide your hand behind your back). Now be careful that you don't mislead yourself here by forcing yourself up against the door or wall and declaring that your posture is okay. This self-evaluation must be done in your

| Sway back / obese | Flatback | Head-forward posture |

relaxed, natural state. If you can force yourself into the desired position, that's a good indication that your posture can be greatly improved. However, don't panic if no matter how hard you try to get all those parts to touch, you fail. There's still potential for corrections.

Next, stand in front of a full-length mirror, again in a relaxed state. Take a close look at the level of your ears, shoulders, and hips. Ideally they should be level. Most people (who have not been addressing the structural aspects of their health) will have distortions here, such as a high ear, low shoulder, or high hip. They may be off a quarter inch or several inches. You might see a combination that crisscrosses like right high ear, left high shoulder, and right high hip. Be careful here again. It's so easy to come up with excuses about this.

 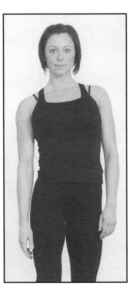 

Level posture   High left shoulder   High right shoulder

Let me ask you: If the causes of the distortions are strictly genetics, or if it's okay to have these distortions, then why do I see them resolve or at least improve with some effort? Some people might even declare that they have scoliosis (curvature of the spine), but even in most scoliosis cases, if properly treated with structural balance methods, the shoulders, ears, and hips should be fairly level.

Most causes of postural distortions are either locked structural imbalances or the accumulated effects of poor postural habits. Does your occupation contribute to your posture? You bet it does. A person who does work that involves repetitively leaning forward will have a permanent slight, or more evident, forward bend if precautions aren't taken. Another common example is seen in those who spend a lot of time sitting in front of a computer. They frequently exhibit head-forward posture. In the case of poor postural habits, the accumulated effects can usually be corrected or at least improved, but a permanent change only occurs when the source is identified and altered.

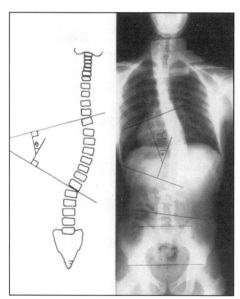

Scoliosis with level hips and shoulders.

Head-forward Posture

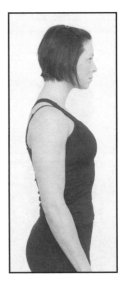

Head-forward posture is the most common of all distortions and is getting even more popular as a result of sedentary lifestyles and desk jobs like computer work. It essentially means that the head is not situated in its rightful position directly above the rest of the spine. Instead, the head is out in front of the spine. Sometimes this distortion is also referred to as "rounded shoulders."

Head-forward posture is on the increase.

The main health ramifications here are spinal chord pressure and pinching. Did you know that your brain does not stop at the base of your skull? No, it extends down to about the middle of your neck, where it is called the brain stem. (See diagram on page 288.) Common symptoms that accompany this posture and its nerve pressure are headaches, lightheadedness, dizziness, low energy, weak immunity, sinus problems, shoulder and arm pains, finger numbness, as well as neck pain and tightness. The developer of the chiropractic profession, Dr. B.J. Palmer, discovered and proclaimed that proper alignment of the neck

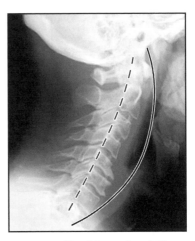

Head-forward neck X-ray.

Incorrect postures

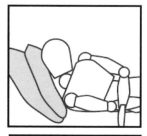

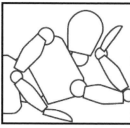

structure is of utmost importance to having good health.

Improving head-forward posture is not that difficult, but does take some time and patience. Start by self-analyzing your positional habits. Do you lie on the couch with your head propped up on the arm rest? Perhaps you watch television or read in this way. Done repetitively, this habit will lead to head-forward posture.

It's a similar story when you're in bed. Your head needs to be level with the rest of your body, not propped up. A general rule is this: when you're lying on your back, your direct line of sight should be the ceiling above you. The incorrect horizontal posture (head propped up) habit can be a difficult one to overcome because it can be very comfortable and convenient. Teenagers seem to have a natural tendency to do this. Quite simply, if you're going to watch TV or read, do it sitting.

Other detrimental positions are leaning back in a recliner, holding a phone to your ear with your shoulder, walking with your head down as if looking for dropped coins, and even leaning back in a chair without your rump up against the back.

I'd advise going a step farther and invest in a special pillow known as a cervical-support pillow. There are numerous varieties available but they all have a unique shape, usually thinner in the middle than along the edges. They are designed to allow your head to lie back, yet support, your neck.

My favorite, and the one I've seen helping most patients, is a pillow with a water-filled insert. There are several advantages here:

♦ The amount of water can be increased or decreased to suit your needs

♦ Water doesn't wear out or get compressed, and

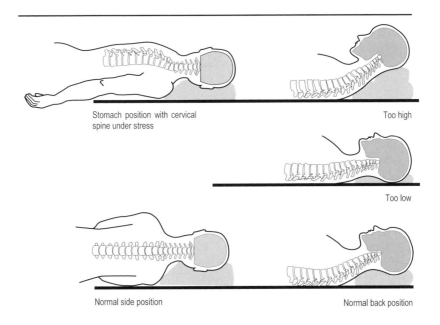

Stomach position with cervical spine under stress

Too high

Too low

Normal side position

Normal back position

Choosing the correct pillow can make a great difference in posture.

♦ The weight of your head displaces the water, pushing it to the places where your neck needs support.

Another common cause of head-forward posture is poor positioning at computers. It's easy to become fatigued and either slouch down in the chair or lean toward the view screen. Having a firm, supportive chair is one necessity here. Also, it's important to get up and move around every 30 minutes or so. Make sure your view screen is approximately at eye level and the keyboard is

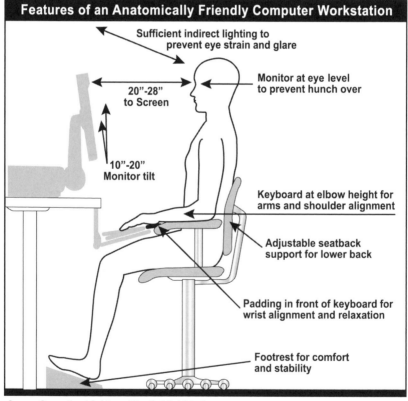

Features of an Anatomically Friendly Computer Workstation

Sufficient indirect lighting to prevent eye strain and glare

Monitor at eye level to prevent hunch over

20"-28" to Screen

10"-20" Monitor tilt

Keyboard at elbow height for arms and shoulder alignment

Adjustable seatback support for lower back

Padding in front of keyboard for wrist alignment and relaxation

Footrest for comfort and stability

Source: Occupational Safety and Health Administration

at a level whereby your forearms remain approximately parallel to the floor.

An excellent exercise to help remedy head-forward posture is called "cervical translation," shown below. It can be performed both sitting or standing. Starting with your head and neck in a relaxed neutral position, slowly draw your head back as far as it will go, hold for a count of ten and then relax. Repeat that five times, three times per day. Take note that when you draw your head back, your head should not tilt up or down. Your line of sight should remain straight ahead. Many people find this move difficult and not surprisingly, those muscles need to be rehabilitated and retrained. It normally takes at least several weeks of doing this consistently to produce permanent change. Don't forget that you must address the source, whether it be positional habits or injuries from a past trauma, and then make changes for the longest lasting results.

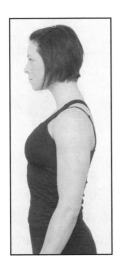 

Left, head-forward posture

Right, drawing head back, keeping head level. Do this five times, three times per day, holding the position 30 seconds each time.

Past traumas, such as sports injuries, whiplash, falls, or even a bump or blow to the head, contribute significantly to head forward posture. Chapter 5, "Structure-Based Healthcare" contains a description of subluxation, a misalignment of spinal bones, and how this is caused by stress and trauma. Subluxations are accompanied by several components like muscle spasms, locked or restricted joints, nerve irritation, and accelerated cartilage deterioration. All of those factors contribute to head-forward posture. When subluxations are present, no amount of exercises or change of positioning habits will fully resolve head-forward posture. Subluxations are only thoroughly treated with chiropractic adjustments.

In my practice, I notice that head-forward posture was more prevalent in females by about 2:1. I don't know why that is, but I specifically remember a young lady named Debbie who came to see me seeking help with severe headaches and a stiff neck. She told me the usual story, that she had tried everything, that it seemed to come on gradually. Her exam and X-rays also showed the usual story: classic head-forward posture and a lot of sub-

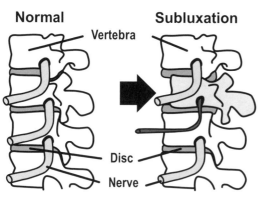

luxations. It took several weeks of chiropractic adjustments, but she finally recovered. When we talked about what might have initially caused the structural disturbances, she said she couldn't think of anything. A few more questions revealed that she had all the usual causes: lying on the couch, reading in bed, sleeping with a thick pillow, holding a phone between her ear and shoulder, and a desk job at a computer. Ladies, does this sound familiar?

The most detrimental effect of bad posture is its cumulative effect of causing vertebral subluxations. These misalignments of spinal bones produce pinching, compression, and irritation of the delicate nerves that exit between each of the 24 vertebrae. Overlooked by most professionals other than doctors of chiropractic, subluxations and their accompanying nerve pressures can produce a variety of dysfunctions in the human body. Left untreated, subluxations then lead to accelerated cartilage deterioration, muscle imbalance, weakness, and eventually disease.

Subluxations can only be found using a combination of diagnostics, and not just on X-rays. Most chiropractors use their hands and the sense of touch as their primary diagnostic tools. This hands-on feeling skill is called palpation, and it reveals locked or abnormal motion of joints, muscular contraction or spasm, soft tissue swelling, and asymmetry. Chiropractors are trained to combine information gained through palpation with a patient's symptoms and other examination findings to determine the locations of structural disturbances and nervous system blockages.

Hundreds of patients have come to see me with X-rays in hand, stating that their medical doctor said nothing was wrong with their spines. When I looked at the X-rays, sometimes the misaligned structure was so obvious, I wondered if anybody had really looked at them previously. Over the years, however, I came to realize several things: it takes special training to analyze X-rays for structural disturbances, the X-rays taken by medical professionals are good but are usually taken in a prone (lying-down) position, lessening the appearance of the misalignments, and lastly, sometimes the subluxations just don't show up on an X-ray and have to be detected by palpation.

How long does it take to improve posture? Length of time varies upon a number of factors like age, severity, patient commitment, and the actual source of the problem. I've seen some patients stand up straighter after one chiropractic adjustment, and I've seen others whose improvement took a full year of rehabilitative procedures. The general rule is that it takes about one month of effort for each year that the problems have existed.

Remember, nothing is going to change if the source of the disturbance isn't dealt with. For example, if a person develops a head-forward disturbance from repetitively sleeping with his or her head propped up abnormally, then goes through treatment or does corrective exercises, but doesn't change sleeping position, I wouldn't expect much long-term improvement.

Likewise, postural distortions won't improve even after finding and correcting the source unless specific treatment is provided. For example; if a person with a neck problem from repetitively holding a phone to his ear with his shoulder decides to stop doing that, and perhaps does some exercises, but doesn't get chiropractic adjustments to restore the alignment, not much improvement could be expected.

Be prepared for postural distortions as a long-term consequence of untreated stress and trauma, for example, from an auto accident injury. Just because you decide that you don't need anything other than rest or time to heal your wounds doesn't mean that your body will ignore these injuries. Something slow and detrimental, called "compensation," occurs in many such cases.

Look at this scenario for example: A person has a minor fender bender. She might feel a little stiff or maybe doesn't feel anything at all. She thinks she's fine, but the delicate spinal bones and joints have been traumatized and misaligned. Months or years go by and compensatory changes slowly accumulate in the form of accelerated deterioration of the cartilage between the spinal bones. The

Don't depend on X-rays alone to show postural distortions or structural misalignments.

body then tries to help itself by slowly and deliberately shifting its weight, movement or posture to minimize the damage (compensation); the person is completely oblivious to what's happening inside.

One day, years after the initial trauma, she bends over to reach for a book and whammo, her neck starts hurting. In her

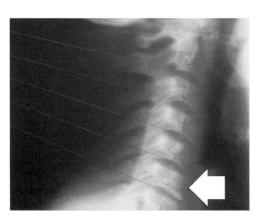

continued stubbornness, misinformed state, or both, she puts a heating pad on her sore neck, which in fact further inflames it. Maybe she takes some anti-inflammatory medication, which only covers the symptoms. Worse yet, she continues to

X-ray of neck showing permanent damage to joints from untreated injury.

wait to get help. Ultimately, a friend sees her continuously rubbing her neck and suggests visiting a chiropractor.

There, the X-ray reveals substantial deterioration of the joints in the neck, as well as head-forward posture that has developed as compensation. She has waited too long and will have a life-long problem.

I've seen thousands of similar situations. It's one of the reasons I had to write this book. When I encounter these chronic pain cases, I inquire what happened to the man or woman suffering from pain. Most don't remember because the trauma happened so long ago, but many eventually recall that fall, accident or other incident that they thought nothing of at the time. Sadly, by the time all this has transpired, the patient has permanent damage, and it's too late to pursue claims through insurance or the legal system.

Thankfully, chiropractic treatment can usually relieve and control the symptoms. Wouldn't it have been easier for everybody if the person would have just gotten his or her structure checked by a chiropractor immediately after the accident? For you eternal skeptics, might I suggest that you at least ask to be

A lady came to my office and said she had neck pain. She said it was from "sports injuries."

"What kind of sport: tennis, golf, volleyball?" I asked.

"No," she said, "My husband was a little too rough with me last night!"

shown where the damage to your structure is? We can easily point it out to you.

I've been to court several times to testify for my patients and their injuries. I see the games played by the critics and adversaries of holistic practitioners, especially insurance companies. They love to use the above-illustrated scenario and point it out as abuse of the insurance coverage; that minor accidents don't cause any structural disturbance, maybe just some sore muscles. But several engineers have investigated and found that a rear-end collision at a speed of just two miles per hour produces damage. Opponents will also say that the long-term compensatory changes like joint deterioration and postural changes are a normal process of aging. Well, it's true that body structure degrades through aging, but it normally occurs rather uniformly. When such degradation is concentrated in a small area—perhaps the base of the neck—it's because that area took a blow and was never treated properly. Believe me, insurance companies profit handsomely on your stubbornness, misinformation, and procrastination! Visit a chiropractor as soon as you can after any accident.

> **Stress or trauma to your body is not to be taken lightly!**

Swayback, Flatback, and Tilted Hips

After head-forward posture, the next most common postural disturbance is a disturbance of the lower back and hips. This can be broken down into three classifications:

1. Too much forward curvature (swayback),

2. Too little forward curvature (flatback), or

3. Unlevel hips (one side higher than the other).

Again, you can check yourself and members of your family using the self-analysis described earlier by standing against a wall or looking in a full-length mirror. As with postural disturbances in the upper body described above, there are several sources of these lower body posture problems.

Some common sources include:

♦ sitting without pushing your butt all the way back in a chair,

♦ sitting with crossed or folded legs,

| Swayback | Flatback | Unlevel hips |

♦   repetitive recliner use,

♦   poor quality shoes,

♦   a short leg, and

♦   a trauma or stressful injury to the lower spine
    and hips.

Sitting

Sitting in a habitually improper position, either with legs crossed or slouching, is a common source of poor posture. Mainly it causes misalignments of the lower spine and hips, locking their motion, contracting muscles, and unleveling the foundation of our frames.

Crossing your legs at the ankles is usually okay, for this doesn't twist or turn the legs enough to do much harm. But when you lift and place one knee over the other, or lift and place your ankle resting on the opposite knee, this produces very abnormal pressures and tensions to the structure of your lower body.

It's best, ultimately, to keep both feet on the floor when sitting. If you must cross your legs, then at least switch sides every few minutes to keep the tension and pressures somewhat balanced.

The closer you keep your butt to the back of the chair you're sitting in, the better. Our frames are not designed for sitting on our tailbones. We are much better off sitting on our pelvic bones.

Better yet, sit on the pelvic bones and have a support pillow that fills the normal gap behind the lumbar curve. The back of

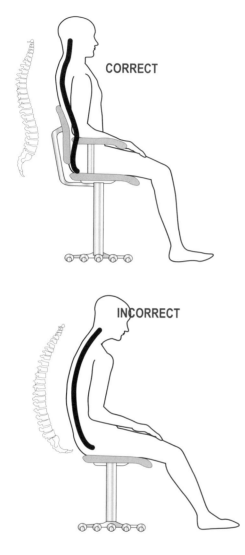

Correct and incorrect sitting positions

the chair should be tilted back slightly. About 115 degrees is good for most people.

Lying back in a reclining chair is certainly comfortable, but looking carefully at the effects on our structures, we see that it places us in a semi-fetal position. This position violates the normal, side-view curves of the spine, encouraging misalignment, abnormally lengthening supportive soft tissues, and promoting both the undesirable head-forward and flat-back posture. At the very least, limit your time in recliners, making sure it is not your primary sitting spot, and make sure you place a support pillow behind your lower back as mentioned above.

Short Leg

Having one leg shorter than the other is actually quite common, but usually not a source of postural disturbances. I've looked at thousands of X-rays and surmise that the majority of the population has one leg a little shorter than the other. The general rule is that if the difference is less than 6 mm (about 3/8 inch), then it's usually nothing to worry about and the body will compensate for the length difference quite well. If the difference is larger, abnormal joint wear, tilted posture, and pain may result.

The solution in the case of different leg lengths is to add a lift under the heel of the shorter leg but doing so only after careful analysis. The only foolproof way of analyzing a short leg is to draw a line across the top of the legs (femur heads) and compare that with a true horizontal line. This must be measured on an X-ray taken when the person is in a standing position.

It might be more complicated as well. For example, misalignment of the lower spine and pelvis can make it look like one leg is shorter than the other. All chiropractors are trained in careful analysis of different leg lengths. Be cautious of anybody measuring off of an X-ray taken in a non-standing position, measuring the legs with a tape measure, or worse yet, just making a visual estimate by looking at a person's posture, hips, or legs; these can all give false readings.

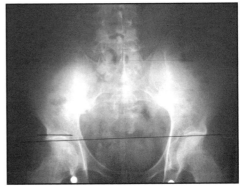

X-ray showing true short leg measurement

Shoes and Feet

Shoes and feet are definitely something to consider with regard to posture. The tailbone and pelvic bones are the foundation of our structure, but looking even lower, our feet are truly our base. Do you have a healthy arch in your foot? Perhaps you're even kind of proud of it? Congratulations, but without proper support that arch means nothing. Ignore the needed support and you're in for trouble. Take a look at the inside sole of your shoe. Now look at the sole of your bare foot. Do the contours match? Probably not. I've observed that the only surefire way to have a properly supportive shoe is to have custom-made inserts (orthotics) designed for your feet and to place them in any shoe you wear.

Over the years, I've encountered many people who have heel lifts placed incorrectly. A 58-year-old lady, who had had polio in her right leg as a child, came to me seeking help for her backaches. She had worn a ¾-inch lift in her right shoe for 44 years, and assumed that her right leg was shorter from the polio. I took an X-ray and was astonished to discover that in fact, her left leg was the shorter leg, and that the lift belonged under the opposite heel.

I showed the X-ray to several of my colleagues to verify my assessment, and they all agreed with me. She had caused her own backache with the poor choice of putting a lift under the wrong heel. When I showed this to her, she was shocked, angry, and sadly, not accepting this revelation. She declined my advice and recommendations; saying, "No, that can't be. I had polio in my right leg!" even though all the evidence was there in front of us on the X-ray.

Chalk up another one for the old adage: "Sometimes the truth hurts."

Make sure your orthotics are custom-made for your feet. Most chiropractors have this capability and will have you stand on a mold or electronic scanner and make impressions of your feet. Then the orthotic is made to match the impressions. These custom-made inserts cost between $200 and $400 but last several years. Usually having one pair is sufficient. Consider that you'll

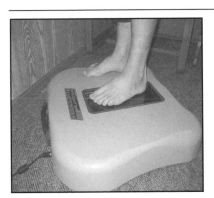
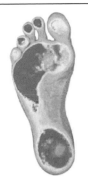
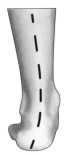

Orthotic scanner

Foot scan

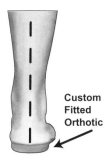

Custom Fitted Orthotic

Orthotic placed in shoe

also save money by not having to buy more expensive, supposedly supportive shoes, not to mention having better health.

If you're not blessed with a healthy arch or have other foot issues, custom-made inserts are even more necessary. Most corns, calluses, blisters, and even arthritic foot joints are the result of walking on feet that are not properly supported. Even a slight alteration of the way a foot moves when walking carries compensatory changes up to the ankle, knees, hips, and spine. The problems and complications multiply and intensify up the body.

> Sometimes I feel like a detective when searching for ultimate causes of the problems patients bring to me. It can get quite complicated. Terry, a 24-year-old secretary, came to me seeking help for chronic headaches. She had them daily, intensely, and told me the common story of having already gone through the mill of X-rays, MRIs, nerve testing, physical therapy, medication, and even relaxation therapy, all to no avail.
>
> The mystery intensified as she told me about her healthy habits of a regular exercise routine, good diet, ample rest, and even prayer. She was frustrated, as was everyone else who tried to help her. I was the last resort before she attempted having some nerves cut. I am known for helping these tough cases, and I did the opposite of what all the other doctors had done.
>
> They had been looking up, at her head and neck. I looked down! I saw that she was wearing what commonly makes a lot of business for doctors—high

heels! Wearing high heels frequently causes slack in the hamstrings. This results in a tipping of the pelvic bones, which causes a swaying forward of the low back. This in turn causes a head-forward posture, which causes misalignment of the top of the spine, which causes pressure on the spinal chord, which causes a short circuiting of the nerves to the muscles and blood vessels, which causes headaches. Whew!!

It took longer to write all that than it took to adjust her upper spine and get her off those high heels and onto orthotics. She's been fine ever since.

Posture is an important factor for real health and well-being. It's a silent troublemaker because you can ignore it with improper sitting, standing, or working habits, and you'll think all is well and then whammo, poor posture catches up with you. The trouble usually arrives in the form of misaligned body structure, particularly of the sensitive spinal alignment and its effect on the nervous system.

The next chapter, "Structure-Based Healthcare," informs you in more detail about the utmost importance of having balanced, aligned bones and joints, how to obtain this ideal alignment, and then how to maintain it for your well-being.

VERTEBRAL LEVELS		Nerve Root	INNERVATION	POSSIBLE SYMPTOMS
Cervical (7)	C1 C2 C3 C4 C5 C6 C7	C1 C2 C3 C4	Intracranial Blood Vessels, Eyes, Lacrimal Gland, Parotid Gland, Scalp, Base-of-Skull Neck Muscles, Diaphragm	Migraine Headaches, Headaches, Dizziness, Sinus Problems, Allergies, Head Colds, Fatigue, Vision Problems, Runny Nose, Sore Throat, Stiff Neck, Cough, Croup, Arm Pain, Hand and Finger Numbness or Tingling, Asthma, Heart Conditions, High Blood Pressure
		C5 C6 C7 C8	Neck Muscles, Shoulders, Elbows, Arms, Wrists, Hands, Fingers, Esophagus, Heart, Lungs, Chest	
Thoracic (12)	T1 T2 T3 T4 T5 T6 T7 T8 T9 T10 T11 T12	T1 T2 T3 T4	Arms, Esophagus, Heart, Lungs, Chest, Larynx, Trachea	Wrist, Hand and Finger Numbness or Pain, Middle Back Pain, Congestion, Difficulty Breathing, Asthma, High Blood Pressure, Heart Conditions, Bronchitis, Pneumonia, Gallbladder Conditions, Jaundice, Liver Conditions, Stomach Problems, Ulcers, Gastritis, Kidney Problems
		T5 T6 T7 T8 T9 T10	Gallbladder, Liver, Diaphragm, Stomach, Pancreas, Spleen, Kidneys, Appendix, Small Intestine, Adrenals	
		T11	Gallbladder, Liver, Small Intestine	
		T12	Colon, Uterus, Buttocks	
Lumbar (5)	L1 L2 L3 L4 L5	L1 L2 L3 L4 L5	Large Intestine, Buttocks, Groin, Reproductive Organs, Colon, Thighs, Knees, Legs, Feet	Constipation, Colitis, Diarrhea, Gas Pain, Irritable Bowel, Bladder Problems, Menstrual Problems, Low Back Pain, Pain or Numbness in Legs
Sacrum		S A C R A L	Buttocks, Reproductive Organs, Bladder, Prostate Gland, Legs, Ankles, Feet, Toes	Constipation, Diarrhea, Bladder Problems, Lower Back Pain, Pain or Numbness in Legs

Diagram showing the relationship between the spine and the organs.

Chapter 5
Structure-Based Healthcare
A forgotten, but important, priority and what it means for your well-being

I've heard the following question thousands of times in my 20-plus years of practice: "I eat healthy, take my prescriptions, I exercise, I take vitamins, so why am I still in pain or unhealthy?" There can be many answers to this question, but most commonly, the people asking have not addressed the *structural* integrity of their bodies. By structural integrity, I mean the *alignment* of bones and joints. It's a forgotten but important priority for your well-being. Structure is often the missing link!

This aspect of health—structural integrity—is so important that it comes innately to most cultures, unless it is suppressed, as in our American society. More about that suppression later.

Evidence of structural integrity's innate importance is supported in historical review. For example, documents existing from the time of the Greek philosopher Hippocrates, long before the birth of Christ, show drawings of crude traction devices used to align the body.

Early Native American drawings show images of spinal manipulations. Many foreign cultures have unlicensed practitioners called bonesetters. I've even heard patients sometimes say they feel like they literally need to be "pulled apart."

So why have you been left out of addressing this important and simple aspect of good health? It's because you've been influenced by biased sources such as the mass media, the medical/pharmaceutical industry, your health insurance, and even misinformed health educators, that's why.

Knock it off and start paying attention to who the advertisers are in the media you've trusted for so long. Unbiased reporting is a rarity. And stop being a victim of health practitioners who don't spell out all of the options available to you. And I mean all the options, not just the ones they or their profession can provide. And most certainly, accept that the recommendations or limitations of your health insurance are economically motivated. Every source of information will be somewhat biased,

> **The doctor of the future will give no medicine, but instead will interest his patients in the importance of *structural alignment*, nutrition, and the prevention of illness.**
> —*Thomas Edison*

based mainly on that source's training and experience. Bias seems to be a natural human trait. However, for your health, it's important to be aware of the selfish ambitions your information sources may have that can leave you out in the cold. Some would say, "Follow the money."

Examples of primitive structural alignment and manipulation

In this book and mainly this chapter, I, being a doctor of chiropractic, have done my best to overcome my bias and present information as I've observed it to be true. My intention is not to get more patients or to grow my practice, but truly to better inform you so you can make better healthcare choices.

> The media reported about a teenager in the southern U.S. who was plagued by the hiccups. The story was main headline news in 2005. She had several per minute, 24 hours a day, and this has been going on for months. The reporters said she has tried everything. I told my wife that I bet she hadn't tried chiropractic.

You see, in years past, Doctors of Chiropractic had reported several cases like hers that responded favorably to spinal adjusting. You'll understand how chiropractic can help this as you finish this chapter.

A few weeks later after reading about the young woman's plight, the same national news channels reported that she stopped hiccupping, never mentioning anything about her cure or what she might have done differently. Later, I heard on my local Christian radio news station that the hiccups stopped after she finally went to a chiropractor. That's certainly no surprise to me. I see this story as a perfect example of how most mainstream media seems to want to keep the public in the dark about holistic healthcare options, such as chiropractic.

What Can You Do?

Your body's structural integrity can be improved several ways such as yoga, postural awareness, chiropractic adjustments, massage, physical therapy, and osteopathic manipulation. Each of these fields has its own take and theory on just how their services can help. Suffice it to say they all strive to loosen, free, unlock and align the bones, joints, and muscles.

When I show my patients the disturbances in their body structure, such as on X-ray, they usually ask, "How did I get this way?" The structural integrity of these body parts is compromised or disturbed through the forces of stress and trauma. These forces can be sudden and strong as in auto collisions, sports injuries, over-lifting, falls, or even birth trauma. Equally

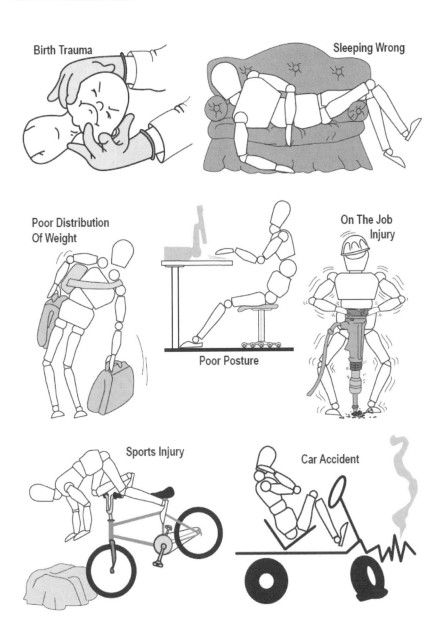

Birth Trauma

Sleeping Wrong

Poor Distribution Of Weight

Poor Posture

On The Job Injury

Sports Injury

Car Accident

Sources of structural disturbance include auto collisions, sports injuries, over-lifting, falls, birth trauma (mother and baby), anxiety, poor postural habits, repetitive motions, and toxic exposure.

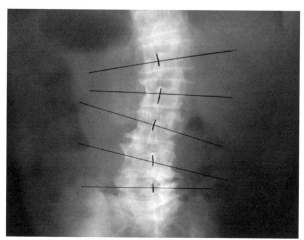

X-ray of crooked spine

common, the forces can come slowly and gradually, accumulating unsuspectingly through anxiety, poor postural habits, and repetitive motions. Sound familiar? That's you and me!

Have you experienced one or more of the sources of structural imbalance? Everybody has to some degree or another. Many people are misled into believing that, since structural disturbances are common, it's okay to ignore them. Adversaries of holistic health and those who feel economically threatened by holistic and vitalistic practitioners, love to use, "Oh, it can be said that every body is out of alignment," as a tactic to push the traditional treatment methods of medications and even surgeries, or at least to discourage people who choose to use more natural, hands-on treatment like chiropractic.

The consequences of leaving your body misaligned are devastating. An analogy I've often shared with my patients is this: you can drive your car quite far with the wheels unbalanced and the front end out of alignment (i.e., negative camber), maybe

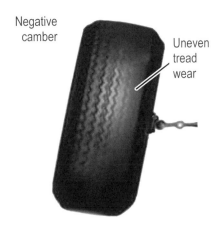

Negative camber

Uneven tread wear

being a bit irritated by the slight shaking of the steering wheel in the short term, but looking long term, you'll be facing high expenses and perhaps breakdowns because the tires, bearings, brakes, and other structural components are wearing out at an accelerated rate.

This concept also holds true for the structure of the human body. For example, most cases of deteriorating cartilage, like an arthritic hip or spinal disc, are due to that particular joint not meshing or gliding smoothly. I'm not talking about a complete dislocation (luxation), but rather a slight disturbance or misalignment of the normal movement (subluxation). That then leads to abnormal, uneven or restricted movement. The result is accelerated wearing of the joint surfaces or cartilage therein.

Image of worn-out spine

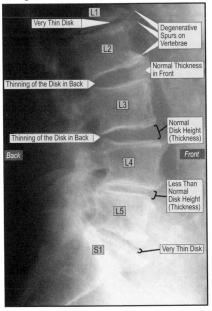

Yes, all joints gradually wear as a normal process of aging;

Don't think you're getting all the information you need about your heath from traditional sources? Question your provider's motivation and training. Gather all facts from several sources before making any decision concerning your health.

that's why most of us end up a few inches shorter later in life. That normal aging process of wear should occur quite evenly and uniformly throughout the body. This we have limited control over, although weight management, good posture, and regular stretching do help. But I'm referring to the devastating premature and accelerated aging that comes with a disturbed joint that grinds away its own cartilage. This is something that can be dealt with. It's what doctors like me, a doctor of chiropractic, can help patients with very effectively. And sadly, traditional medical care has little to offer other than expensive and risky joint replacement surgery.

A few years ago, a middle-aged lady named Nancy came to see me seeking help for the symptoms she was having from an automobile accident. Her case was a fairly standard rear-end collision: neck pain, headaches, tingling in arms, and difficulty sleeping scenario. She said she came to me reluctantly, not knowing where else to turn. She had tried every other treatment option like physical therapy, medication, and injections. I was her last resort, she said.

When I explained the simplicity and common sense behind the chiropractic treatment I suggested and offered, she was stunned. When she finally felt the relief she was seeking after her first chiropractic adjustments, she was delighted. When Nancy came to realize she should have taken this less invasive route first, but wasn't told about it and had suffered for months, she was angry, especially because she had been trained as a registered nurse and never heard chiropractic mentioned!

Self-Testing for Structural Misalignment

Following are some simple methods to test yourself or your family members for structural misalignment. A general indication is restricted or uneven movement. It is easy to self-administer this range-of-motion evaluation. As you perform these self-testing movements, pay close attention to evenness (symmetry) from one side to the other. Listen for popping or grinding noises, which are also indications that something is not lining up properly.

Signs of Misalignment

♦ Restricted movement when comparing one side to another

♦ Grinding, cracking, or clicking sounds when moving

♦ Pain and/or stiffness

♦ Swelling

♦ Weakness

♦ Hips, shoulders, or ears appearing unlevel

Start by sitting or standing in front of a mirror. Slowly tilt one ear toward your shoulder until you feel some resistance, keeping both shoulders level. In other words, don't tilt your whole body. As you look at yourself in the mirror, drawing an imaginary line from between your eyes, down across the tip of your nose, and to the center of your chin. This line should be at least 45 degrees to an imaginary line drawn across the top of your shoulders. Now repeat this exercise on the other side. Does your head tilt at least that amount? Is the movement equal on each side? If either answer is no, it's a general indicator that your neck is structurally imbalanced. The uneven movement is the stronger of the two indicators.

Now stand in front of a full-length mirror. Bend your entire upper torso to one side, keeping your hips level. You should be able to bend at least 30 degrees. Now bend to the opposite side. Once again, pay close attention to any difference from one side to the other.

Neck tilt in front of mirror (sitting or standing)

Body tilt in front of mirror

You can utilize this general simple testing method for range of motion and symmetry on most movable/jointed parts of the body such as wrists, elbows, shoulders, knees, and ankles.

Another way to see if your body is structurally aligned or misaligned is simple observation. Once again, stand in front of a full-length mirror. Look closely at the level of your ears, tops of your shoulders, and crests of your hips.

Most people will have some amount of unevenness between the two sides of their bodies. Even though it's common, it shouldn't be ignored, especially if it's accompanied by one or more of the other signs of body structure misalignment listed earlier. Rather, it ought to be evaluated by a properly trained professional with structural integrity training.

| Aligned body | Unlevel shoulders | Unlevel hips |

Why is structural alignment so important? Because the musculoskeletal structure of the body is its foundation and framework. As an analogy, think of a house. If the foundation and framework of a house are not level, all kinds of problems follow:

doors squeak or don't open and close properly, cracks appear in the plaster, floors slant and creak, the roof may leak, there might be openings that let unwanted critters in, and more! Technically, you could push a crooked house straight (treat the symptom), as they have been attempting to do with Italy's Tower of Pisa for years, but it won't stay that way unless you level the foundation (address the cause).

The famous "Leaning Tower of Pisa"

In a similar fashion, unbalanced body structure leads to a host of dysfunctions, including restricted circulation, not only of blood, but also of cerebrospinal fluid (the extremely important liquid that bathes the brain and spinal chord), constricted organs, stagnant lymphatic flow (another very important body fluid that helps fight illness), and, most importantly, pressure on nerve tissues like the brain stem and spinal chord, and the nerve roots that branch from it. I emphasize that the nerve tissues are most important for reasons I'll explain later, but suffice it to say for now, the nerve tissues make up the control center and wiring system of the body. Think Grand Central Station and the entire train track system of the country!

My specialty, chiropractic, has as its primary objective, treatment focused on changing body structure to release nerve pressure. Herein lies the secret to the tremendous success and high patient satisfaction with chiropractic. Our premise concerning the extreme importance of a free-flowing nervous system for optimum health and performance is unique, often overlooked, and frequently misunderstood. Chiropractors are not muscle, bone, or joint doctors. We are not back specialists or pain-relief professionals. We are nerve specialists.

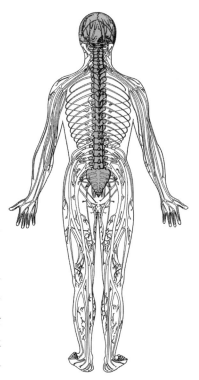

Nerve diagram

Fundamentally, chiropractic is an art, science, and philosophy focused on adjusting body structure, mainly the joints of the spine, to release nerve impulses for better internal communication. Kind of important and needed, don't you think?

Your nerves are like an electrical system. They carry mental impulses from your brain (generator) through your spinal chord (main cable) to all your organs and tissues via nerves (wires). Your nerves also carry signals from your organs and tissues back to your brain. It's a complete cycle (loop). Any disruption of that flow results in malfunction. Nerve signal flow or mental impulse flow is a major component of well-being, if not the life force itself.

In all my years of studying biology, health, nutrition, exercise, and human physiology, I've not seen any concept or principle more simple, true, and helpful to a human being than that!

Here are more reasons to start paying more attention to your nervous system and getting chiropractic treatment. What body system controls and coordinates all the other systems of the body? The nervous system. What system is the first identifiable

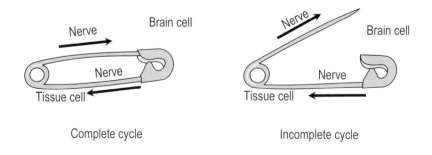

Complete cycle   Incomplete cycle

structure in a human embryo? The nervous system (neural streak or neural fold).

What system senses your environment and then adapts your body to it? The nervous system. Lastly, the function of what system is used to determine the legal definition of being alive versus being dead? The nervous system. In other words, science possesses machines that can keep your heart beating and your lungs breathing, but according to legal definition, you're not really alive unless electrical activity (nerve impulses) are detected in your nervous system. On the flip side, you might have stopped breathing or have no heartbeat, but you're not truly legally dead unless all electrical activity has ceased in your nervous system. That's what an EEG (electroencephalogram) is used for.

The nervous system—how obviously important for your health and wellness, yet frequently taken for granted or forgot-

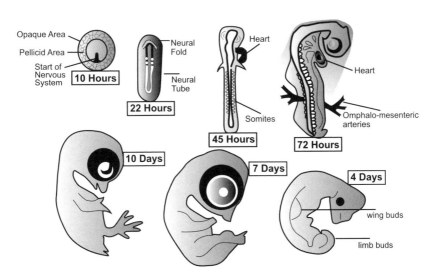

Neural fold in human embryo. Note its development within 22 hours of conception.

ten! The most important system and function of your body—unhindered flow of electrical impulses from our trillions of tissue cells to and from our brain—yet most people don't consider its

Consider the importance of a free-flowing nerve system for your ultimate well-being.

importance or that something can be done to improve and maintain it, except as a last resort or grasping at a final straw that "maybe something can be done," or "I've tried everything else." It makes sense to me that ensuring a free-flowing nervous system is the *first* thing that should be addressed in non-emergency situations concerning healthcare and preventive care. Does it make sense to you?

So where and how does the nervous system and its flow of life force get disrupted? It happens most commonly when body structure is imbalanced or out of alignment, particularly the structure of the spine. We chiropractors call this phenomenon *vertebral subluxation.*

If you take a closer look at the human spine and its intricacies, first notice its incredible engineering. It not only protects delicate nerve tissue, but also holds us upright and allows us movement. The spine's complexity leaves it vulnerable to any number of traumas and stresses. It's been said proof of God can be found in His creation, and the complexity of the human spine is a good example.

Notice particularly the close relationship to spinal alignment and the flow of nerve impulses or life force. There is enough room around the nerve tissue to allow for normal movement, but not enough to allow for both misalignment and normal movement. The most common interruption of internal commu-

Spine diagram

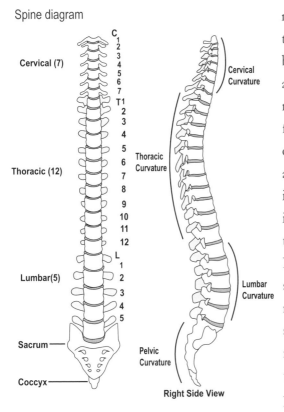

nication occurs when the vertebra (spinal bones) become misaligned subluxated), making the openings for the nerves smaller, constricting the nerve and interrupting or impeding the flow of impulses to and from the body and brain. New scientific research shows that the mechanisms of spinal subluxation are much more complicated than the simplistic explanation I give here, but the bottom line is:

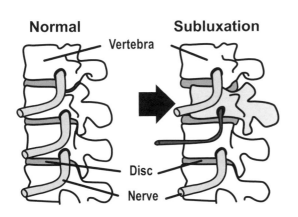

Structure affects function.

A young adult who struggled with school and had dropped out at a young age, came to my office seeking help for her headaches. An exam and X-ray revealed misalignment of her neck, which put pressure on the brain stem, a common cause of the headaches for which she was seeking my help.

I explained to her that she had a subluxation, treated her with an adjustment, and sent her off feeling better.

A few weeks later she came to me with a new problem and asked, "Doc, can you fix this by cracking my sub-sub-submarine again or whatever you called it?"

The Controversy

The concept of stress/trauma, structure/misalignment, and nervous system importance ultimately influencing health underlies the practice of chiropractic and makes it unique. The objective is a healthier you. The principle of structure affecting function is one of the simplest I know of. Unfortunately, it has been the target of constant attack by our adversaries and competitors since chiropractic was discovered and developed over a century ago.

Why the controversy? Well, imagine you were a medical doctor and had gone deep into debt with eight or more years of training. Suddenly, a patient suffering from headaches tells you that she would rather go to a chiropractor and get an adjustment for approximately $50.00, than go through thousands of dollars of diagnostic testing (X-rays, MRIs, blood tests, and urine samples). The doctor may resort to scare tactics, such as warning her of the possibil-

Insist that your doctor, no matter what kind you choose to see, cooperate with other professionals, even if there are opposing viewpoints.

ity that she might have something serious, perhaps a brain tumor. The patient, having had excellent results with chiropractic treatment previously, tells the doctor she wants to try the conservative, less invasive, drugless route first. The chiropractor she chooses examines her, determines that she likely will benefit from chiropractic care and provides treatment. If she is like most chiropractic cases, she responds well. Who then looks like the fool in this situation?

No, I'm not implying that the problem here is always about the money, or that all doctors are greedy. I'm sure it's sometimes, if not more often, lack of understanding, improper training, pride, and even market competition that are responsible for patients getting misled.

One might argue, "Well, what if it turned out that she did have a tumor?" Hidden pathologies like tumors are always a possibility, but they are rare and much more the

The pill-popping route?

exception than the rule. Keep in mind that properly trained and licensed holistic/vitalistic practitioners, like chiropractors, are thoroughly trained to refer patients they cannot help, or those they suspect might have problems like tumors. Also, in most cases, waiting a few days or even a few weeks to give natural healing a trial period, is not a harmful delay of medical treatment. If after a few treatments using the safer, more economical natural approach, the patient is not any better, then a referral to the more risky, more expensive diagnostic testing and treatment would be warranted.

Do you see the struggle here? How difficult it is for the two sides, holistic/vitalistic vs. traditional medical, to work together? The conflict described here has been occurring frequently at least since the chiropractic profession was founded over a century ago, and it's increasing as the economics of the healthcare marketplace tightens (higher insurance deductibles, higher co-pays, and other restrictions on what's covered and what's not) . One of the main reasons for this book is to help you, the consumer of healthcare services, make more informed decisions, utilizing the best that both sides of healthcare have to offer.

To those of you who think that, if it were you in the above scenario having frequent headaches, you'd want to go through medical testing first, especially because your health ("sickness") insurance would cover it, I say "Shame on you!" Your selfishness and irrational behavior has nearly bankrupted the entire healthcare economic system to a point where people can't afford to see a doctor if they don't have insurance, and worse yet, some can't even afford to have the health insurance.

> I've tried everything I know of in an attempt to communicate and connect with medical doctors. When building my practice, I wanted a network of other doctors to whom I could refer patients if they needed additional help. On one occasion, I called up a local doctor and invited him to my office for a tour. He gladly accepted and seemed impressed with me and my facility. He even invited me to set up a small chiropractic service in his own medical clinic.
>
> "Now I'm getting somewhere," I thought. Following through with his invitation, it soon became apparent that he and the other doctors in his office liked having my name on their sign, but didn't refer any patients for treatment! I soon had to shut the operation down.
>
> I was even more disappointed when I found out that years later, the doctor hurt his back, and instead of coming to me seeking chiropractic treatment, underwent two risky spine surgeries!

The same goes for any of you in the medical profession who have this same selfish, irrational behavior. I'm referring here to the concept of taking the more expensive options for your healthcare simply because somebody else (your insurer) is footing the bill. Also, consider the higher risks with medical care and even medical diagnostic tests. Just this morning, there was a front page article in my local newspaper describing the dangers of the high doses of X-rays from a CT-scan (Computerized Tomography, a very detailed X-ray using several times more radiation than a conventional X-ray). More radiation means higher incidence of cancer.

Personally, I don't see this mess getting vastly better anytime soon. More cooperation and communication between all the professions would only partially solve the problem. The ultimate solution would involve medical doctors referring more patients to holistic/vitalistic providers. That is unlikely. As a consumer, be wary; the medical profession is already trying to capture a share of the holistic/vitalistic market by attempting to provide natural care like acupuncture and nutritional advice. Be aware that, in most cases, their training on these subjects stems from a few weekend seminars. It's up to you, the patients, to vote with your feet and take control. Don't be afraid to question a practitioner's training or knowledge and seek other opinions if you're suspicious.

The History of Chiropractic

The concept and benefits of structure-based healthcare are best illustrated with the history of the development of the chiropractic profession. I never get tired of telling it.

Chiropractic started in 1895 when a holistic, hands-on healer named David Daniel Palmer thrust on the upper spine of an African-American man named Harvey Lillard. He did so for good reason. The place was Davenport, Iowa, and Harvey was D.D. Palmer's janitor. Harvey was deaf, but managed to communicate to D.D. Palmer that his hearing difficulty began a few years earlier when he was crouched under a wagon in an awkward position and heard a popping sound in his upper spine. After having Harvey lie face down on a table to examine him, D.D.

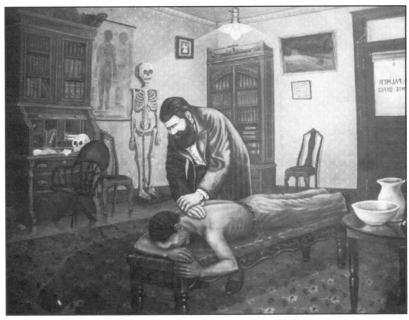

First chiropractic adjustment in 1895 by David Daniel Palmer
with patient Harvey Lillard.

noticed an abnormal protrusion, or bump, on Harvey's upper spine. Reasoning that there might be some connection to Harvey's hearing loss, D.D. thrust upon it, inducing a loud cracking sound that startled both of them. Jumping up from the table, Harvey began wildly shaking his head while tugging his ears, proclaiming, "I can hear, I can hear!"

News of Harvey's remarkable recovery soon spread. D.D. Palmer assumed and proclaimed he had discovered a cure for deafness. Harvey testified that D.D. was a miracle worker, and the medical community accused both of snake oil tactics. As a result of the publicity, dozens of deaf people showed up at D.D. Palmer's Davenport office. Upon applying the same technique,

David Daniel Palmer

feeling for abnormal bumps in the spine and thrusting upon them, there were no further deafness cures. Instead, D.D. Palmer observed that many other health benefits were reported by these deaf people.

The frenzy continued as D.D. Palmer gained a reputation for curing, or at least relieving, many conditions that could not be ameliorated by conventional medical care of the times. Patients began showing up with a wide range of illnesses and ailments. As D.D. Palmer investigated and deduced the nerve system/spinal alignment connection and refined the treatment techniques, the chiropractic profession was born. He began the first chiropractic school at his office.

An elderly lady named Vira came to my office one day seeking help for her neck pain. I noticed she had two hearing aids. After performing an examination and taking X-rays, I began chiropractic procedures on her neck.

She returned in a week. When I walked into the treatment room, there she stood with tears in her eyes and a clenched fist! I was tempted to run. She slowly opened her hand to reveal the hearing aids, explaining with joy that not only did her neck feel better, but unexpectedly her need for the hearing aids was gone!

Since Palmer's time, the chiropractic profession has experienced rapid growth. There are now twelve chiropractic schools in the United States and even more overseas, with thousands of practicing chiropractors worldwide. Treatment methods are being continually refined with numerous options available, all with the same intention: balancing and improving body structure to improve the nerve system communication, resulting in better internal communication and improved health.

During the flu epidemic of 1917 to 1918, both chiropractors and osteopaths noticed that their patients with the flu had a lower fatality rate, 0.25 percent, compared to that of the medical professions at 5 to 6 percent. The conclusion of a research paper written in 1919 was that subluxations suppressed the immune system, and that removing them assisted the immune function.

Newer research verifies this, showing that white blood cells increase with chiropractic adjustments. So remember, the next time you're sick, a chiropractic adjustment is just what the doctor ordered.
(Source: J. Selano, *Chiropractic Research Journal*, 1994: 3(1):32-29.

The prospering of the chiropractic profession has not come easy. It's been driven by patient referrals, meaning satisfied patients tell others. Acceptance by insurance companies, government regulators, and the medical profession; although improved, is still

Joint Effort by M.D.s, D.C.s
Praised at Trial
American Medical News, June 26, 1987

U.S. Judge Finds Medical
Group Conspired Against
Chiropractors
New York Times, Aug. 1987

Judge hits AMA on
Chiropractors
Chicago Sun Times, Aug. 29, 1987

Should Chiropractors be
Granted Hospital Privileges?
Physician's Weekly, Aug. 31, 1987

Chiropractors find Judge
with Backbone
San Francisco Examiner, Aug. 29, 1987

What Happens When Chiros Get
Hospital Privileges
Medical Economics, Jan. 4, 1988

'80s Chiropractors in Sync
with Demand
Oakland Tribune, Jan. 10, 1988

Physicians Working with
Chiropractors:
A Growing Trend
Back Pain Monitor, March, 1988

Chiropractors Cite
Progress in Bid for Place
in Medicine
Medical World News, Sept. 12, 1988

Hospital Allows
Chiropractors to Treat Out-
patients on Physicians' Turf
Los Angeles Times, June 18, 1989

Chiropractor a Hero after
Taking on AMA
Hayward Daily Review, Feb. 14, 1991

A few of the headlines that appeared
during the antitrust lawsuit won by
chiropractors.

lacking, and mostly gotten by legal and political force. In the early 1980s, a group of chiropractors was inspired to file an anti-trust lawsuit against the American Medical Association (AMA), when documents were discovered outlining the latter's covert plan to "discredit and ultimately eliminate the chiropractic profession." The lawsuit proceeded all the way to the United States Supreme Court. Details of the AMA's antics read like a novel, bringing to mind thoughts of an evil empire, with threats of bodily harm, spies with code names like "Sore Throat," and hidden research studies, all in the name of eliminating competition.

Some of their tactics were quite laughable. For example, the AMA sharply criticized chiropractors for advertising their services, yet a few years later, medical-related advertising is just about everywhere you look—on buses, TV, radio, newspapers, magazines, and so on. In another example, AMA leaders were so convinced that chiropractic was worthless, they financed several research studies investigating its effectiveness, hoping to use the results to discredit. When the results showed more benefit from chiropractic treatment than from medical care, they were furious and quickly shelved the studies.

Another foolish tactic of theirs was to order their members to refrain from communicating with any chiropractors, either professionally or socially, essentially blackballing the chiropractic profession. This meant that an MD, a medical doctor, was neither allowed to accept from nor refer patients to chiropractors. It also meant that if a chiropractor joined a community service group like the Lion's Club or Kiwanis, any MD members of that group were ordered to resign.

One hospital in Illinois, uniquely utilizing chiropractors and chiropractic treatment with tremendous benefit for their patients, such as producing shorter hospital stays, was severely ridiculed and threatened by the AMA. The list of the AMA's selfish atrocities is a long one. Amazing!

> Marty, age 30, was quite incapacitated from years of chronic illness. It had left him limping, with deformed legs, lots of pain, and difficulty performing most of the tasks we all take for granted. He came to me consistently about twice monthly because he found that although chiropractic treatment didn't cure him, it did give noticeably more strength and

relieved his pain. This allowed him to live independently, hold a part-time job and even drive.

He proudly told me how he recently encountered a critical MD who waved a finger and scolded him for utilizing chiropractic care. Marty said he enjoyed waving his own finger in response and explaining that chiropractic helped him more than anything modern medicine has been able to. I thanked Marty for standing up to those who are misinformed.

Of course, not all MDs adhered to these archaic rules of membership in the AMA; many did, but a handful of free-spirited MDs came to chiropractic's defense once the lawsuit was underway. Ultimately, the Supreme Court awarded the chiropractic profession a victory, declaring the AMA guilty of an anti-trust conspiracy, and issuing a "cease and desist" order to the AMA.

Thankfully, relations have improved since. But some adversaries still persist today. Most chiropractors, including me, feel a stronger responsibility to bring the principles of good health through natural means to the masses as a result of the AMA's antics. Their plan backfired.

Some would argue that the anti-trust lawsuit is water under the bridge, and I certainly agree that life must go on. But lessons from history are important, and the battle between chiropractic

History is a guide to navigation in perilous times. History is who we are and why we are the way we are.
—*David C. McCullough, two-time Pulitzer Prize winner*

and traditional Western medicine is one that needs to be remembered as much as the Holocaust, world wars, and epidemics because as many, if not more, lives were lost due to the foolishness of one group trying to dominate a market. Consider, for example, the thousands of patients who were misled into submitting to possibly unnecessary surgeries and medications and exposed to the high risks involved. These patients might have been

> Let's not forget the lessons from history, especially this one. When one group attempts to eliminate competition for strictly economic reasons, the public suffers.

able to avoid costly and risky procedures had they chosen chiropractic treatment instead. History might indeed indicate that the thousands mentioned above may turn out to be a very conservative count! Scarily, the number of misled individuals is still growing. Look carefully at most medical information and you'll see that mention of holistic/natural treatment methods is still lacking.

I enjoy looking at health-related books. I'm sure my patients appreciate my staying informed and caught up on current information. I just noticed a new book, *The Mayo Clinic Book of Alternative Health*. While the book did a good job of explaining the many different alternatives like massage, acupunc-

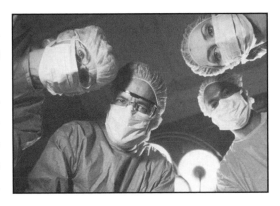

ture, naturopathy, and chiropractic, I chuckled upon noticing that each description included a highlighted box of text that essentially said the same thing each time: "This type of treatment has not been scientifically proven, has had little research, and contains some risk." Were the authors really trying to inform people or rather scare them away from alternative treatments?

Not surprisingly, no mention was made of the much higher risks with medical care. Nor did they note that only around fifteen percent of medical procedures are validated through scientific research. Just how dumb do they think we are?

Not convinced that the current power brokers of healthcare aim to keep you in the dark, particularly when it comes to info about chiropractic? Take a look at the January 2008 copy of *Newsweek* magazine. It features a front cover story about alternative healthcare. Guess what? Not a single mention of chiropractic!

> *The word chiropractor is a compilation of the Greek words "chiro" meaning hands, and "practices," meaning practitioner. Thus, a chiropractor is a doctor who works with his or her hands.*

Seeking Chiropractic

So how do you go about getting structure-based healthcare, such as that which a doctor of chiropractic would provide? Well, if one or more of the many satisfied chiropractic users has not already suggested it and referred you to one, simply ask around.

You'll find many of your co-workers, neighbors, and friends are already utilizing or have utilized chiropractic care.

Your first visit will start with a consultation/history, examination, and perhaps X-rays. The information being sought addresses several questions:

- Can chiropractic help you?
- What is the source of your trouble?
- What is the best treatment?
- How long will it take?

In most offices, the information will be gathered directly by the chiropractor, the examination will be very hands on, and the overall encounter will be much more personal than what you've encountered on the allopathic/medical side of healthcare.

Treatment options may be explained immediately or it may take a day to compile them. The treatment is usually performed hands-on, although more mechanical devices are being used lately. The treatment is called "chiropractic adjustment." It's a very safe procedure when performed by a highly trained and licensed practitioner. Most times, particularly when the hands-on method is used, clicking or cracking noises may be heard. This noise is technically called "cavitation," and is caused when the joint moves and produces a slight vacuum phenomenon. This is safe and a similar process occurs when the vacuum of a suction cup is released.

You may see several odd-looking tables and equipment around the chiropractor's office, shown on the following pages.

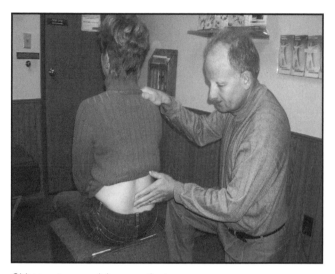

Chiropractor examining a patient

A chiropractic table called flexion/distraction. This type of table is mainly used for treating disc problems.

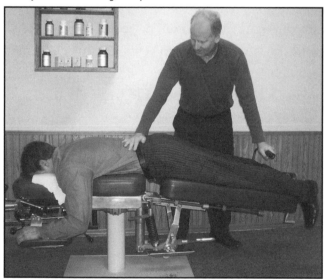

Don't let them scare you; they are designed to make your treatment as comfortable as possible. There is a wide selection of treatment variations being utilized depending on the chiropractor's training and preference.

Pro-adjuster

Vectra
GeniSys
Laser
Therapy
Unit

Knee-chest Table

Chiropractic Hylo Table

Chiropractic
Hylo Table

C.A.T.
Chiropractic
Adjusting Tool

Chiropractic treatment tables and instruments

The Gonstead Method

If you heard of a legitimate doctor who attracted patients from all over the world, had so many patients coming that he had to build an airstrip and a hotel next to his office, worked seven days a week, 16 hours a day, for over 50 years, would it interest you? It interested me so much that I chose to study intensely what this unique doctor did to help so many patients.

CLARENCE GONSTEAD BUILT A CHIROPRACTIC MECCA IN A SMALL WISCONSIN TOWN AND REDEFINED THE NATURE OF HIS PROFESSION.

The miracle man of Mount Horeb

Dr. Clarence Gonstead
(photo used with permission from the Mount Horeb, Wisconsin, Museum)

His name was Dr. Clarence Gonstead, and he was a doctor of chiropractic practicing in a very small town called Mount Horeb, Wisconsin. Dr. Gonstead was originally a mechanical engineer. In his early 20s, he developed a severe case of rheumatoid

Dr. Gonstead's nervoscope, a heat-sensitive device

arthritis. Helped by chiropractic treatment, he changed careers, applied his engineering background to the chiropractic training he received, and developed a special chiropractic adjusting system called "The Gonstead Method." He soon had one of the largest and busiest offices in the world.

Patients came from all points of the globe as word of his seemingly miraculous abilities spread. It was not uncommon for patients to wait several hours for their treatment even at 1 a.m.!

The secret of Dr. Gonstead's success? Accuracy. He combined the sense of touch (palpation) with use of a special heat-sensitive instrument (nervoscope) and insisted on analysis of the spine with weight-bearing, full-spine X-rays. In addition, he designed three unique adjusting tables, each for a specific part of the spine. Thankfully, before he passed away in 1978, he taught and wrote extensively on the details of his method. I am blessed to have spent hundreds of additional training hours, listening and learning and training in The Gonstead Method. I utilize all of what he taught and advocated in my own prac-

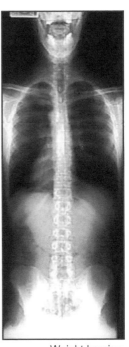

Weight-bearing, full-spine X-ray

tice, and The Gonstead Method is my main method of providing adjustments.

The number of treatments varies widely with the patient's age, severity of condition, and goals. Severe conditions may require daily treatments for a week or two to produce relief as quickly as possible, and then a gradually decreasing frequency to produce stability. Most cases start with

Gonstead-type chiropractic treatment table

two or three treatments weekly for three to six weeks. Those seeking preventative or health maintenance care may be seen once weekly or monthly. A patient's response also varies; some experience immediate relief, others not. Still others may have minor to moderate worsening of their condition temporarily as the structure goes through changes. What is important to remember is that the goal has to be more than just symptom relief; focusing *only* on that repeats the mistakes of medical/allopathic type treatment.

A better goal would be to focus on making a thorough structural improvement in the alignment; improving your body's well-being, and of course, then feeling better as a result. Now that's real healthcare with long-term benefits! And better yet it's low risk and economical especially when compared to the alternatives of injections, medications, and surgeries. Do you see why I'm so glad to be a Doctor of Chiropractic?

> I'm not trying to sound mean, but sometimes I think I should be sending patients to a financial counselor as part of their treatment. Better yet, maybe a math refresher course.
>
> Joe, for example, 39 years old, was a patient who came to me for help with a variety of moderate to severe problems like back pain, headaches, and multiple arthritic joints. He had more frequent health troubles than most. He'd always responded well, needing 8 to 10 chiropractic adjustments for each of his episodes to get back to normal. This happened to him 4 to 8 times each year. Numerous times I suggested he'd be better off just routinely getting an adjustment about once per month to pre-

> vent these health problems. That protocol works
> best for most chronic, repetitive troubles such as
> his.
>   He'd always say that he couldn't afford that, like
> it was a luxury. You do the math!

Regulations vary by state. You may be required to sign a HIPPA form (Health Insurance Privacy Protection Act) and an informed consent form. All chiropractors in the United States are licensed by their state, are graduates of accredited chiropractic colleges, and pass proficiency exams at both the national and state levels. It takes approximately eight years of college to become a Doctor of Chiropractic (DC). Some chiropractors specialize in such matters as pediatrics, orthopedics, radiology, or sports injuries. All doctors participate in post-graduate education through license-renewal requirements.

Pediatrics? Chiropractic for children? Oh, yes! Even infants have spines and these young people are just as likely to have spinal misalignments and benefit from chiropractic treatment as we adults. You can read more about the details of holistic healthcare and specifically chiropractic care for infants and kids in Chapter 10, "Raising Healthier Children."

In most cases, there are no significant risks from chiropractic treatment. Chiropractors enjoy the lowest liability insurance rates of all healthcare providers. Keep in mind that any activity

Chiropractic treatment is generally 1/3 the cost of medical care for the same condition.
—*The British Medical Journal, 1990*

involves some level of risk, whether it is sports, driving, chiropractic care, and so on. In very rare instances, broken ribs, ruptured discs, and strokes have been reported. The excellent and high level of education required of chiropractors results in better and safer treatment.

Many types of insurance cover chiropractic services, including Medicare, Medicaid, group health, auto accident insurance, and worker's compensation. Individual plans vary by state, so check the details of your policy. Chiropractic services are very economical when compared to other alternatives. A typical chiropractic office visit may cost $40 to $60, versus a typical physical therapy visit of $80 to $100, or a spinal injection of $1,500 to $4,000, or a typical spinal surgery of $20,000 to $40,000. There exist multiple studies concerning which choice is best and they all conflict greatly. The general rule worth following is: always try the least invasive method first and that is usually chiropractic.

> Cynthia, a 39-year-old medical technologist, came to my office reluctantly only after much prodding by her family and friends. She had neck and shoulder injuries that stemmed way back to her teenage years as a gymnast. She had spent thousands of dollars on physical therapy, cortisone injections, neck and shoulder surgery, and even had gotten severely addicted to the pain medications she had been prescribed for so long. She admitted her health was a mess, but had always resisted holistic care like chiropractic, explaining that "I've always thought you guys must be quacks when I've heard about you treating things like ear infections and asthma."

> Holding back my scream, I calmly explained the principle that we really don't treat any specific condition, but rather focus on balancing body structure to improve nerve system function. And since the nerve system controls and coordinates the entire body, things like ear infections often respond well due to the favorable immune system response (stronger infection-fighting ability).
>
> She seemed embarrassed by her lack of understanding, but soon was delighted when after several treatments, not only did her neck and shoulder problems respond well, but so did her long bothersome sinus congestion.

Adversaries of the chiropractic profession love to say that our motivation for recommending consistent treatment, perhaps once per month, is that we just want to keep patients coming back forever. In reality, we benefit far more financially when patients wait until their need is greatest, and that's because the patient will need more treatment visits, an examination, maybe X-rays, and perhaps even some adjunctive therapies like massage, ultrasound, and so on. We're actually "shooting ourselves in the foot" when we advocate consistent, periodic, preventive treatment.

I've often wondered just how recommending preventive chiropractic care is any different or less beneficial than a dentist recommending regular teeth cleanings? The truth is: there is no difference, just lack of understanding by the critics. Consider this also: no one is immune from the myriad sources that can cause spinal misalignments. The stresses and traumas are a part of everybody's life, so why fight it; just get yourself straightened out on a regular basis.

My friend and colleague, Dr. Jerry Zelm, from Oconomowoc, Wisconsin, loves to tell this story:

"I was sitting in a restaurant with three other people, one of whom has been a patient of mine for years. The subject of chiropractic treatment came up.

One gentleman said, "I'm afraid to go to a chiropractor because I heard that they just want to keep you coming."

My patient put his arm around my shoulders and said to the group, "I get chiropractic treatment from Doc twice a month. He doesn't keep me coming; he keeps me going!"

Chiropractic treatment won't help everyone, I must admit. Some problems will need the more invasive, higher risk, more expensive options in the medical industry. Often though, when I've encountered the few who are dissatisfied with their attempt at chiropractic care, I notice a significant number of them did not go about it correctly, such as not following the chiropractor's recommendations in regards to treatment schedule, exercises, or lifestyle changes.

Possible reasons for failure to improve with chiropractic treatment

♦ Unrealistic expectations

♦ Impatience

♦ Failure to follow treatment schedule

♦ Failure to make suggested lifestyle changes

♦ Lack of understanding, and

♦ Irrational fears.

Most of these reasons are due to poor communication between doctor and patient. Don't be afraid to ask for more information about the source of your health condition, the type of or duration of treatment, and the expected response. More help with this kind of dialogue is provided in Chapter 7, "Talking to Your Doctor."

As logical as the chiropractic story sounds, few people ever really "get it." Sure, most people understand that chiropractic treatment may help their back pain, but the principle of having better overall health if your spine is aligned involves quite a stretch even for those who regularly use it for pain relief. You see, the chiropractic profession is still comparatively young and practitioners are greatly outnumbered by those involved with the allopathic/medical world. When we try to disseminate our message, we are usually easily drowned out. This is very frustrating to many of us chiropractors. I'm not kidding when I tell you that at least half of my patients have come seeking my help as a last resort. Many of them have had tens of thousands of dollars of medical care involving prescriptions, injections, therapy, and surgeries. I call these patients "ones who went through the mill" or "medical rejects." I frequently see surgical scars on people's backs even though it's well known and accepted now that the long-term success rate of spinal surgery is shockingly low.

At the beginning of this chapter, I gave you a wild story about a young woman who went to a chiropractor and was cured of her persistent hiccup problem. It was said she tried everything else. Well, as usual in chiropractic healing, the results can, at times, appear magical, but the truth is there's a logical explanation. In the case of hiccups, its cause is always a spasm of the diaphragm. The diaphragm is a large, very strong muscle at the base of the lungs that compresses the lungs for breathing. As everything else in the body, it doesn't just work on its own. No, it too has a nerve supply (wire) connecting it to the brain (generator) so it can be controlled with signals (vital force). Specifically, in the diaphragm's case, its nerve exits the spine between the 4th and 5th cervical vertebrae (mid-neck). If structural imbalance (misalignment) occurs there and irritates or pinches that nerve, the diaphragm malfunctions with repetitive spasming and voilá, it's one possible cause of hiccups. Unpinching that nerve with chiropractic treatment can resolve the problem.

There are thousands of examples like this illustrating the importance of body structure and how it influences your health and well-being, especially the alignment of your spinal bones. It's not that chiropractic treatment is the only answer to all that ails you, it's all about keeping your nervous system free flowing your entire life for optimum health. It's been much too overlooked for far too long. Whether you're battling a health problem or just interested in maintaining your good health, I urge you to make structural balance a priority and support it with good eating, proper rest, and exercise.

Chapter 6
Help For Your Ailments
Common Questions and Practical Answers

The following chapter contains the most common questions I've received from my patients during the more than two decades I have been practicing chiropractic. The table on the following page provides page numbers for your ease of reference. Each question is followed by a synopsis of mostly self-help, natural treatments. When appropriate, I've also included a visual spinal road-map for each topic, providing information on the likely nerve system connection described in the previous chapter.

The spinal nerve system connection is provided because every health malfunction needs to be assessed with structure in mind, for it is the commonly overlooked and most easily treated source. Always keep in mind that this information is in no way a substitute for any needed medical care. All of the holistic products mentioned below and **highlighted in bold** are available on our website, www.WholeHealthHealing.com.

You'll find more information on the following ailments on these pages.

DISCLAIMER: The information provided in this book is not intended to replace or provide any necessary medical treatment.

Acne

Q Both my teenagers have acne. They are very self-conscious about it, for it affects them socially. They have tried the typical prescription medications given them by their dermatologist but are bothered by the side effects. I am concerned about the ramifications of the long-term use of these drugs, not to mention the costs. Are there any non-drug remedies available?

A Acne can be devastating to many young adults and yes, you should be concerned about the side effects of those drugs. There are several considerations that can be taken to help these teenagers.

Everyone's skin should be exposed to a few minutes of daylight daily, particularly acne sufferers. Don't be alarmed by the exaggerated reports in the media about the harmful effects of sunlight. Of course, overexposure is a concern, but ten minutes daily on the face, or other body parts with acne, is adequate even if it's just daylight and not sunlight. Not only does sunlight assist in the body's production of many wonderful things it needs, like vitamin D, it also kills undesirable bacteria on the skin. Natural sunlight works best, but don't hesitate to utilize an approved sun lamp or tanning booth, making sure you follow the manufacturer's instructions. I've observed improvements for some acne sufferers who do no more than this one step to help their complexion. Others need to follow several of the next steps.

The troubled complexion must be cleaned at least twice daily and only with a non-deodorant, more natural, gentle soap like Ivory®. Light scrubbing with a soft, loofah sponge or washcloth is adequate.

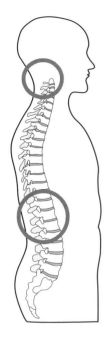

A good night's sleep shuts down the oil production factory in the skin's sebaceous glands. This promotes healing. So set a schedule of regular bedtime without interruption.

Avoid rubbing, touching, or scratching the areas of infection and pimples. This habit just grinds the heavy skin secretions into the pores.

Meals heavy in fat, especially the saturated fat found in most meats and snack foods, promote profuse skin oil production. Avoiding these fatty foods greatly aids in skin care. Also, refined (white) sugars, and foods that are processed, packaged, and containing unnatural chemicals are responsible for much skin distress during the adolescent years. Devitalized dietary habits upset the endocrine balance and greatly stress the body and its skin. Seek a more natural, organic diet of quality proteins and greens.

Our skin functions as a secondary elimination organ. Make sure the main elimination process is functioning optimally by periodically cleansing the intestinal tract. This can be done through short periods of fasting, or with intestinal cleansing products, like **Ultraclear**® and **Chiroklenz**® tea.

Act now with these young adults. Acne is typically outgrown, but can leave permanent scars, both physical and emotional.

Arthritis

Q I was taking Vioxx® for about two years and was recently advised to switch to another drug. I've read about the dangers associated with this type of drug. Is there any natural alternative? I'm 68 and have arthritic pains in my hands, knees, and shoulders.

A The drugs you name are anti-inflammatory medications in the cox=2 inhibitor category. They were hailed as wonder drugs because they did not cause the characteristic gastro-intestinal bleeding associated with many other anti-inflammatories. However, Vioxx® had been found to significantly increase the risk of cardiovascular problems. Many lawsuits have been filed charging the risks were hidden from the public.

I believe we're just beginning to see the tip of the iceberg in regard to the many problems associated with the changes the FDA made in the 1990s. In that decade, they reduced restrictions on mass media advertising and research on all new drugs. This resulted in a shocking increase in advertising of drugs to the public, release of new drugs, and, of course, record profits for the pharmaceutical industry. We chiropractors, the only primary healthcare provider group that advocates a reduction in drugs, watched helplessly as we were unable to voice our stance in the media. Suffice it to say: "Buyer beware!"

There is plenty you can do on your own to reduce inflammation in your joints. Reducing your intake of processed, poor-quality carbohydrates is the most important step. This means reducing candy, soft drinks, white bread, pastries, pastas, and alcoholic beverages. Replace them with honey, purified water,

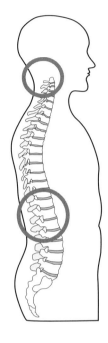

whole grains, organic fruits, vegetables, and juice. There are several facilities around the country that specialize in natural arthritis treatment; their protocol, like mine, essentially helps clean you out and encourages a change in your lifestyle, mainly your eating habits. By the way, artificial sweeteners found in diet drinks may reduce some of the caloric intake, but I've observed that they have some long-term negative health ramifications so don't go there. Take a look at the preferred anti-inflammatory eating guidelines in Chapter 3, "Enjoying Eating."

Light, regular exercise is also recommended. Some people with arthritis avoid exercise, saying it hurts too much, but this is one of many times where you must push yourself somewhat. I'm always amazed at how little exercise it takes to produce benefits, but it must be done consistently. Even a few minutes a day of gentle calisthenics or a brisk walk can work wonders.

For arthritis sufferers, the key is to get movement into those sick joints. For this reason, my answer is always "yes" when I'm asked if chiropractic treatment can help arthritis. Adjustments loosen joints.

Consider taking a food allergy test. Hidden food allergies can be a source of inflammation in joints and muscles. The test I suggest to my patients is an easy self-test from an organization called **U.S. Biotek Laboratories**.

I also suggest nutritional supplements to my arthritic patients. Such supplements include natural anti-inflammatories and joint support such as **Omega-3, glucosamine, chondroitin, hyaluronic acid,** and **MSM**. Two products I frequently recommend to my arthritic patients are **Chondrorelief**® and **Ultrainflammax**®. But the goal is to change your lifestyle enough so you need nothing more than good-quality food, rest, and exercise.

I've heard all the excuses in the world for not managing arthritis naturally, like heredity, no time, costs too much, and so on. However, in 20-plus years of practice, I've never heard any one, when committed to the changes above, say the effort is not worth it.

Baby Colic

Q My 9-month-old daughter cries frequently. Her pediatrician has examined her but has found nothing wrong, and said she'd grow out of it six months ago. My mother-in-law calls it colic. What is colic and what can be done holistically?

A Colic is uncontrollable crying in babies, more than three days a week for three weeks or more. Although many babies seem to grow out of colic, it can last up to a full year and is suspected to be a precursor to neurological problems later in life, such as ADHD, autism, learning disabilities, and so on. Babies with colic have normal weight gain, thrive, and are otherwise healthy. Colic affects 20 percent of newborns, is destructive to family life, and puts the child in a high-risk group for possible central nervous system damage.

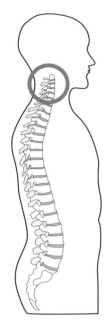

Colic needs to be taken seriously. In some extreme cases, constant crying can even lead to the death of the baby from being violently shaken by parents and/or sitters (also known as shaken baby syndrome); up to 30 percent of babies shaken die from these injuries, and 30 to 50 percent have severe cognitive or neurological defects. In Milwaukee County, where I practice, five to ten infants die each year from Shaken Baby Syndrome.

No causative factor or successful medical treatment has ever been found. Many folk remedies, such as music and different sounds or vibrations (like driving a baby around in a car until it falls asleep) have been investigated but none has been shown to consistently be an answer. Infant massage can bring temporary relief.

Traditional medical treatment is with a drug. Several respected controlled studies have shown that this is no better than a placebo treatment and can have side effects.

Doctors of Chiropractic have long reported frequent success in their treatment of colic using chiropractic manipulation.

Chiropractic treatment involves gentle pressure applied to specific spinal areas and is often performed while the infant lies on the mother's lap. Three studies since 1985, including a randomized controlled trial in 1996 published in the *Journal of Manipulative and Physiological Therapeutics* (October 1999), have verified that these clinical observations are correct.

The first study in 1985 reported successful results with chiropractic management of infantile colic in 90 percent of infants. The second study in 1989 was a multi-center study of 316 cases of infantile colic that revealed chiropractic treatment produced a 94 percent success rate within two weeks and an average of three treatments with no side effects.

The third study in 1996 was a randomized, controlled study of 50 infants with colic. Twenty-five were assigned to drug treatment and 25 were assigned to chiropractic treatment. This study produced the same outcome as the second study, with the chiropractic-treated group far surpassing the results obtained in the drug treatment group. Nine of the 25 drug-treated infants dropped out of treatment with the parents indicating their babies had worsened. None of the babies in the chiropractic group were withdrawn and no adverse side effects were reported.

Critics of the chiropractic profession, especially medical critics, often hold up infantile colic as a graphic example of a condition treated by chiropractors outside their scope of practice. Some have argued that chiropractic management of infants should be illegal or only done on the basis of medical referral. However, the research cited above makes infantile colic the best current example of what might be called the fundamental principle of chiropractic care: improving the functional integrity of the neuro-musculoskeletal system.

From the patient's perspective, chiropractors may be said to be treating specific symptoms or disorders, in this instance infantile colic, but from a chiropractic perspective, practitioners are primarily treating spinal dysfunctions or lesions, traditionally termed subluxation. These subluxations in infants, simply known as misalignments of their spinal columns, are most likely the result of birth trauma. These may be a significant factor in many disorders apparently remote from the spine because of changed biomechanics, referred pain, and other altered neurophysiology.

For infantile colic, the logic and success of the chiropractic approach has now been demonstrated. All chiropractors have training in treating infants and children. Some practitioners even pursue extensive post-graduate training in this area. Most health insurance plans cover this gentle, noninvasive method of improving an infant's well-being.

Back Pain

Q I'm 45 and my back hurts virtually all the time, both my lower back and mid-back. I don't understand why because I don't do heavy lifting, have had no accidents, and exercise regularly. What could be causing this?

A There can be many causes of back pain, sometimes even serious ones like cancer and fractures. When back pain persists such as in your case, it needs to be evaluated by a professional. As a chiropractor, I have found that most times persistent back pain is a result of spinal misalignment. I've seen thousands of patients come through my clinic just like you, some who had even gone through CT scans, MRI, physical therapy, injections, and even spinal surgeries, and then finally finding relief through chiropractic. The spinal misalignments, referred to as subluxations, are not easily found through conventional medical testing, and don't go away with exercise, massage, therapy, or stretching. These subluxations are locked joints that must be released with a specific force applied appropriately. Chiropractors have unique training in finding and reducing these subluxations.

Other structural factors involved in back pain can be improved by practicing proper posture, avoiding slouching and sitting with your legs crossed, losing weight, having supportive inserts in your shoes, and being ergonomic (safe and optimum form) when performing repetitive movements, on the job or at home.

I assume your occupation involves frequent sitting since you said you don't do any heavy lifting. Review the chart on proper posture for sitting occupations in Chapter 4, "Your Posture." Consider using a proper lumbar (back) support cushion whenever you sit for more than a few minutes, for example, in your car and at work. The best one I know of is the **Sitback-Rest Cushion**® from Core Products.

Be wary of labeling. By this, I mean embracing an excuse for having back pain such as genetics ("my father had back pain"), arthritis, a bulging or ruptured disc, "everybody's back hurts," or even age. I have observed that none of these labels warrants ignoring proper evaluation and treatment.

Bed Wetting

Q My 8-year-old son wets the bed most nights. We've tried the usual solutions such as restricting liquids in the evening, and setting an alarm to waken him about midnight for a potty stop. These had limited, minor benefits. I've heard chiropractic treatment can help. How does the back affect bedwetting?

A Bedwetting, also known as *enuresis*, is devastating to children and their self-esteem. Luckily, most do grow out of it eventually, but attempts must be made to remedy this as soon as possible because of the potential emotional ramifications.

Chiropractic has a long history of helping bedwetters. The

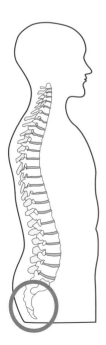

connection is nothing mysterious. The nervous system controls all body functions, including the contraction and releasing of the bladder muscles. Those nerves are closely connected with the spine. Disturbance of spinal structure such as misalignment from trauma and stress like falling, sports, poor posture, and even general horseplay, can produce disruption of vital nerve signals. Chiropractors call this condition vertebral subluxation. There need not be any pain in or around the spine for this to exist. Most definitely take your child to a chiropractor for an evaluation.

On rare occasions, the source of bedwetting is an allergy. A qualified holistic practitioner like most chiropractors or naturopaths can evaluate this, though usual allergens are dairy, wheat, and food additives. A food allergy test is recommended. **U.S. Biotek Laboratories** provides a good one.

Carefully explain to the child that this problem is not their fault and that many other people have had the same trouble. Never scold, ridicule, or criticize them for this problem; instead, encourage them with much love and kind words regularly.

Blood Pressure

Q I am 48 and my friends are also in their 40s and 50s. It seems that most of us have been placed on prescription medication for high blood pressure. We are wondering if there is something we can do to control it other than the drugs?

A There are several non-prescription medicine methods of controlling blood pressure. According to a four-year study of hypertension in the *Journal of the American Medical Association*, "Study findings demonstrated that nutritional therapy may substitute for drugs in a sizable proportion of hypertensives (those with high blood pressure), or if drugs are still needed, can lessen some unwanted biochemical effects of drug treatment." Here are ten things you can do.

1. Increase your intake of Omega-3 fatty acids. Studies indicate that oils in fish may help lower blood pressure. The best fish containing Omega-3 are salmon, tuna, trout, and sardines. Taking a quality supplement is also recommended. The one I suggest

is called **EPA/DHA**. It contains the fatty acids needed to assist in combating blood pressure problems.

2. Increase your intake of foods containing calcium, garlic, magnesium, and potassium. Studies show that these minerals and herbs may be more helpful in lowering blood pressure than salt restriction.

3. Control your caffeine intake. Coffee, tea, colas, and many pain killers contain caffeine, which can elevate blood pressure.

4. If you are overweight, increase your leanness. Implement an effective weight loss program.

5. Get more exercise. Try to be physically active every day.

6. Quit smoking. Cigarette smokers not only drive up their blood pressure, but also run twice the risk of heart attacks as non-smokers.

7. Cut down on salt. Instead of salt, use substitutes such as herbs, lemon juice, and mint. If you must use salt, use only sea salt because it contains a better variety of minerals. Look at the sodium content of every food item you buy.

8. Avoid alcohol. A pint of beer or about half as much wine has about as many calories as a pat of butter. Also, alcohol adversely affects the diameter of the blood vessels.

9. Get regular chiropractic adjustments. They reduce mechanical stress to the nervous system, thus lessening vasoconstriction (choking) of the cardiovascular system. The benefits are validated with research.

10. Relax more. Manage your stress with daily practice of prayer, meditation, and just taking a few minutes for yourself.

For years, I've watched patients successfully manage their blood pressure with the aid of two nutritional supplements called **Vasotensin**® and **Cardiogenics**®. These contain the micronutrients necessary for an optimally functioning cardiovascular system.

If you're currently on blood pressure medication, don't stop without cooperation from your medical physician. Use the dialogues provided for you in Chapter 7, "Talking to Your Doctor," if you would like to alter or discontinue any prescription.

Contrary to popular belief, the genetic connection for those with high blood pressure is not common. The source is much more likely a structural blockage like spinal misalignment, maligned lifestyle choices, or both. If you are overweight, start your focus on that.

Cancer

Q I'm on my second round of cancer. I've had breast and colon cancer that required surgery. I've recovered but feel weakened from the chemo and radiation therapy. I'd sure like to know what can be done to help me avoid another episode?

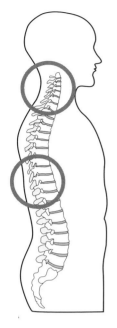

A There are several things to be doing in regard to cancer from a holistic perspective. Crisis situations of cancer identified by the medical practitioners certainly need to be dealt with swiftly and strongly, but whether one is seeking help in recovery or prevention, focus needs to be put on strengthening the immune system. The immune system, a complexity comprised of blood cells, organs like the spleen and liver, and even nerves, is the body's protective mechanism against foreign and mutated cells. We all depend on the immune system immensely but it's easily taken for granted. Strengthening and maintaining optimum immunity involves all the aspects of good health covered in this book. Review the following checklist from Chapter 8, "Strategies for Prevention." Choose one or two points that you feel are your "weakest link" and focus on making the associated lifestyle changes to improve them.

- Minimize your exposure to media news by watching or listening no more than once daily. (Chapter 1, What is *Real* Health?)

- Do some focused deep breathing regularly. (Chapter 1, What is *Real* Health?)

- Learn to see the positive and humorous side of everything. (Chapter 1, What is *Real* Health?)

- Set specific times to do nothing but totally relax at least 30 minutes daily. (Chapter 1, "What is *Real* Health?")

- Engage in a fun, physical activity for at least 30 minutes daily and vary it frequently. (Chapter 2, Exercises that Really Work)

- Eat several (4 to 6) small meals per day of wholesome, organic food, growing some of it yourself. (Chapter 3, Enjoying Eating)

- Stretch your body structure for at least ten minutes daily. Practice good postural habits. (Chapter 4, Your Posture)

- Get a chiropractic adjustment every week or at least monthly. (Chapter 5, Structure-Based Healthcare)

- Have the responsibility of doing some work every day whether it's paid or volunteering. (Chapter 9, Growing Older and Really Enjoying It)

- Learn something new every day by reading or attending classes. (Chapter 9, Growing Older and Really Enjoying It)

- Grow spiritually through prayer and study daily. (Chapter 9, Growing Older and Really Enjoying It)

- Give and receive compliments freely every day. (Chapter 9, Growing Older and Really Enjoying It)

- Lead by example and teach the holistic lifestyle to your family (Chapter 10, Raising Healthier Children)

Many people with cancer easily and rightfully become very absorbed with the medical abilities of dealing with it. The tremendous joy and satisfaction of finding that the cancer is in remission or better yet, has been overcome, are fantastic; but can blind cancer sufferers to the realization that the cancer is likely a symptom of some major disruption in the workings of the body, most commonly of the immune system. But a proactive, holistic approach, combined with the medical intervention, will produce better real health, a stronger immune system, and give you the best chances of recovering from and preventing cancer. The significant lifestyle changes, as described in this book, are the best prevention of cancer I know of.

Chancre Sores

Q I've been bothered for the last two years by chancre sores in my mouth. They come and go in various places, even on my tongue. I'm 16 years old. I've been told I get them because my body is too acidic due to the food I eat, but I've tried altering my diet to no avail. Are there any natural solutions to this?

A Your attempt at altering your diet was a good first step toward solving this problem. Quite often, today's typical diet of highly processed, nutritionally deficient foods is a con-tributing factor to frequent chancre sores. A deficiency of B vitamins is something to consider. Don't give up eating better quality, more nutritious foods, especially organically grown ones. The benefits of doing that will serve you well in many ways.

Your next attempt should be to change your toothpaste. Frequently I have recommended my patients give up their standard, brand-name toothpastes and switch to a natural-based one. This has many times solved these chancre sore problems. I believe this success occurs because most standard toothpaste brands use quite strong artificial mint or peppermint flavorings that can irritate the mouth membranes. Also, these standard toothpastes commonly contain a jumble of other chemicals including perfumes, preservatives, artificial coloration, and soaps. Any of these can be irritants to the mouth membranes. Look for natural toothpaste at any health food store. A reliable brand is **Tom's Natural Toothpaste**®. Make sure you brush (using a soft brush) not only your teeth with this natural toothpaste, but your tongue, gums, and the insides of your cheeks as well.

Chest Pain

Q I've suffered with chest pain for several years. My heart has been checked thoroughly and nothing has been found wrong there. What else can I do?

A Chest pain is definitely something to get checked out medically to rule out heart malfunction. Beyond that, the answer usually lies with addressing the structural imbalance of the neck, ribs, shoulders, and middle spine. The *Journal of the American Medical Association* featured an article covering a report from a meeting of the American College of Cardiology. At that meeting, a condition called cervicoprecordial angina was discussed. That condition with the long scary name is just a fancy term for "pinched nerves causing chest pain." The physicians and researchers at that meeting discussed several things relating to angina (chest pain), specifically noting the following.

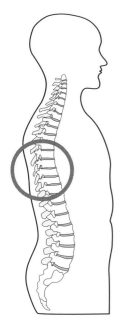

1. Lots of people suffer chest pain and angina with no heart problems.

2. Most of these people suffer from cervicoprecordial angina (the fancy name for pinched nerves in the back).

3. Many people are being treated for heart disease, using lots of drugs for years, when all they are really suffering from is pinched nerves.

So, give strong consideration to structural balance and alignment as discussed in Chapter 5, "Structure-Based Healthcare." Stretch your body daily, particularly your neck, upper back, shoulders, and chest. Practice good postural habits at all times. And visit a Doctor of Chiropractic for a spinal alignment evaluation.

Childbirth

Q I am eight months pregnant and have been searching the Internet for information on pregnancy, birth options, infant care, and so on. I am amazed at the controversies about conventional hospital births versus home births, circumcision, breast feeding, and immunizations. Are these alternative ideas true?

A There are many alternatives to the conventional "hurried hospital birth, circumcision, shoot-'em-up with immunizations, and drug them" routine of pregnancy and delivery. The United States has one of the highest infant mortality rates in the developed world. Some Third World countries have better infant survival than we do. Could it be that conventional medicine intervenes too much and treats pregnancy and childbirth more as diseases than the natural processes they are?

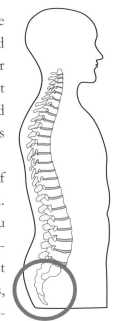

One example of the controversy is that of having your baby at home versus at a hospital. The hospital personnel will most likely tell you that home births are risky, perhaps even danger-ous. The facts and statistics actually show that home births are quite safe for healthy mothers, especially when assisted by a qualified, experi-enced midwife. Most mothers of home-birth children will tell you that the experience was amazingly calm, relaxing, and that they needed no pain medications. Home births are not for every-one, but it is important to get the facts straight so that you can make intelligent decisions. At the very least seek out one of the new hospital birthing centers staffed by midwives. I've observed that some of the overly abused medical services are avoided there.

Breastfeeding is undeniably very important. Imagine the ar-rogance of whoever decided that man and his science can pro-duce milk for a baby better than the mother's body. Breastfeed your baby for as long as possible, until the baby no longer wants it.

Circumcision is an easy decision when you consider this question: Do you think God made any mistakes with the creation of the human body?

I'm not afraid to say this boldly and confidently: You're a fool if you're not getting chiropractic treatment weekly throughout your pregnancy. Research indicates and we chiropractors observe clinically that pregnant women who get chiropractic treatment have less complicated births. That means less discomfort, less need for risky medical intervention, and a healthier mother and baby. And get your newborn to a chiropractor as soon as possible after birth. Read more about childbirth in Chapter 10, "Raising Healthier Children."

I advise you to continue researching and asking questions. Make your choices after considering all the options, not just on what you're told by conventional medicine.

Cholesterol

Q My doctor put me on a cholesterol drug. Since I began taking it, I have had muscle aches throughout my body. Two of my friends report the same experience from their cholesterol drug. Is there a connection and are there any alternatives?

A These drugs are intended to inhibit the activity of enzymes necessary for the body's production of cholesterol. I've observed several known side effects from this type of drug, including multiple muscle pains.

The first line of treatment for cholesterol imbalance should be dietary/lifestyle modifications, including adding more exercise to your lifestyle. That exercise needs to be consistent and at least 20 minutes three times per week. Too much sugar, especially white, refined sugar, and drinking excessive alcohol can increase blood fats. Following a typical Mediterranean diet, meaning adding more foods like almonds, fish, olive oil, fresh fruits, and vegetables, will help you manage your cholesterol.

If adjusting diet and exercise don't work to lower your "bad" cholesterol, a good nutritional alternative is a supplement called **Red Yeast Rice**®. It contains at least nine substances that are similar in chemical structure to the active ingredients in statin-type drugs, and costs a fraction of the prescriptions. With the scientific name of *Monascus purpureus*, red yeast rice has been shown in clinical studies to be effective. It should not be taken by pregnant or nursing mothers. The only reported significant side effect is that two percent of the people who used it reported some heartburn or gas. A properly functioning liver is essential for cholesterol management so consider a liver cleanse like **Ultraclear**®, and don't forget the liver's nerve supply.

Cold and Flu Prevention

Q Just what can a person do to lessen the frequency and duration of typical cold and flu infections?

A As winter approaches, it's a good time to put into practice some practical cold and flu prevention methods, but better yet, keep them going year round. Many of these suggestions are not only common sense, but are frequently recommended by many natural healthcare practitioners.

Preventing many health problems is really a choice. Common sense is easily overshadowed by technology and expediency. You see, we don't really catch cold and flu germs. They catch us when our resistance is weak. These suggestions below, followed routinely, will produce a stronger immune system and a happier, healthier you.

#1 Wear a hat outdoors. Approximately 40 percent of our body heat is lost through the scalp. Any lowering of body temperature can weaken our immune systems. If you are worried about the dreaded "hat head," or have a child who consistently loses hats, consider a hooded coat as a close alternative.

#2 Monitor the humidity level in your home. Low air moisture is common in closed, heated environments. Many viruses love to make their attack through the mucous membranes of the mouth, nose, and eyes. If these membranes are even slightly dry, you are inviting the viruses into your body. A humidifier hooked directly to the furnace with a humidistat is the best defense against dry mucous membranes. An alternative is to set out one or two pans of water in frequently used rooms, especially sleeping quarters. Check your home by inspecting the inside lower corners of windows on cold mornings. Proper humidity leaves minor condensation there. At a minimum, make sure you are drinking an adequate amount of water, at least 4 to 6 glasses daily.

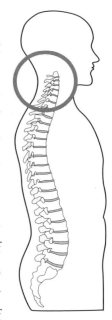

#3 Take multivitamin/mineral supplements daily. The hard-line stance of getting "all you need" from the food you eat is rapidly becoming antiquated. You're likely deficient in essential vitamins and minerals if you eat a lot of meals at fast food restaurants or highly processed and preserved "corporate grown" foods. Make sure the supplements you buy are organic, not synthetic. Synthetic supplements are made by mixing chemicals, are less expensive, and called "bedpan bullets" by nurses because they frequently pass though our systems intact and are poorly absorbed. On the other hand, organic supplements, derived and concentrated from actual food may cost more, but are highly absorbable. My favorite mutivitamin/mineral supplement is called **Multigenics**®.

Vitamin C is the most important vitamin for the immune system. Dr. Linus Pauling, world-renowned vitamin expert, says the average adult needs to supplement at least 2000 mg. daily. In my practice, I frequently recommend a brand called **Mark V**® **Vitamin C**. It is a timed-release variety.

#4 Slow down. Many health problems are self-induced. Weak immunity is frequently the result of an overburdened lifestyle. Take time to organize your responsibilities by making lists and then prioritizing them. Make sure one of your top priorities is getting plenty of sleep and relaxation time. Living in this world does not require being a part of the madness to overachieve, overproduce, and "over-acquire" each other. Strive for inner peace; you will know you are getting there when you find yourself choosing your own direction instead of following that of others.

#5 Get regular chiropractic treatment. Research has shown a close relationship between the immune system and the nervous system. Chiropractic aims to maintain a proper functioning nervous system through spinal adjustments. Many chiropractic patients report fewer infections and faster recovery from colds and flu.

Cracking Sounds

Q My neck makes grinding sounds every time I turn my head. I'm 48 years old and this has been happening for the last 2 years. My 19-year-old son forcibly twists his back until it makes a cracking sound. He does this several times per week and tells me it's just a nervous habit. Should either of us be concerned about these noises?

When you turn your head and hear those grinding noises, it is called "crepitus." Crepitus can occur in any of our joints, and the noise comes from the abnormal movement of damaged or deteriorating cartilage. I believe it is quite normal to experience some crepitus as a person ages, particularly beyond age 45. It is generally not a concern, but if it is accompanied by pain, weakness, swelling, or is progressively getting louder, I would suggest consulting a healthcare professional; especially one with structural training like a chiropractor. The noise is often an early sign of arthritic changes in the joint or can indicate joint misalignment. At the very least, read the information provided about arthritis prevention and control. Put those measures into practice.

When a person exercises or stretches, an occasional popping or cracking sound may be heard or felt. This is looked upon as good and is generally the joint adjusting or realigning itself to some degree. If the noise is repeated with every movement, stop the activity and get the joint evaluated.

Interestingly, I've noticed that crepitus usually is found in joints that were injured or traumatized years ago, such as in an auto accident, sports injury, or other accident. This is another good reason to visit a chiropractor periodically; doing so slows down and prevents premature joint deterioration.

Your son's habit will eventually catch up to him and become a problem. I've observed this time and time again whereby young people develop a habit of cracking fingers, neck, or back. They then start to develop pain or stiffness, necessitating even more self-cracking. Eventually they develop instability in the joints and cracking no longer relieves the symptoms. An X-ray would then reveal that they have literally been grinding away at the cartilage, unknowingly creating a permanent problem. Your son should stop his habit immediately.

Occasionally, the above example of repetitive cracking is used as an analogy against repetitive chiropractic treatment. Misguided critics use that as a fear tactic to smear the chiropractic profession. Unfortunately, this attitude can scare people away from the more conservative treatment of chiropractic and lead them to higher risk treatments such as injections, prescriptions, or even surgery. These misguided critics fail to realize that no chiropractic treatment is made without a thorough prior analysis to determine joint misalignment. Only then is a specific force applied to accurately reduce the imbalance. Furthermore, it's easy to observe that those who receive regular, periodic chiropractic treatment have less joint deterioration, better posture, more endurance, and generally enjoy better health. Have no fear to get regular chiropractic treatment through your entire life.

Depression

Q I've fought light to moderate depression for many years. I'm now 60 years old and am still looking for a solution. The medications prescribed to me have been disappointing because of poor results. What can a natural approach offer?

A Depression is a serious condition at any age. The natural approaches are well worth pursuing but need to be combined with professional medical treatment in the moderate to severe levels. One of the first things to consider is this: your brain/mind is much like a computer, garbage in equals garbage out. Take a close look at what your exposing yourself to each day. I truly believe that if you frequently read, listen, or watch standard media news, it can contribute to depressive thoughts.

Most of what the media presents is bad news that you and I can't do anything about. We can get very frustrated by programming our minds with negative information day after day, week after week. The same goes for frequent exposure to addictive violent and/or pornographic materials. Keep putting garbage like this into your mind and you're bound to get garbage out in the form of negative, depressing thoughts.

Instead, feed your mind with positive, uplifting, even humorous, motivational information. And yes, you must keep that up on a regular, hopefully daily, basis. In my opinion, if you're reading the newspaper once a day or tuning into the news once a day, that's more than enough media exposure. Remember, the media are businesses and they'll take whatever measures they can to keep us interested and coming back. Unfortunately that means a focus on bad news.

In combating depression, exercise is also extremely important. There is a tremendous mind/body connection. If you focus on keeping your body fit and feeling good, your mind benefits. As I spelled out in Chapter 2, "Exercises that Really Work," find a variety of physical activities you enjoy and strive to spend at least 30 minutes daily on them. There is a group of chemicals your body produces when you exercise that can help make you happy. Don't miss out on this natural high.

Consider your diet. If you are frequently partaking in all the no-no's of eating discussed in Chapter 3, "Enjoying Eating," your mind suffers as much, if not more, than your body. This is particularly true of poor quality carbohydrates like candy, bakery, soft drinks, and most fast foods. When you're depressed, it's a

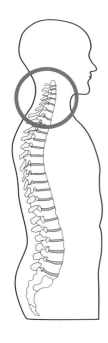

sign that your brain is essentially starving. Eating that stuff is like putting rocket fuel in your car; it may give you a great temporary boost but you won't go far.

Taking a daily organic multi-vitamin/mineral supplement is essential. I recommend **Multigenics**®, as it has the best combination of nutrients in a very absorbable form.

Get outdoors. Your mind and body are a lot like a solar energy cell. It's very important to get out in the daylight for at least several minutes daily. Go to a park or a scenic viewpoint and breathe deeply. Notice the beauty of the trees, plants, birds, and all the rest of God's wonderful creation. Give thanks for being a part of it. Even in winter, don't miss the show.

Speaking of God, how is your spirituality? Some experts even make the argument that part of depression is a call for exploring your connection with your creator. Kind of like an alarm. As a Christian, I feel your spirituality is as important, if not more so, than your physical and mental self. And that your spirituality has a close personal tie to your emotions. Are you sure of where you came from and where you are going when you die? I believe those answers are best found in the words of a man who walked on water, fed thousands with a small basket of food, healed the sick, and rose from the dead. His name was Jesus. Check out my testimony of this on my website, www.WholeHealthHealing.com.

And yes, structural balance of the spine is not to be forgotten. Our moods are very dependent on our hormone balance and the nervous system plays a vital role. Keep your nerve channels open and free-flowing with regular chiropractic adjustments.

Media marketing so easily leads us to believe that all one needs is to pop a pill and feel better with depression or whatever ails us. Whether you need medication or not, make sure you're not missing out on these simple, easily forgotten basics of wellness.

Digestive Problems

Q My medical doctor has diagnosed me with GERD (gastro-esophageal-reflux-disorder) and placed me on an expensive prescription that only provides temporary and partial relief. She said I need to take this medication for the rest of my life. I am 45 years old. Are there any natural remedies available?

A In a case of GERD, and many other digestive problems like bloating, the acid in the stomach is rising too high in the esophagus, sometimes coming up all the way to the throat and/or mouth and irritating the sensitive membranes there. Some say that such reflux might increase the risk of throat cancer.

There are several common-sense remedies that may help and sometimes stop GERD and other digestive maladies.

First and foremost, consider that the acid that is coming up is rarely from overproduction of the normal acids produced by the digestive system. Normal aging processes mean that most people produce fewer stomach acids. The problem of GERD and abdominal bloating usually stems from acids produced by the putrefying, undigested food that remains in the digestive tract for too long.

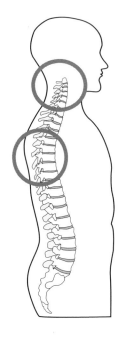

Start by slowing down your eating. Many patients with GERD swallow their food in gulps, with little chewing. This means that larger pieces of food stay in your stomach longer than desired, and requires more churning to break up the food. Take small bites and thoroughly chew all food into a paste or mush before swallowing. Also, eat several small meals thru the day rather than a few large ones.

If you don't have ulcers, take hydrochloric acid supplements with your meals, 1300 mg per meal for the average adult. I suggest a supplement to my patients called **Metagest**®. Do not drink any liquids immediately before, during, or after meals. Any liquids will dilute the normal stomach acids, further weakening them. If you must have liquid during eating, take it in a few small sips, then wait at least 15 minutes after eating to finish any beverages.

Third, sit up straight during and after eating. Slouching compresses and constricts the digestive mechanisms. It also impinges on the vagus nerve, which controls digestion. Regular chiropractic treatment will keep body structure balanced and the nerve supply to digestive function normalized.

Last, do this exercise three times daily between meals. While standing, quickly drink a large glass of warm/semi-hot water to load up and weigh down the stomach. Then immediately rise up on your toes and quickly drop onto your heels hard enough to cause the stomach to be pulled downward via momentum. Do this jarring motion every three seconds for 1 minute. This helps to reposition the stomach into its more natural, less troublesome position.

GERD and many other digestive maladies are a consequence of our society's trend toward high-stress, fast-food, no-time-to-eat-or-relax lifestyle. In slower-paced cultures, the prevalence of such maladies is far lower.

Ear Infections

Q I've been considering taking my child to see a chiropractor. My 2-year-old has repetitive ear infections. Standard medical treatments of antibiotics, and ear tubes have not produced the help we've hoped for and I refuse to medicate my son any longer. Can chiropractic treatment help the ear infections?

A After 20+ years of practicing chiropractic, I am still amazed at the wonderful results children receive from chiropractic care. Critics of the chiropractic profession scoff at this, but the truth is that chiropractors have been treating children successfully since its beginnings in 1895, and all chiropractors have training in how to work with youngsters. Some chiropractors, like myself, have even taken many hours of post-graduate training in the treatment of children.

Obviously, children also have spines. Misalignments of the spinal bones is commonly caused by trauma. What child does not experience trauma from falling, sitting and lying in awkward positions, sports activities, roughhousing, and even the process of being born. These structural disturbances of the spine can disrupt the flow of nerve impulses to the body, resulting in poor health. Commonly, the symptoms manifest themselves in weak

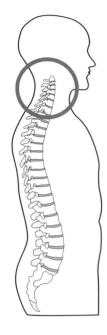

immunity, such as in the case of your 2-year-old's frequent ear infections.

Many common childhood complaints are dismissed by the medical profession as a normal part of growing and are covered up by medications, whether those are antibiotics for ear infections or pain killers for growing pains. If improper treatment continues, your child risks not only side-effects of the medications but likely will have further health problems down the road.

Chiropractic care seeks to address the cause of these problems and produce a better functioning nerve system and improved health. My own three children are perfect examples. I've checked and treated them since they were born and they have not yet had a need for any medications. So, yes, take your children to a chiropractor and congratulations for seeking out what makes sense instead of following the crowds.

Fibromyalgia

Q I have been diagnosed with fibromyalgia. I have the typical chronic multiple pains, fatigue, poor concentration, weak immunity, and depression. I've been to several medical doctors and have tried numerous medications, only to find myself slightly relieved, having side-effects, having a smaller bank account, and getting more frustrated. What non-medicine things can I do?

Many in the medical profession use the term "fibromyalgia" as a "garbage-can diagnosis," meaning "we don't know what's wrong with you so let's call it this." Some say this group of symptoms is caused by the long-term side effects of past medication usage. I wouldn't be surprised because I've always said there is a price to pay for putting any chemicals in the body that don't naturally belong there. Sometimes those bad effects don't show up for years.

Albert Einstein said, "A problem can never be solved by the same thinking that created it." If you've been skeptical of holistic healthcare and have ultimate confidence in medical science to solve all your problems, you won't get over your fibromyalgia until you let go of that way of thinking. If you're going to try holistic healthcare to see if it helps, hoping it will convince you, you'll end up back where you started if you don't make the major changes necessary in your lifestyle and have the patience for it. With fibromyalgia, you've gotten yourself into quite a mess and it's going to take considerable effort and time to get out of it.

Sometimes I hear people say they don't believe lifestyle is the cause of their fibromyalgia because other people who drink, smoke, eat junk food, don't exercise, and so on, feel fine. If you're not yet convinced, go back to the first paragraph and re-read what Einstein said. In other words, you're not going anywhere with the same old thoughts and opinions. Then thank God you have fibromyalgia. It is your wake-up call before you end up with something more life-threatening, like cancer. Many of those "other people" you mention get worse problems like that first.

Read and learn about holistic healthcare before diving in. Healing over the long term involves gaining faith first because this has to be a permanent lifestyle change and that won't happen unless you understand how and why holistic care works. When you're ready to start, welcome to the other side and here is what you need to do.

#1 ***Detoxify.*** Your body has an accumulation of toxins that must be cleaned out. These toxins are chemical residues from past drug usage (prescription and recreational), smoking, alcohol usage, food preservatives, artificial flavorings, artificial colorings, environmental pollution, and even stress. Many fibromyalgia sufferers have "Leaky Gut Syndrome," meaning these toxic chemicals have damaged their intestinal walls, which allows many nasty things such as large protein molecules, undigested food particles, and more toxic chemicals to enter their blood stream. These undesirable substances irritate and inflame many of your internal organs and tissues, not to mention accumulating and resurfacing under stressful circumstances.

The only way out of this mess is to stop the intake of the poisons and remove what has already accumulated. There are numerous ways to detoxify, including fasting, chelation, colonic irrigation, allergy elimination, and juicing. The fastest, most thorough method I recommend is a program called **Ultraclear**®. It involves a step-by-step program of diet changes and a powdered drink mix.

It is important to avoid excitotoxins in your diet. These are food additives that affect your nervous system. MSG (monosodium glutamate) and some artificial sweeteners are the most common ones. You must examine every label and ask at every restaurant to make sure you avoid these dangerous substances. Get a food allergy test performed. Certain foods can be secretly contributing to abnormal inflammation in your body. This is very common in those with fibromyalgia. A kit for this is available on our website, www.WholeHealthHealing.com.

#2 *Improve your body structure.* A crooked house can't be made straight without leveling the foundation. In the human body, unbalanced structure causes impingement, irritation, and interference with the nervous system. This is particularly true when the spinal column is unbalanced. The nervous system controls and coordinates all body functions. It is the first visible structure in a developing embryo. It senses your environment and adapts your body accordingly. If you don't think a free-flowing nervous system is important to your well-being, then that alone means yours probably needs help. A flexible mind goes with a flexible body.

There are several ways to increase structural balance and improve nerve flow, including yoga, chiropractic adjustment, massage, osteopathic manipulation, and posture control. Disturbed body structure is caused by stress, physical and mental trauma, and toxins. Excuse my bias but chiropractic practitioners have been advocating this and practicing it since 1895. As far as I know, chiropractic is the safest and most thorough method of balancing body structure and improving nerve flow.

#3 *Learn how to relax.* The Bible says even Jesus and God rested. Don't be afraid to pamper yourself. Are you

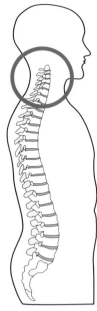

having fun every day for at least a little while? Are you pursuing your dreams, hobbies, and aspirations? Learn how to laugh with others and at yourself. Have you discovered your spiritual side? Don't forget that a human being is a physical, mental, spiritual, and emotional being. All four need regular attention, improvement, and maintenance. I believe that the fastest, most thorough method of obtaining that feeling of "at ease" with yourself and the world is by reading the Bible and studying the life of Jesus.

#4 *Exercise.* The human body is made of hundreds of bones and joints because it was made to move. This is difficult when you're in pain and low on energy but it is important even if you start with very little. Begin by taking short walks. Gradually increase the speed and distance.

There are many other choices such as aerobics, calisthenics, bicycling, and so on. The most thorough exercise I am aware of is swimming. Personally, I find I must constantly choose different exercise methods because boredom discourages me. Whatever you choose must be done regularly and consistently. There is no need to push yourself to exhaustion. Raising your heart rate for 20 minutes three times per week is sufficient.

#5 *Take supplements.* There is some excellent research, reasoning, and clinical observation that certain nutrients, taken in supplement form, provide relief to fibromyalgia sufferers. Malic acid, magnesium, and 5-hydroxytryptophan are key nutrients that every fibromyalgia patient should try for at least 60 days. I suggest a supplement called **Fibroplex®**, which contains many nutrients specifically for conditions like fibromyalgia.

#6 I highly recommend getting a *food allergy test.* Hidden food allergies are a known source of inflammation of joints and muscles. Many fibromyalgia sufferers have recovered doing nothing more than this procedure and then modifying their diet accordingly. The food allergy test I administer to my patients is from a company called **U.S. Biotek Laboratories**.

Gout

Q I have severe pain, redness, and swelling in my big toe. These symptoms come and go. I've been diagnosed with gout and given prescriptions. Are there any natural alternatives?

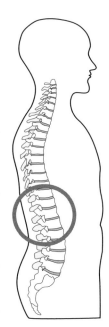

A Gout can be very debilitating and can strike elsewhere in the body beyond the big toe. Gout involves an excessive build-up of uric acid and is usually triggered by poor diet and inadequate exercise. In addition to improving those two aspects of your lifestyle, I suggest purchasing some natural, unsweetened cherry juice from your local health food store. Take one shot glass of it every two hours until the symptoms abate, and then one or two shot glasses each day for prevention.

Remember that your gout is not the result of deficiency of cherry juice, any more than it is not the result of deficiency of the prescription you've been prescribed. Look deeper for the underlying cause: poor diet and inadequate exercise. You must make lifestyle changes because further more serious trouble will lie ahead for you if you continue your former habits. Consider your gout troubles to be a blessing as an early warning sign. Also, uric acid control is performed by the kidneys and liver, so consider the integrity of those organs and their nerve supply in searching for the ultimate solution.

Growing Pains

Q My eight- and ten-year-old boys have frequent leg pains at night that keep them awake. Their pediatrician said they have normal growing pains and suggested an over-the-counter painkiller. Is there any other help for them?

A I've seen many children with so-called growing pains in my practice. Most of the time, the source of the pain is spinal misalignment at the lower end of their spines. Kids acquire these structural disturbances from stress and trauma through sports injuries, horseplay, and general poor posture like slouching in chairs. The delicate nerves that exit the lower spine easily get pinched and irritated by the misalignments and contribute to leg pains and cramping sensations. These discomforts are usually quite manageable with chiropractic treatment.

What are they eating? I've also observed that this type of pain often has a nutritional source: a poor diet usually consisting of soft drinks. These poor dietary habits, especially the frequent intake of soft drinks literally leach the minerals from the bones and joints, causing pain, especially at night. Take your children to a chiropractor, restrict their intake of soft drinks, improve their diet, and give them a high-quality multivitamin/mineral supplement like **Multigenics**®.

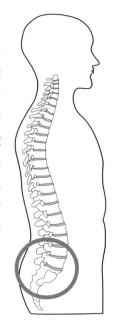

Headaches

My 15-year-old daughter has headaches several times per week. The headaches are so bad that she must sometimes miss school. She also has abdominal pain, which seems related to her headaches. We have taken her to several medical doctors whose testing has revealed nothing. The only treatments they prescribe are medications like pain killers and laxatives but I know this is not getting to the cause of the problem. Is there anything else we can do?

You are on the right track by trying to get to the cause of the problem. Chiropractors and other holistic-type practitioners view symptoms as clues or warning signs of malfunction. Covering symptoms with medications is only a

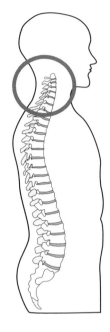

short-term solution and ultimately leads to further trouble. The problems you are describing usually indicate that there is a toxic build-up occurring in her body. Assuming her diet is typical of most 15-year-olds, she is likely lacking adequate fiber and protein and consumes too many carbohydrates. Modify her diet accordingly, make sure she drinks plenty of water, and perhaps have her follow a cleansing program to rid her body of the existing toxins. This usually makes a wonderful difference.

In many cases, headaches, and abdominal pain also have a postural component. The slouching, poor sitting and lying habits of many young people or trauma from sports contribute to a certain sequence of spinal misalignments that can cause headaches and abdominal pain. The spinal misalignments may need to be treated by a chiropractor. Improving her postural habits will help prevent reoccurrence.

Hernia

Q I have pain in my right groin. It becomes quite sharp when I lift something or move a certain way. My medical doctor diagnosed an inguinal hernia and suggested I visit a surgeon. Are there any ways to avoid surgery?

A I am not aware of any natural or holistic methods to alleviate a true hernia, whereby a portion of the intestines is protruding through an opening of the abdominal or other trunk muscles. Surgery is usually necessary in the most severe cases such as when the pain of a hernia is debilitating. A traditional hernia support belt may help. I've also observed that realigning the pelvic bone structure can be helpful in some cases.

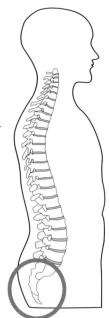

Heel Spurs

Q I have severe pain around the edge of my heel especially in the morning. It gets better as my day goes on but comes and goes, hindering activities like walking. What can be done to avoid surgery?

A Heel spurs and the discomfort associated with them is also referred to as plantar fasciitis, once known as "policeman's heel." It is almost always structural in source, meaning that the cause is misalignment or malfunction of some part of the foot's bones, joints or soft tissues. There are plenty of holistic methods that should be tried before undergoing any conventional surgery or taking medication. In some cases, an actual spur of bone, visible on an X-ray of the heel, will form.

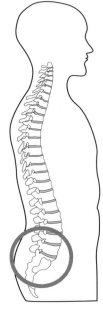

Obtain a high-quality, custom-made shoe insert called an orthotic. This insert needs to be flexible, made from a cast of the bottom of your foot, and address and support all three of the foot's arches, not just the main instep. I recommend one called **Foot Levelers**®. You can obtain a casting kit from our website, www.WholeHealthHealing.com. Orthotics always come in pairs and need to be inserted in any shoe you wear. The support obtained from doing this is very important in helping to correct the structural imbalances of your foot. Wear them as often as possible.

Have a chiropractor check the alignment of your heel bone (*navicular*) and ankle bone (*talus*), along with the alignment of your lower spine. Get adjustments to these areas until structural balance is obtained.

Losing weight will also help remove substantial pressure on the affected spinal and foot structures.

Some simple exercises include rolling your foot on a rolling pin against the floor with moderate pressure, going from the heel to the toes twelve times, three times a day.

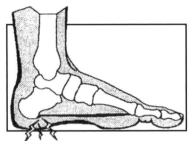

Heel spur (plantar fasciitis)

Be patient in the recovery of this painful condition. The problem was likely accumulating for a some time, long before you noticed it.

Injections for Pain

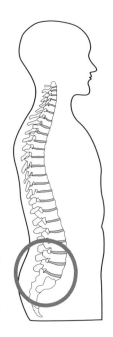

Q My family doctor referred me to a pain management specialist. This doctor wants to give me an injection into my spine to ease my sciatic nerve pain. Would this be wise?

A Injections are medical procedures and I can't advise you directly on this decision. I have observed that sometimes pain management injections can be helpful, but they should only be considered after all less invasive treatment procedures have been exhausted, such as nutrition, chiropractic care, lifestyle changes, and weight management.

To help you decide, you should be aware that a study recently outlined in the *New England Journal of Medicine*, showed very little benefit of spinal injections in a group of patients with sciatic nerve pain. The study concluded: "Although epidural injections of methylprednisolone may afford short-term improvement in leg pain in patients with sciatica due to a herniated disc, this treatment offers no significant benefit, nor does it reduce the need for surgery." Also, according to the literature, the side effects of such injections include headache, accidental puncture of nearby tissues, aseptic meningitis (a serious infection), and neurological problems.

Give chiropractic treatment a try. I've observed it to be a great help to many patients with sciatica.

Insomnia

Q I've been troubled with sleeping difficulties. I've been learning and utilizing holistic healthcare more than ever and I was wondering if there are any natural approaches to getting better sleep?

A : Several non-medicinal protocols can help improve sleep. We spend about one-third of our lives sleeping, so it's important to do it well.

Don't eat anything other than a light healthy snack 3 hours or less before you go to bed. Digestive activity, particularly by the stomach, can disrupt sleep patterns.

Invest in the best mattress and pillow you can find. I recommend a water-filled support pillow called **Chiroflow®**. Make sure you both rotate and flip your mattress at least seasonally.

If your sleep difficulty stems from unwanted thoughts, keep a paper and pen handy near your bed. Put those thoughts on paper and out of your head. Deal with those thoughts another time. You may want to consider doing this routinely; start a diary or journal, making entries each evening. It's no coincidence that a high percentage of historically great people kept diaries.

Move the furniture around in your sleeping quarters, particularly your bed position. I don't know why this works but many report that shifting the position of the bed can improve their insomnia.

Avoid taking naps during the day. Naps can be refreshing but they generally just steal time from your regular night's sleep.

Many chiropractic patients report more restful sleep after receiving chiropractic adjustments. The treatment not only relieves pain but calms the nervous system.

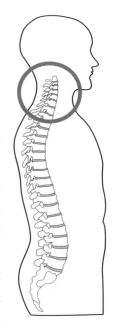

The one nutritional supplement that commonly helps insomnia is magnesium. Take 300 mg before bedtime. It is a mild relaxant and can be used during the day also for nervousness and anxiety. It is non-addictive and has no side effects. I recommend a supplement called **Myocalm**®.

Keep control over the situation. Don't watch TV or read until you fall asleep. Have a regular bed time and give it a lot of priority. Always set an alarm clock even when you can sleep later than usual. Having a regular, consistent wakening time is much easier on your health.

Get more exercise, both mentally and physically. Do it to a point when you feel the need for rest. Lack of exercise is the single most common cause of poor sleep. If you have become quite sedentary, remember that everyone needs to have goals and challenges every day. Keep at least your mind active if not your body.

Lastly, accept that some people may not need 8 hours of sleep daily. Many people do fine with six or fewer hours of sleep. You might be one.

Knee or Ankle Problems

Q My knees hurt when I walk a block or more. Both my knees and ankles make cracking sounds when I move them. I'm only 49. What can I do besides taking arthritis medication?

A Plenty. If you're overweight, any weight loss always pays off in providing relief. I've been amazed at how loss of even a few pounds makes a world of difference. Take natural anti-inflammatory supplements like glucosamine and chondroitin. Eat more anti-inflammatory foods as are described in Chapter 3, "Enjoying Eating." Obtain and wear a custom pair of shoe inserts (orthotics) with any shoes you wear.

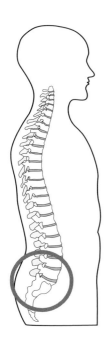

Misalignments can occur just as easily in joints like the ankles and knees as they do in the spine. The disrupted structural balance is readily detected and treated by a doctor of chiropractic. Arthritic problems are rarely genetic. Don't fall into the trap of accepting that you have to live with the pain and take medication to cover it.

Consider also that lower spine alignments sometimes cause pain to be referred into the knees and ankles. Get your spine, knees, and ankles checked by a chiropractor.

Do this knee-stretching maneuver, gently, three times a day: place a rolled up towel (about four inches in diameter) in back of your knee. Next, slowly and gently flex your knee on the rolled towel, making a slow, gentle pumping motion about 12 times. The towel acts as a wedge or fulcrum, producing gentle traction in the knee joint. This is a painless maneuver when done properly. As with all exercises and stretches, stop if you sense any significant pain or difficulty.

Leg Pain / Sciatica

Q I have severe pain running from my back down to my leg. The pain in my leg is mainly along the back side and outer shin. This has bothered me for 6 months. I am 48 years old. The pain killers I've been prescribed are expensive and making me drowsy at work. Acupuncture has provided some relief. Anything else I can do?

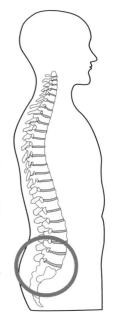

A This sounds like you have pinching, pressure, or irritation of your sciatic nerve. Some call this condition sciatica. The sciatic nerve is both the longest and thickest nerve in the body, making it the most commonly pinched. It usually is pinched at the lower spine, generally at the 4th or 5th lumbar vertebrae. That's about beltline level. The most conservative, efficient, economical, and safe route to recovery is to visit a chiropractor. Over the years, I have observed that more than 80 percent of people suffering from this condition can be resolved with chiropractic care alone.

Beyond chiropractic, some people opt for epidural injections (shots into the spine) or surgical decompression (laminectomy, discectomy, or spinal fusion). These more invasive procedures involve much more risk and expense.

A chiropractor will listen to your history, examine you, and take X-rays to determine the misalignment complex as precisely as possible. A treatment plan is then recommended to relieve, correct, and control the spinal disturbance. Make sure that you follow these recommendations accurately because your problem has existed at least six months and will take considerable effort to resolve fully. Shortening treatment, perhaps when initial relief is obtained, usually results in later relapses that are then more difficult to resolve.

The spinal disturbance in these cases is what we chiropractors call "vertebral subluxation complex" and is usually due to some kind of trauma. The trauma may have been the result of a fall, accident, or lifting improperly. Most often, the trauma is cumulative, coming from such habits of sitting with crossed legs, lying in awkward positions, having poorly supportive shoes, or even being overweight. I mention these examples because you should spend some time examining your lifestyle and make appropriate corrections to prevent this and other similar troubles from returning.

Recovery and prevention can be aided by wearing a back support belt during strenuous activity, like heavy lifting or digging. The only back support belt I recommend is called a **Sheik Support Belt**®.

Menopause / Hot Flashes

Q I am 58 and have hot flashes that are very uncomfortable. I also have multiple joint pains, some swelling, difficulty concentrating, insomnia, and low energy. I've been told these are symptoms of menopause. My doctor wants me to take hormone replacement therapy. Is there a way to avoid it?

A Menopause involves fluctuating estrogen levels and can cause a host of problems for some women. The National Institutes of Health and numerous additional studies, including several published in the *Journal of the American Medical Association*, have indicated that the risks of hormone replacement therapy far outweigh the benefits.

There are basically three types of menopause. Natural, or physiologic, menopause is caused by ovarian slowdown as a normal part of aging. Surgical or artificial menopause refers to the woman who has had both of her ovaries surgically removed, which dramatically reduces estrogen production. These women possess the same capacity to suffer from the clinical symptoms and complaints associated with natural menopause. Premature menopause refers to ovarian failure before the age of 40. Possible contributing factors include radiation exposure, surgery, drugs, poor diet, smoking, alcohol abuse, and structural disturbances.

There are several non-medicinal things women with menopause symptoms need to do

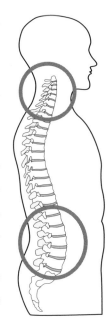

to reduce the severity of those symptoms. Basic good nutrition, exercise, and structural balance efforts as detailed throughout the book are essential. Specifically, in regard to structural balance, I've observed that chiropractic adjustments to key areas of the spine can help normalize the hormonal balance, easing many symptoms.

Supplementation with several nutrients and herbs like black cohosh and magnesium have been helpful. I've consistently recommended a supplement called **EstroFactors**®.

Menstrual Problems

Q I'm 29 and have moderate to severe cramping, pain, swelling, headaches, low energy, and difficulty concentrating just before and during my menstruation. I exercise two to three times per week at the gym. Do you think that the exercise is disrupting my cycles?

A I doubt that exercise, at the level you describe, is the source of your menstrual difficulties. The source of menstrual dysfunction is usually either nutritional or structural or both. In terms of nutritional sources, the symptoms you describe are commonly due to a lack of essential oils such as Omega 3 and 6. If you're partaking in the typical American eating style, you are likely lacking these. As I describe in Chapter 3, "Enjoying Eating," the fast, convenient, processed and corporate-grown foods are sorely lacking in the nutrients we need. The ramifications of poor nutrition show up in people just like you.

Try adding at least a few organic fruits and vegetables to your daily fare together with a meal of oily fish (tuna, salmon, sardines, or trout) at least twice weekly. Use nothing but olive oil for your cooking and snack on things like almonds and walnuts. Sprinkle a teaspoon of ground flax seeds on your morning cereal. These modifications are generally enough to supply your daily needs of essential oils.

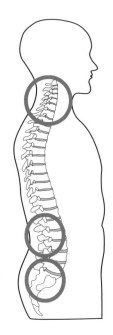

The structural sources are not to be ignored. You may have a spinal misalignment in one or more areas, impeding the nerve supply to the ovaries and uterus, short circuiting their functions. Most of these spinal imbalances come from past traumas and stresses like sports injuries, car accidents, accumulated poor postural habits, and even from birthing children. The disrupted nerve supply is only part of the story. Misaligned pelvic bones and the tailbone result in torqued soft tissue connections (muscles and ligaments) that make it difficult for the uterus to contract properly during menstruation. Get evaluated by a chiropractor.

I've commonly supplied my patients with menstrual problems with two supplements called **Fem-Premenstrual**® and **EstroFactors**®, both of which contain the nutrients to aid in healthy menstruation.

Obesity

I've tried all the diets and lost some weight with each one, but the weight never stays off. I am about 65 lbs. overweight and 49 years old. Am I missing something?

What you're missing is an understanding that weight loss is only permanent with lifestyle changes. These lifestyle changes are the result of choices we make. There may be some influence by hereditary factors and nationality but these are more minor than most people think. Getting excess weight off is easier than keeping it off. In my 20-plus years of practice, I've observed several factors that will lead to permanent weight control. These factors are all based on the principle of eating fewer calories and burning more. This principle must become a habit and followed for a lifetime.

Some tips to lose and maintain a healthy weight include:

♦ Have regular eating times. This can be difficult in our hurried world but this priority needs to be made. Inconsistent meals result in greater calorie intake. Aim for six regular, small meals per day.

♦ Eat more slowly. Chew your food into a fine mash before swallowing. Focus on the taste of each bite. If a typical meal of bread, vegetable, meat, and salad is eaten in less than 20 minutes, then you're eating too quickly. Eating quickly encourages gorging and gulping. Food that is not chewed properly results in poor absorption of the desirable nutrients and high absorption of the fats.

♦ Avoid eating out. The reason that restaurant food sometimes tastes better is because it is laced with sugar…yes, even the vegetables! If you must eat out, be very selective and choose the salads, soups, and higher-quality proteins like broiled chicken or fish, and grilled steak. Do not supersize! If the restaurant serves a large portion (I believe they are all too large), immediately ask for a container and place half the meal out of sight. Take it home and eat it for another meal.

♦ Seek more natural, organic, fresh foods. They cost more in the short term but pay off greatly in the long term by preventing expensive illnesses and joints worn out by obesity. More wholesome foods have a much higher nutritional value and thus are more satisfying to your hunger. One of the reasons for food cravings is caused by deficiencies of vitamins and minerals. If your fruits and vegetables look pretty, shiny and unblemished, they are probably corporate grown. Such eye-pleasing produce is likely to be grown in mineral-depleted soils, sprayed with dangerous pesticides, and even artificially ripened.

I don't approve of radical diets that advocate extremely high protein intake and few or no carbohydrates. I know you can lose weight by following such regimens, but as you've noticed, the weight comes back. I do advocate eating fewer carbs, and to especially avoid refined carbs (processed foods, white flour, white sugar). Add more quality proteins like lean meats and fish, broiled or grilled. I also encourage my obese patients to use a weight-loss aid called **Ultrameal**®. It is a powder mix taken twice daily to cleanse internally and get them started on some better eating habits. It has a wonderful balance of protein, fiber, and micronutrients.

Get a food allergy test performed. Hidden food allergies can contribute to unusual food cravings and fluid retention. The test I prescribe to my patients is from **U.S. Biotek Laboratories**.

If you must snack, choose wisely. Plain or lightly salted almonds, good quality protein bars, raisins, or whole wheat crackers are good choices. Read the label on those protein bars; many are high in carbohydrates to improve the taste. For nervous snacking, replace the eating with a hobby, craft, or exercise.

To burn more calories, don't overdo it. Small changes in your daily activities will go a long way. When shopping, don't look for the closest parking spot, and use the stairs instead of escalators and elevators. Walk or bike to work or school whenever possible. Strive for at least 30 minutes of steady, aerobic activity at least three times per week. Most importantly, vary the type of activity because boredom is the primary reason people stop exercising.

If you are in pain and can't exercise, then go to a chiropractor. We have special training in treating large people. A common side effect of many pain medications is weight gain. A common side effect of chiropractic treatment is weight loss, because it allows people to move better and become more active, burning more calories.

Being overweight or underweight is better evaluated in terms of body composition, in other words, what is your body fat percentage. This is best measured with an impedance analyzer, which is a device that sends a small electric current through your body and registers the resistance of that signal. The National Institutes of Health indicates that a healthy fat percentage for females is 20 to 25 percent and for males is 10 to 15 percent.

Some people might look at developing good weight control habits as hard work. Keep in mind the body is the temple of the spirit. Its well-being must be a top priority. The best investment of your time and money is taking care of yourself.

Osteoporosis

Q I'm in my early fifties and worried about my bones. I am very physically active and hope to stay that way. Is there anything I can do to avoid the stooped posture some older women have, also hip fractures and osteoporosis?

A Bone is a hard substance that forms the framework around which the body is built. That framework, or skeleton, contains over 200 separate bones that support and give shape to the body and protect its vital organs. Contrary to a common misconception, bone is a living substance! In fact, bone is one of the most active tissues in the body. It is constantly being dissolved and rebuilt in a process called remodeling and, like any other living tissue, needs nourishment to stay strong and healthy.

Since nutrition is so important, I recommend that any woman over 45 take calcium supplements. But be careful, because the kind of calcium you take can make or break you. Many people are falsely led to believe that any kind of calcium supplement will suffice. Some even take Tums® because it contains calcium. Big mistake! Many of these calcium supplements are either poorly absorbed into your system, or are not a complete bone food. Microcrystalline Hydroxyapatite Concentrate (MCHC) is the best calcium supplement to use. A good source of MCHC in supplement form that I've been recommending for years is called **Cal-apatite®**.

Regular exercise, a wholesome diet, and at least ten minutes daily of sun exposure are also very important. The stooped posture you mentioned can be caused by weak bones resulting from poor calcium intake, as well as by poor posture. To check for posture problems, stand with your back against a wall or door. Your heels, buttocks, upper/middle back, and head should be touching the wall. Walk away and try to hold that position. Also, sit with your butt all the way back in a chair and place a small pillow in the hollow of your low back. Avoid sleeping in chairs and avoid recliners altogether. Good glandular function, especially the adrenal and thyroid glands are critical to calcium processing in the body. That is why chiropractic treatment to the related spine-nerve connections will help.

Please also see the chart of "Calcium Supplements: Their Advantages and Disadvantages" in the Resource section at the back of this book.

Prostate

Q I'm 55 and have been diagnosed with a swollen prostate. My PSA test is above average. I've been told this can become cancerous. The surgeon wants to remove my prostate. What can I do to avoid surgery?

A Medical treatment of prostate problems is quite controversial, especially with regard to when and when not to consider surgical intervention. In most cases, "watchful waiting" is the best approach. Be aware that PSA tests have a high false positive rate. This means the test can show a problem that may not exist. I have observed numerous cases that have benefited from holistic practices. I believe they should be tried before anything more invasive. For one, I recommend a combination of nutritional supplementation containing zinc, pumpkin seed extract, and saw palmetto. The supplement I know of that contains all that in good quality is called **Ultraprostagen**®.

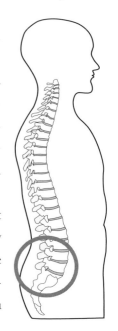

Converting to and being consistent with a more holistic/vitalistic diet is also important. As detailed in Chapter 3, "Enjoying Eating," this involves better quality carbohydrates and proteins, more raw, fresh, and organic fruits and vegetables.

The prostate, like all other organs, does not just function by itself. It has a nerve supply from the lower spine. This connection is all the more reason to address spinal alignment regularly, rather than simply chalking up back pain to pulled muscles and self treating with heat or pain killers. There are occasions whereby the lower spine can be out of alignment, which in turn can cause prostrate malfunction, but the person has no back pain.

Of course, regular exercise, adequate sleep, stress control, and overall holistic practices are not to be taken lightly both in the recovery and prevention of any kind of prostate trouble.

Psoriasis

Q I am 33 and have dry, red, scaly patches of psoriasis on several areas of my body. What natural procedures can I do to help this?

A I've seen numerous patients improve their psoriasis, sometimes dramatically, by doing two things simultaneously: improving their nerve system through chiropractic spinal adjusting, and thoroughly cleansing their digestive tract. I've heard it said that the health of a person's skin is a direct reflection of the inner lining of their digestive tract. I believe this to be particularly true in the case of psoriasis. Our skin is an excretory organ just like the digestive tract. A fully functional and unimpeded nerve supply is important because it's the body's wiring system and control center for many things we rarely consider including the skin and digestive system.

The best internal cleansing program I'm aware of is called **Ultraclear**®. This is a powder you mix and drink over a six-week period.

Improving your relaxation skills through meditative prayer, recreation, deep rhythmic breathing, and stretching is also important especially in preventing recurrences. Follow the same advice I provide for acne sufferers in this chapter.

Shoulder Pain

Q My shoulder hurts every time I try to raise my arm. I hear some grinding sounds during movement and I can't lie on the side of my sore shoulder. I'm only 60 and want to stay active but my shoulder is holding me back. What can I do?

A Shoulders are very complicated joints involving several muscles, nerves, and bony connections. Most respond quite well to holistic treatment unless the joint is severely arthritic or contains large tears in the ligaments. An MRI (magnetic resonance imaging) test needs to be performed to rule out the possibility of tears. Many shoulder pains really have their source away from the shoulder itself, meaning disturbances in the alignment of the neck, upper spine, collar bone, and scapula can make a person feel referred pain in the shoulder. The same goes for myofascial trigger points in the same areas. These small pockets of lactic acid or knots in the muscles can easily refer pain to the shoulder.

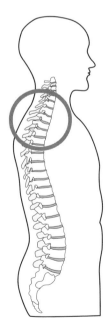

Many times, structural disturbances of the shoulder are caused by a stress or trauma like a sports injury, accident, or a fall, although it's not uncommon for shoulders to start hurting for what seems like no reason at all. Some patients even say they just woke up with it. The source could also come or accumulate from repetitive motions. Sometimes an improper sleeping position, particularly if habitual like using the arm as a pillow, can be a source. See Chapter 4, "Your Posture," for the proper positioning.

As in all joint pains, increasing intake of nutrition that minimizes inflammation is helpful as detailed in Chapter 3, "Enjoying Eating." In seniors, a common source of shoulder pain is from myofascial trigger points that form in the deltoid muscle. These can be felt as small, painful nodules on the side of the arm. Heating them and rubbing them out regularly usually produces fast relief.

The common medical approach is to prescribe anti-inflammatory drugs. These can provide relief but do not address any underlying sources of the disturbance, and carry a significant risk of adverse side effects.

Both the alignment of joints and disturbances in the muscles need to be evaluated by a person trained in structural problems like a massage therapist, physical therapist, or chiropractor. You'll know you're in the right place when the practitioner places his or her hands directly on your shoulder and the connections I mentioned above. Scans like X-rays, MRI, or CT can be helpful but usually won't reveal the misalignments or muscular sources.

Don't fall for the usual medical excuses of bursitis, tendonitis, or rotator cuff problems without trying a holistic approach first. Don't even bother trying to exercise a painful shoulder thinking that will help; movement will only increase the damage to the shoulder complex. Strengthening should only follow structural change like chiropractic adjustments or myofascial release.

Sinus Problems

Q I have persistent sinus pain, congestion, and drainage. At age 45, I've never had any allergies. Decongestants help but not permanently and the side effects make me feel tired or spacey. What natural remedies exist to help this?

A Sinus problems can certainly be annoying. They seem to develop by surprise and have several sources. The most common causes are weak immunity, allergies, and misalignment of the cervical spine (neck). Your cause may be one or a combination of these.

If the discharge shows any substantial discoloration such as yellow, red, or green, you must immediately seek medical help. If your discharge/drainage is clear/white and relatively free-flowing/dripping, then the source is likely something you can deal with naturally. Start by eliminating or at least decreasing your intake of substances containing common allergens for sinus problems: dairy, beer, wheat, orange juice, smoke, and food additives. I call these mucous formers. Even though you claim never to have

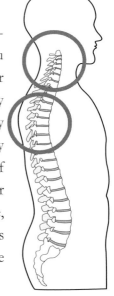

had any allergies, they may be there but well hidden. Consider taking the food allergy test shown on our website: www.WholeHealthHealing.com.

Obtain and place an air cleaner in your home and work place, preferably an ionizing air cleaner. These type air cleaners will reduce or eliminate any irritants that may be present.

Quite often, we chiropractors observe that misalignment of the cervical spine (neck) produces irritation of some nerves called the cranial plexus. These delicate nerves control the tiny mucous glands and cells lining the sinuses. When the nerves are compressed or irritated due to spinal misalignment, a sort of short circuit occurs, causing excessive mucous discharge, and then frequent infections.

Nutritional supplementation can help. The supplement I frequently recommend is called **Sinuplex®**. It contains a variety of nutrients helpful to healthy sinus function.

Perform this sinus-opening procedure daily: curl both your index fingers and place then on your cheek bones close to your nose. While pressing firmly, slowly pull your hands laterally (sideways away from your nose). This helps to open up the delicate sinus drainage passages to prevent clogging. Consider a sinus cleansing technique. I recommend a product called **Sinucleanse®**. It involves mixing a warm solution and literally pouring it in one nostril and letting it run out the other. This is performed while leaning over a sink.

Sleep Apnea

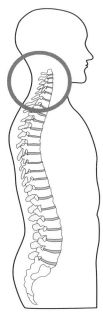

Q I suffer from sleep apnea and utilize the nightime breathing machine. What can be done naturally to help me?

A There are three highly effective things to consider for sleep apnea sufferers. First, consider weight management. Excess body fat can accumulate in unusual areas and one of them is around the breathing/throat/uvula structures, constricting air flow especially when sleeping.

Second, consider getting a food allergy test. Hidden food allergies can cause swelling of the throat structures and also have an effect of disrupting breathing mechanisms in the brain. The test I administer to my patients is from a company called **U.S. Biotek Laboratories.**

Last, but important, brain stem pinching and compression due to misalignment of the uppermost spine can cause or contribute to breathing problems; a chiropractic evaluation is also recommended.

Spinal Surgery

Q I have had surgery on my spine twice, both in the neck and back. One was a discectomy, the other was a laminectomy. I have pain daily; it radiates from my neck into my arm, and from my back into my leg. Can I still go to a chiropractor and receive treatment even though I have had these surgeries on my spine?

A Chiropractors go through six to eight years of training to attain their degree. Part of that involves learning how to help people who have had spinal surgery. It is not uncommon for patients to continue having problems after spinal surgery. The changes made to one part of the spine to relieve pain can ultimately lead to damage in another part, especially long term. Make sure you explain to your chiropractor the details of the surgeries you have had, bring along any X-rays, MRI, or CT scans, and ask for an explanation of what the treatment will involve. The treatment you receive may be lighter and more gentle than that given to other patients. If your condition appears to be untreatable, your chiropractor is also trained in how and where to refer you to another professional.

Robert Mendelsohn, MD, author of *Confessions of a Medical Heretic,* stated, "No one should ever have spinal surgery without first undergoing chiropractic treatment." Many spinal surgeries can be avoided by first visiting a doctor of chiropractic.

Vaccinations and Immunizations

Q My wife and I were recently married and we are planning on having three children, God willing. We are wondering about whether to vaccinate/immunize our children. What do you recommend?

A Congratulations on your marriage and may God grant you healthy children. My position on vaccinations/immunizations is that these are medical procedures and the decision for immunization or vaccination should be between you and your medical physician. As a chiropractor, I can't directly advise you on this issue for legal and ethical reasons. However, I am concerned about, and you should be informed that, the medical information provided to you may not be all that you need to make a rational decision.

I recently met with a medical doctor over lunch and the subject of vaccination/immunization was discussed. The physician initiated our discussion about this topic by mentioning that a lady with three children had recently come to his office for their annual examination. Apparently, she told the physician that she has not immunized/vaccinated her children because she read a book about the subject. He was aghast!

This was a perfect example of the one-sided thinking on this subject that I believe many medical doctors possess, particularly with regard to immunizations and vaccinations. They are programmed from day one of their medical education that everyone should receive vaccinations and/or immunizations, never or rarely looking at the information on the other side.

The famous bumper sticker, *QUESTION AUTHORITY*, definitely applies here. Wouldn't it have made sense for that doctor to ask if he could read the book she mentioned? Or at least inquire about some of the facts or principles there. Perhaps this is why MD in some circles stands for "Medical Deity" (god) rather than medical doctor. Of course, there are many exceptions to that arrogant colleague, some medical professionals are aware of alternatives to pushing pills and shots.

What I can legally and ethically tell you is that my wife and I made the decision not to vaccinate or immunize our three children, who are now ages 12, 10, and 7. We made the decision after studying the facts on both sides of the issue. Doesn't that seem like a rational way to make a decision like this? I constantly monitor the latest information on this subject and continue to feel strongly that we made the right decision. Our decision may not be right for you. I encourage you to study the subject thoroughly. You will find lots of information both pro and con on the Internet.

By the way, I mentioned earlier that the decision should be made by both you and your medical physician. There are many efforts underway to pass legislation that takes away your rights to decide what can be injected into your and your children's bodies. Some states have already taken your freedom of choice away. In Wisconsin, where I have my practice, the choice is still yours, but that choice is under attack. To currently avoid vaccinations/ immunizations here, you merely need to sign the back of the child's vaccination/immunization record, stating your choice not to immunize for personal, religious, or medical reasons.

I feel strongly that this choice be respected and upheld. It not only makes sense, but also when historians review the origins of Germany's Nazi Party, it is as clear as day that some of the atrocities began when German citizens' rights to make their own decisions about their personal healthcare were taken away and placed solely in the hands of medical physicians. This of course led to an avalanche of atrocities like mass sterilization of certain groups and extermination. Let's not let that happen again.

Whether you decide to immunize or not, take at least some of the holistic preventive measures outlined in Chapters 8, "Strategies for Prevention" and Chapter 10, "Raising Healthier Children." There are many non-pharmaceutical things to do to build and maintain strong immunity.

Weak Immune System

Q My diet is very good. I eat balanced meals of fruit/vegetables/grains and meat/fish. My snacking is light and usually consists of something like popcorn or nuts. I drink mainly water or fruit juice (unsweetened). I exercise regularly, mainly by swimming, walking, or bike riding. I get several colds per year, which consist of sinus congestion, coughing, fever, and weakness. Each cold lasts about two weeks and I usually have to go and get antibiotics. I don't understand why I get sick like this with my lifestyle as healthy as it is. Is there anything more I can do?

There are many more things you can do. Although your diet might seem good, our food supply is so depleted in vitamins and minerals that your body may be lacking the nutrients it needs particularly for a strong immune system. It's very possible to be eating plenty yet be malnourished. For example, if your fruits and vegetables look "pretty" (meaning shiny, unblemished, well shaped, and colorful), they are probably corporate grown. These fruits and vegetables lack many necessary nutrients because they are grown in depleted soils using synthetic fertilizers. They may be genetically modified and/or artificially ripened. Buy or grow organic fruits and vegetables. They are not as "pretty" but do a lot more for you.

Take a good organic multivitamin/mineral supplement daily rather than a synthetic variety. Most popular, brand-name vitamin and mineral supplements are synthetic, meaning made out of chemicals instead of derived from foods. Synthetic varieties are poorly absorbed or utilized by the body. Many nurses call them "bedpan bullets" because they pass through the body without dissolving or being absorbed. Any holistic professional or health food store can guide you in your purchase. I'm a fan of the multivitamin/mineral supplement called **Multigenics**®.

Your frequent use of antibiotics concerns me. Infections of the type you describe are usually viral. Antibiotics only kill bacteria. You may be killing or at least diminishing the normal natural bacteria that belong in your body. Such repetitive antibiotic use can contribute to a weakened immune system. If you must utilize antibiotic medications, make sure you follow their use with probiotics. Probiotics are foods or supplements that contain and rebuild the normal, natural bacterial flora in the digestive tract. Yogurt is a good example of a food that helps rebuild the normal flora.

Have you considered your body structure? The immune system is controlled by the nervous system. The nervous system is easily disturbed by faulty spinal alignment. Many chiropractic patients report less frequent infections and faster recovery from them with regular chiropractic treatment.

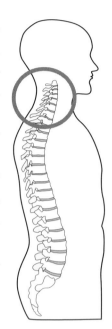

There are several other issues to consider such as: the humidity level in your home and workplace, getting enough sleep, stress level, and washing your hands frequently. Any holistic-minded doctor can help you sort through these possible causes of your weak immunity.

Whiplash / Neck Pain

Q I was involved in a rear-end collision about two years ago. My neck still does not feel right even after going through an extensive course of physical therapy and rehabilitation. I still do the neck exercises I was taught. I also get more frequent headaches and numbness/tingling of my fingers. What am I missing?

A You're missing chiropractic adjustments. Pardon my boldness here but I've seen thousands of cases like yours over the years and truly believe that without chiropractic treatment, you'll never recover as fully as possible. Sadly, now that two years have passed, there may be some permanent damage to your ligaments, nerves, and cartilage. I strongly

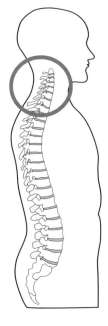

advocate that anybody involved in an auto accident be evaluated as soon as possible by a doctor of chiropractic.

Physical therapy, medication, and other medical care may also be necessary, but the trauma and stress involved in an auto accident almost always produces misaligned spinal structure that is best addressed with chiropractic care. Don't be misled by attorneys, insurance companies, medical personnel, or therapists who insist that the pain is "just muscles." The symptoms you have of headaches and finger numbness/tingling are present due to the nerve flow interference as a consequence of the spinal misalignments.

This condition of spinal misalignment and nerve pressure, which we call subluxation, is progressive when left untreated, ultimately contributing to accelerated disc degeneration, not to mention more future symptoms. Get to a chiropractor as soon as possible. Many times the med-pay portion of your own auto accident insurance may cover the chiropractic care you need. Often, an accident like this leaves the victim with a permanent vulnerability or weakness in the injured areas, so following the posture and stretching instructions in this book is paramount to minimizing future disability.

Wrist or Hand Pain

Q I've been bothered with wrist and hand pain for about eight months. There is also some tingling and numbness at night. I do a lot of work on computer keyboards. My medical doctor says I have carpal tunnel syndrome. Are there any holistic methods to help this?

A Before resorting to surgery, make sure you try the following for at least six weeks:

#1 Rearrange your work station to change the angle of your elbows, wrists, and neck. Keep experimenting with different angles until you feel a noticeable change. Generally, your forearms should be parallel to the floor when your hands are at the keyboard. Your wrists should be straight. Your monitor should be at eye level when you're sitting erect.

#2 Take Vitamin B6 supplements daily. The recommended dietary allowance is determined by an individual's daily protein intake. Adults need 2 milligrams of B6 per 100 grams of protein per day. The need for B6 increases during pregnancy, lactation, exposure to radiation, cardiac problems, and the use of oral contraceptives. B6 is water soluble so it's unlikely that any harm can result from overdosing. Daily doses of 100 to 300 milligrams have been administered without side effects. I recommend a supplement called **EZFlex**®.

#3 Wrap a rubber band around the first joint of your fingers and thumb. Spread your fingers and thumb apart, making the circle of the rubber band as large as possible, repeating to expand and feel the resistance of the rubber band until you feel fatigue. Repeat this exercise at least three times daily. This exercise strengthens a group of forearm muscles that opens up the compressed tunnel of the wrist. See Chapter 2, page 57, for pictures and a description of this exercise. Our website also offers a more elaborate exercise tool for this called a **Carpal Care Kit**®.

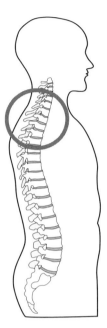

#4 Have your neck examined by a Doctor of Chiropractic. Many wrist and hand troubles are really a referred problem from compressed nerves at the base of the neck and upper back. This spinal component is often missed by medical practitioners and is one of the reasons that carpal tunnel surgery at the wrist is often unsuccessful.

Chapter 7
Talking To Your Doctor
Using the power struggle to your advantage

T his is my favorite chapter. I believe the information given here, when used by patients, will change the course of healthcare and give patients the control of their well-being that's been lacking for a long time.

If several 747 jetliners, loaded with hundreds of people, were crashing every week, with no survivors, or about a hundred thousand casualties annually, you would not get on a 747. Yet an equal, if not greater, number of casualties results from the side effects and errors of modern medical care, approximately 100,000 per year according to the World Health Organization. That's considered a low estimate because many mistakes are not reported. And people keep submitting to medical care, usually without questioning it.

> **People vote with their feet.**
> —*Joseph Stalin*

Are you one of those people? Where's the outrage? I'm not talking about avoiding surgeries or medications that are necessary in life-threatening or emergency situations. Modern medicine does excellent work with those cases and I hope they will help me someday if I need it.

I'm talking about making wiser choices when high risk, costly procedures are recommended to you when other alternatives exist. Remember from discussions in prior chapters that most medical treatment is really "sickness care" (covering symptoms), not real healthcare (addressing your mental, physical, and spiritual well-being). It's important to keep that difference in mind when communicating with any doctor. If you follow through on my suggestions in this chapter, you'll no longer be a potential victim of the current insane system.

Since it wouldn't be wise to ask a Ford dealer about a Chevy, some will ask, "What is a chiropractor like me doing talking about medical care then?" The answer is simple. I'm not giving medical advice anywhere in this book, nor have I done so at any time in my career. If you need medical treatment, you should get it. But I stand firm on my suggestion that there is much abuse, that medical doctors shouldn't give out advice about holistic/natural care, and that patients like you need to have the information from books like this to navigate your way through the conflict. I can't provide the information you need without

Let people feel the weight of
who you are and then let them deal with it.
—John Eldredge

pointing out the shortcomings of medical care and how you need to be cautious with what they tell you when it comes to anything other than emergency or life-threatening situations.

Read this next sentence out loud: "I understand what you're recommending, Doctor, but I want to give the more natural route a try first." This is what you need to say to your doctor to avoid being a victim of the medical holocaust. Many people will feel uncomfortable speaking up to their doctors with that sentence, because they are used to being led like sheep to slaughter. Dealing with the medical industry can be very intimidating. Repeat the above sentence until you feel comfortable saying it to your medical doctor.

> Be bold and use your enlightenment about the benefits of natural health methods to demand cooperation from your medical doctor.

You must take back control! It's your body and your health! A really good doctor will answer "okay" to the above statement and work with you. Others will be shaken, upset, maybe even abusive, or try to talk you out of it. You, being wiser with the help of this book, will see through the arrogance, and the threat to their economic dominance of the healthcare marketplace. If your doctor turns out to be one of the uncooperative ones, remember, there are lots of other doctors out there and it's okay to switch. Your courage and persistence with this, when shared by enough others also, will transform the healthcare system, and it will happen fast.

Sometimes you'll come across a medical professional who has taken notice of the current trend of people seeking more natural solutions to healthcare. Some of these doctors try to combine the best of both worlds—holistic and medical. Don't be fooled! Both involve years of in-depth training and licensing. I've never met any doctor who can do both very well, even the few with dual degrees. There are simply too many details to keep straight. Most medical personnel who attempt to provide some holistic care are doing so with very little training. Maybe they've read a book or two, or maybe they've attended a few weekend seminars. I do believe many of them mean well, but they fail to acknowledge or respect the real training and licensing necessary to provide holistic care properly.

> An elderly lady, aged 74, sheepishly told me that her medical doctor had recently performed a bone density test on her, diagnosing osteoporosis, and placed her on one of the popular osteoporosis drugs.
>
> "Did he advise you to get a few minutes of sun on your skin each day, perform light exercise regularly, or add more calcium-rich foods to your diet?" I asked.
>
> "No," she said. "He just handed me a prescription."
>
> I wanted to scream, but I stayed calm, gave her some printed material about osteoporosis, its natural prevention and treatment, and became even more motivated to write this book!

The rift between medical doctors and holistic/vitalistic practitioners like chiropractors has been lessening. I'm hearing and reading about more frequent cooperation. The two sides are working together more often, not only on individual cases, but also with professional athletic teams, in hospitals, and even writing books and research articles together. Quite often, unfortunately, the holistic/vitalistic side, when employed by or at least overseen by the medical, produces a watered down, overly controlled "squeak" of the more logical, safer, and economical choice. I'm happy to report that, perhaps somewhat due to my outreach efforts, each year produces more patients coming into my office who say, "My medical doctor told me to come here." Hurray for both you and me! The rift, however, is still large.

I always encourage my patients to tell their medical practitioners about any holistic care they are receiving, but to not necessarily expect approval. The MDs need to know about it and I believe most want to know. If you do tell, and receive a not-so-pleasant response, I suggest you say, "Thank you for your opinion, Doctor. Now let's get back to talking about what *you* have to offer me." I believe this is the best and most respectful way to get what you need from them.

> **Always inform your healthcare professional about all the treatments you are receiving or practitioners you are seeing.**

Much of the rift between the two sides of healthcare stems from the illegal boycott orchestrated by the AMA a few decades ago. It took a Supreme Court judge to issue a cease-and-desist order in 1984, based on AMA documents that clearly stated their covert plans to "contain and eliminate the chiropractic profession." Under those archaic AMA decrees, a medical doctor was forbidden not only from referring patients to chiropractors, but also from even associating with them. Some MDs broke ranks, and did whatever was best for their patients, but then faced ridicule from their peers and perhaps even were barred from medical seminars. More details of this suppression by the medical industry can be read in Chapter 5, "Structure-Based Healthcare."

> Surprisingly, nurses and other medical assistants make excellent chiropractic patients and love other holistic/vitalistic methods. Many do so somewhat secretly. It's because even though they are trained allopathically/mechanistically, they observe first hand the many downfalls there.
> One of my patients, Barb, a 33-year-old RN, said to me, "If you ever meet the doctor I work for, please don't tell him that I come here."

Putting my bias as a chiropractor aside, you deserve to know some of the accusations that were made against chiropractors and other holistic/vitalistic practitioners. Some of these are still repeated to this day. Most commonly, natural healthcare adversaries claim that we put patients in danger because we might miss something that needs medical attention. Second, they accuse the holistic professions of lacking research to support our claims and methods. Last, they claim that the quality of education in the natural healthcare fields is lacking.

With regard to putting patients in danger, the best place to judge that would be by looking at both the lower malpractice insurance rates of holistic practitioners and the higher patient satisfaction surveys. Both show that the holistic care is statistically safer and preferred by patients. There is and always will be some risk in any kind of healthcare procedures. The medical establishments and the media have a habit of over publicizing the rather rare, unfortunate complications of holistic care. In my field of chiropractic, much of the education involves learning to detect cases that are outside the scope of our treatment, and then refer them to someone that can help them.

It's important to consider the arguments on both sides of the healthcare marketplace. You be the judge.

Stanley, age 85, was another victim of the current osteoporosis game being played out frequently in the medical world. Now understand that osteoporosis is not to be taken lightly, for it affects the structure and foundation of your body.

Stanley's doctor told him to take an over-the-counter, common antacid tablet because it's a cheap form of calcium. I nearly fainted when I heard that. I promptly explained to Stanley that taking any antacid increases your risk of osteoporosis because antacids decrease digestive acidity, inhibiting the absorption of calcium. Also, such products contain a form of calcium not very helpful for bone density. He was stunned but happy to get the real story.

The accusation of lack of research among holistic treatment methods has some substantiation. Dollars spent, and papers published on research is certainly dominated by the medical community, but the holistic side is rapidly making gains here. One detriment has been that the allocation of research grants has traditionally been controlled by the medical establishment. It's only been in the last few years that the federal bureaus administrating research have opened divisions on natural health methods.

It's also important to consider that much of the medical research is financed by the pharmaceutical industries. Recently there have been several reports that much medical research is flawed because of that economic connection, producing a tremendous conflict of interest. Modern medicine prides itself on the claim that its methods and procedures are based on scientific evidence. In a perfect world that would be great, but the evidence seems to be just as often disproved soon after it is proven. As I'm writing these very lines, the headlines in today's newspaper tell of new research regarding a popular drug, formerly shown to help depression, has been proven to greatly in-

Comparison of classroom hours required to obtain a Doctor of Chiropractic (DC) degree and a Doctor of Medicine (MD) degree		
D.C.	*SUBJECT*	**M.D.**
540	ANATOMY – EMBRYOLOGY	508
240	PHYSIOLOGY	326
360	PATHOLOGY – GERIATRICS-PEDIATRICS	401
165	CHEMISTRY	325
120	MICROBIOLOGY	114
630	DIAGNOSIS – DERMATOLOGY EYES, EARS, NOSE THROAT	324
320	NEUROLOGY	112
360	RADIOLOGY	148
60	PSYCHOLOGY – PSYCHIATRY	144
60	OBSTETRICS – GYNECOLOGY	148
210	ORTHOPEDICS	156
3,065	*TOTAL*	2,706

Source: Palmer School of Chiropractic

crease the risk of suicide among young people! Also, reliable sources within the medical field itself acknowledge that only about 30 percent of medical procedures have substantial research to support them.

> Question the training and education of any professional giving you advice about your health.

The claims of poor quality of education are half true. Some holistic practitioners have very little education in their fields. For example, some states are quite unrestricted in who is allowed to claim the title naturopath, massage therapist, and nutritionist. Many states lack licensure for these titles. Part of my advice involved in inspiring people to make wiser choices about their healthcare is to question the credentials of the holistic practitioners they consult. I recommend being skeptical taking advice from someone who read a few books or attended a few weekend courses.

I'm happy to report that all states have strict educational and licensing requirements for Doctors of Chiropractic. All the chiropractic colleges adhere to strict academic requirements and credentialing. It takes at least six years to obtain a DC degree. Then there are four national board exams, a state board exam, and yearly post-graduate training requirements for maintaining a chiropractic license in any state.

> I always ask my patients how they heard about me. Most tell me they were told by another patient. That is the best compliment I can get—a satisfied patient recommending me to someone else.
> One young lady named Julie told me she found me in a surprising way. She was at a medical diag-

nostic center, getting an MRI scan ordered by her medical doctor to find the cause of her headaches. During the setup for the scan, she conversed with the technician, explaining her health problem and her frustration getting any relief other than with the expensive prescription pain killers that made her feel dizzy and tired.

At the end of the scan, as Julie lay on the scanner's table, the technician leaned over and whispered, "Go see my chiropractor, Dr. Potisk. He helped me with the same trouble you're having."

As painful to my pride as it's been, I've tried hard to objectively listen to critics of holistic methods, both from the medical establishment and from the few patients who claim to have tried it and didn't like it. I've noticed that quite often, the expectations of those critics were too high. For example, with most holistic/vitalistic methods, results can come more slowly than results with medications. Quick, dramatic results are more the exception than the rule with natural methods. Lifestyle changes, nutritional supplementation, and structural improvement techniques often involve several weeks and sometimes several months of persistence to obtain thorough desired results.

A substantial portion of my time and energy in helping patients isn't consumed by the application of the treatment itself. Instead, it's in reassuring patients, encouraging them to have patience, to stick with it, to allow their body to have the time it needs to heal. For the average human being, especially in this continually accelerating society, the time factor can be a real deterrent to choosing holistic/vitalistic health methods. It's a lot easier and quicker to swallow a pill, get an injection, or have something cut out. When I carefully question the few people who tell me natural methods didn't help them, invariably it turns out that they didn't give the natural methods enough time.

> **Be prepared to allow plenty of time for your body to fully heal when utilizing natural methods.**

I can easily relate to those who are in a hurry because I'm quite impatient in many respects myself. However, age and experience have taught me that really good things don't usually come quickly or easily. That lesson sometimes has to come the hard way.

> I'd estimate that at least half the patients who have come to my office over the years have come as a last resort. I could fill another book with some of the stories patients have told me about what they've gone through in their search for better health. Thousands of dollars spent, multiple surgeries, dozens of medications, and countless hours spent in medical waiting rooms are common experiences of those patients I label "medical rejects," or those who have "gone through the mill."

We chiropractors almost enjoy getting patients like that ("medical rejects") only because, at times, it's almost too easy to help them. We simply find the blockage as I described in Chapter 5, "Structure-Based Healthcare," remove it, and then watch them get better. Since nearly everything else has been tried, we easily look like heroes. The truth is that they should have taken the holistic path first. Sadly, some have waited too long. Scar tissue, degenerating cartilage, or a body literally poisoned by medication can hamper natural healing.

> Tears filled my eyes as I wrote the preceding lines, remembering those poor souls who waited too long. For those of you I was not able to help, I apologize. Please teach your children, grandchildren, neighbors, and friends the simple, but overlooked concepts in this book, so they don't make the same poor choices you did.

Another common complaint I hear from critics is that there is inconsistency in treatment methods with natural practitioners. Here lies another significant difference between the two sides of healthcare: art. The art of practicing has declined greatly in modern medicine. The skills, intuition, and knowledge gained by doctors from the school of hard knocks have been hampered by economic and government regulations, economic pressures to spend less time with patients, as well as marketing pressures in the medical world. For example, more and more medical doctors are contracted by insurance companies like HMOs (health maintenance organizations). These are big businesses and they routinely require their employee doctors to limit time spent with patients. Think "assembly line" healthcare! At the World Health Organization (WHO) Convention in 2008, the Director General, Dr. Margaret Chan, MD, stated: "Medical care has become depersonalized, some would say *hard-hearted.*" Yikes!

In the holistic/vitalistic world of healthcare, art is alive and well. That means that different practitioners of the same holistic profession will have varying approaches to helping the same problem, perhaps even in treating the same person. This drives science-minded scholars crazy, motivating them to label us artists as voodoo practitioners. The last laugh is on these scholars. They fail to notice that in other countries, where medical care is still rendered with much art, people on average live longer and are generally healthier. I'm not saying all science in healthcare should be abandoned; but when it replaces human compassion, a warm loving touch, unique talent, hard-learned skills, and a concerned, warm-hearted practitioner, together with intense concern for a patient (art), then I say science is out of control.

As I revealed in previous chapters, I initially considered becoming a medical doctor. Because of this, I have several personal friends from those earlier days who now are MDs. I've come to the conclusion that, when we get together, it's better if we not bring up any discussions about health. On the few occasions when we've tried, it's like we are speaking different languages. Combining that with our natural high egos and pride, you can imagine how feelings easily get hurt. It all comes down to the reality that God made some of us to think holistically/vitalistically and some others to think mechanistically/medically. Patients need us both.

Not only MDs but patients also need to be aware of the prevalence of art in holistic/vitalistic treatment and respect it. Most patients, not surprisingly, love it, but on occasion some are confused by it, especially in regard to variations in treatment methods. That inconsistency is a godsend from the perspective of finding treatment you're comfortable with. In other words, if you're not happy with what one holistic provider suggests to you, another will likely have a different approach that may be more to your liking. Seek another option in the medical field, and you're likely to encounter a similar white-coated doctor using the same prescription pad and pen from the local pharmaceutical salesperson, the same diagnostic tests, and probably the same advice. They pride themselves on consistency and that certainly has value at times, especially in life-threatening or emergency situations, but apply that to real health and wellness as discussed in earlier chapters, and you get an awfully cold feeling, just when you need a warm smile and touch.

> **Expect a lot of "art" when seeking care from holistic/vitalistic practitioners. It's refreshingly wonderful! Some even say it's the biggest part of real healing.**

In my field of chiropractic, for example, a practitioner like me, focusing on structural treatment, will start adjusting from the tailbone and work up. It's just the way I've been taught to do it. My associate, also a DC, usually starts adjusting at the top of the spine and works down. It's the way he was taught. Still another DC may provide most of the structural treatment using a small, hand-held adjusting instrument. There are numerous approaches, each taught slightly differently, but with the same goal in mind—

to change the structural integrity of the spine and improve nerve function.

Consider the very first vertebra in the spine, located immediately below the skull, called the *atlas*. That bone can be adjusted with patients sitting, lying on their backs, lying on their sides, lying face down, with a small instrument, with the chiropractor's thumb, with the chiropractor's wrist, with the chiropractor's first knuckle, and these are just some of the variations. Each chiropractor will apply his or her art differently. For those of you hard-core, scientific, consistent medical personnel who freak out about this, let me remind you about the numerous studies that show our artful approach has higher patient satisfaction ratings. You'll find just as much variation in visiting massage therapists, acupuncturists, and nutritionists.

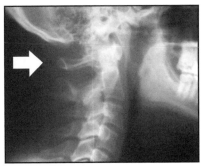

The atlas bone

Now, what can I tell you about how to talk to your holistic/vitalistic practitioner? For one thing, in contrast to the challenges mentioned above when talking to a medical practitioner, don't always expect us to be gleeful of the decisions you may have made in choosing medications or even surgeries. For example, when I take patients' histories, trying to get information on how best to help, and they pull out a list of several prescription medications they take daily, I do everything I can to keep from sighing and rolling my eyes. I can't help but at least suggest that there may be alternatives.

Expect bias from us just as you would from them. Neither side has all the answers, yet you, the patient, deserve the best from both. Cooperation from your practitioner is the key. Although difficult, it is possible for a practitioner to be respectful and understanding, yet disagree. You, the patient, must insist on that, even if it means choosing another provider. As with medical providers, there are many natural practitioners to choose from. I encourage you not to be afraid to choose another if you sense anything other than complete concern for your well-being.

Thus, your dialogue with holistic/vitalistic practitioners is essentially similar as I suggested earlier with your medical provider. Based on my contacts with many holistic/vitalistic providers, I truly believe you'll find much easier discussions, more cooperation, and more logical suggestions from our side. Be wary of any practitioners making unrealistic claims, promises, giving medical advice, or even telling you to stop using any medication. If suggestions are made about alternatives to medications or even surgeries, seek cooperation from your MD first by commenting, "I'd like to try a trial period of natural treatment to see if I can eliminate the need for this drug, will you help me?" Remember, don't expect understanding, but insist on cooperation.

Nurse: 'Doctor, Doctor, the man you've just treated collapsed on the front step. What should I do?' Doctor: 'Turn him around so it looks like he was just arriving, then call 911!'.

The improvements in your health from holistic/vitalistic treatment can be quite impressive. But be wary of expecting too much too fast. It's certainly okay to ask when you might expect to see progress, but don't ask continually or you'll drive us both crazy. Likewise, don't be alarmed if your natural practitioner does not ask you how you're feeling on each visit. Remember, the goal in holistic/vitalistic care is not to cover symptoms, it's to make a change that allows your body to heal, to get at the true source of your symptoms. A general rule is that some noticeable improvement should be seen in a trial period of one month. Thorough changes require an average of 90 days and sometimes, a full year.

If you're not pleased with the treatment plan or frequency of visits recommended to you, there may likely be a miscommunication in regard to what your goals are. Are you seeking some temporary relief, thorough correction of your problem, preventive/maintenance care, or just want some advice? Make yourself as clear as possible. Don't be afraid to ask for a couple of options to choose from. I've always operated on the idea that I want to be my patients' chiropractor for the rest of their lives. That doesn't mean I'll treat them continually. It means I'll serve their needs, on their terms. Not all patients have the same goals.

All treatment should include instructions in lifestyle changes, exercise, nutrition, and posture/ergonomics. Patients need to take those suggestions seriously to avoid treatment dependency. In the event that you're seeking help for multiple problems, do your best to direct the focus of your treatment on just two, at the most three, top issues.

Feel welcome to tell your practitioner if any of the treatment feels uncomfortable. Quite often alterations can be made for your comfort. By all means give us your input, particularly if you've had care previously from another holistic practitioner and know what worked for you before. In the case of any practitioner giving you the "it's my way or the highway" routine, take the highway.

Most of the difficulties between patients and doctors and even between doctors and doctors are communication issues. This chapter has empowered you to be in control and have more responsibility for your well-being. Use it to your advantage!

The power of the human mind is quite amazing, especially when it comes to a person's health and wellness.

If you're a hard-core skeptic about the things I write about here, but decide to try it anyway, I really suggest you wait. Read, study, and investigate these natural healing concepts until you have more understanding and belief. I've observed that intense doubt can overpower natural healing. I've had a few cases like that over the years.

One guy, in his mid-forties, boldly told me, "The only reason I'm here is because my wife made me come in. She's tired of hearing me complain about my pain."

You can imagine the pain I had in trying to help this guy!

Copy the following page and take it with you on your next doctor's visit.

SOME QUESTIONS TO ASK YOUR DOCTOR

Use the tools you've acquired from this book to communicate well with your healthcare provider.

❑ Do I really need this test?

❑ Where would you send your spouse or children with my problem?

❑ This treatment is uncomfortable. Is there an option?

❑ Is there a discount available if I pay upfront?

❑ How many of these procedures/surgeries do you perform each year, and what's your success rate?

❑ Are there any significant risks?

❑ What can I do on my own to help my condition and prevent future trouble?

❑ What does this prescription say?

❑ Do you earn bonuses/gifts based on your performance or from salespeople?

❑ From where and when did you receive your degree?

❑ What is the goal of the treatment you recommend?

❑ Will you work with me as I pursue natural options?

Chapter 8
Strategies for Prevention of Illness
Saving time and money on your healthcare

S o, you'd like to avoid illness and injuries. What happened? Did you get enlightened and motivated by the preceding chapters, or did you skip it all and turn here first, looking for magic answers? Either way, you'll find this to be the shortest chapter, yet probably the most challenging to you.

Just how perfect can you get? Can a person have a life completely free of illness and injury? Absolutely not! I am 100 percent sure that you, and future generations, will never, ever have that.

Can you accept the concept of real health?

If you lead an injury-free life, I'll say you are too inactive.

If you never feel ill, I'll say your immune system is not fighting properly against the endless onslaught of microbes.

However, I'm equally sure that you can have 100 percent health. The difference here goes back to definitions as explained in Chapter 1, "What Is *Real* Health?", *the concept that REAL health has little to do with how you feel.* The ideal situation, the one you and I must strive for, is for all of our parts—not just the physical parts, but also the mental, emotional, and spiritual ones, to work at 100-percent capacity. This is most certainly a worthy goal.

To start with, you must have a clear understanding of the holistic concept of what "real health" means. This understanding involves knowing that, at times, you might feel absolutely horrible, yet be completely healthy. And vice versa: you might feel wonderful, yet have terrible health. If the difference and what it means for your well-being is not crystal clear to you, don't read any further in this chapter. Instead, go back and re-read Chapter 1. This understanding is paramount to both prevention and recovery from illness.

We already discussed how fever and other symptoms of colds and flu are examples of how you can feel lousy, but your body is producing those symptoms, doing exactly what it needs to do to correct its well-being. I know—both from my understanding of the principle, and from watching thousands of patients—that if you show some restraint and don't immediately reach for medications to suppress the symptoms, you will get over these illnesses faster and have fewer of them in the future.

To achieve real health, you must stop short-circuiting your God-given, innate healing abilities. Taking medication when relief is needed or monitoring your cholesterol and blood pressure all have their place and time, but nothing overshadows respecting your body's abilities.

Let me repeat myself and remind you again here that I'm not talking about neglecting emergency or life-threatening situations. If you suspect you're in danger, seek immediate medical help, but if you've read and understood the previous chapters, especially chapters 1 and 7, then you are prepared to navigate your way through the healthcare marketplace and make wiser choices.

I've noticed several health programs on my local public television station. I enjoy watching these and suggest you do, too. Last night there was a medical doctor on, and he was giving some great advice about healthier eating like consuming smaller portions and having more variety. But then he began to recommend hormone replacement for men and women as a general health preventative measure. Not! I immediately lost respect. There are many reasons a person's hormones will fluctuate, especially as a normal part of aging. Altering them with prescriptions may produce some seemingly anti-aging benefits in the short term, but both common sense and several studies show that long-term troubles are inevitable. We all need to be wary of holistic health advice from medical/allopathic practitioners.

You shouldn't be surprised by the holistic concept of prevention: regularly engaging in deliberate measures to improve and maintain your physical, mental, emotional, and spiritual well-being *before* symptoms are noticed or medical tests show abnormalities. The how-to's of these measures are covered in previous chapters. What made you think that maintaining your body was much different than maintaining your car, house, or other things? Investing a little time, money, and effort on a regular basis saves you a lot of trouble later. You don't wait until your car's engine is smoking before you change the oil, do you? You don't wait until your home's wood is rotting before you paint, do you? Maintaining real health for prevention of illness is no different.

I have respect for the medical/allopathic model of health prevention: getting cholesterol, blood pressure, colon, and heart exams regularly, but few people seem to see what's missing. What's missing is the recognition that by the time testing reveals abnormalities with any of those things, the person's already long been unhealthy. A better name for these would be "early detection," rather than prevention. High cholesterol, high blood pressure, heart disease, and polyps in the colon don't just drop out of the sky to get you, they've been developing over a long period of time, long before they were detectable, because of some underlying malfunction, irritation, impingement, or imbalance. Addressing those underlying sources is where real prevention takes place, and doing so is relatively easy if you embrace the fact that most of those underlying sources are really the result of making poor choices.

> Cardiovascular problems are not to be taken lightly. But several sources reveal that medical methods performed here, especially in regard to prevention, are way off the mark.
>
> I'll never forget a wonderful patient, Charlie, who was full of energy and enjoying lots of activity during his retirement. I was treating him with chiropractic to help his neck.
>
> One day, he told me that his doctor had found some blockages and that he was going in for bypass surgery, even though he had no symptoms. I tried to suggest he at least ask the doctor to delay the operation so he could try some well-known altera-

tions in diet and lifestyle that have been known to reverse coronary blockages.

Too late. He was already convinced he needed the surgery and it was scheduled in a few days. After the surgery, he regretted going through with it, and he was never the same again. His energy, ambition, and willingness to live had been removed along with the blockages. The information provided in this book needs to be taken seriously.

Yes, the strategy that allows us to win at obtaining good health, therefore, is making wiser choices. Doing so is only possible when you have all the information. I truly believe that the self-proclaimed leaders in healthcare, the medical/allopathic machine, have not been providing you with all you need to know.

How about those of you reading these pages who claim to feel good? Are you judging your health by that alone? Are you willing to invest the time, money, and effort to maintain true health? I'm convinced it's not that difficult. The real barrier lies between most people's ears.

The excuses I hear from people concerning their actions about maintaining their health are truly amazing. Quite often I've heard people say they don't have time to exercise, and in the same sentence, tell me they watch a lot of television. Another common excuse is that they can't afford it, but they are able to pay for cable television, have a big-screen TV, high-speed Internet access, and buy bottled water. Or worse yet, they tell me they're saving for retirement. I'm sorry to be the one to tell you

> **Even if you're on the right track, if you don't keep moving, you'll get run over.**
> —*Mark Twain*

that you won't be enjoying retirement if you're pinching pennies on your healthcare now, especially preventive healthcare.

Congratulations to you if you've got your priorities correct and you're enlightened to the concept of investing in yourself. It really is the best investment you can make. I've observed over and over that doing so will pay off in the long term.

> **Get your priorities in line. Preventive healthcare needs to be at the top of your list!**

Just as in the treatment of an actual health problem (trying to get better), medications or even surgery for preventive measures may be necessary. If you need them, you should get them. But not before considering the many natural/holistic methods available that may produce a result that is just as good, if not better. You'll find all those details in the preceding chapters.

Just what would be the optimum measures a person should take, to have the best chance of maintaining his or her health through holistic methods? See my "Healthy Living Checklist" on the following page. Copy it and hang where you can see the list every day!

Notice that none of the measures are impossible and certainly not difficult. Several can be combined; for example, can you bike, walk, or rollerblade to your job, stopping along the way for your chiropractic appointment, while listening to a motivational speaker on a small cassette/CD player or iPod with an earplug? Can you stretch while you pray? Can you read the Bible while you eat a small, nutritious meal? Can you share some laughs with a friend while you take a walk? Focusing on one

Dr. Tom's Healthy Living Checklist

☑ Engage in a fun, physical activity for at least one half hour daily and vary it frequently.

☑ Eat several (4 to 6) small meals per day of wholesome organic food, growing some of it yourself.

☑ Get a chiropractic adjustment every week or at least monthly.

☑ Do some focused deep breathing regularly.

☑ Stretch your body structure for at least ten minutes daily. Practice good postural habits.

☑ Have the responsibility of doing some work every day, whether it's paid or volunteering.

☑ Learn something new every day by reading or attending classes.

☑ Grow spiritually through prayer and study daily.

☑ Minimize your exposure to media news by watching or listening no more than once daily.

☑ Learn to see the positive and humorous side of everything.

☑ Lead by example and teach the holistic lifestyle to your family

☑ Set specific times to do nothing but totally relax at least 30 minutes daily.

☑ And lastly, give and receive compliments freely every day.

aspect of prevention is far less productive than doing a little of all of it. And, can you do a lot of this with your family?

The greatest challenge with prevention may be changing your belief system. It's easy to fall into the trap of making excuses, being misled by the "worldly way of healthcare" I described in Chapter 1, "What is *Real* Health?", or just being plain stubborn.

> **Devise a strategic plan to have and maintain real health. Failure to plan is planning to fail.**

Surprisingly, the most difficult patients I've encountered have been those with the most education, especially those trained in exacting sciences like accounting, engineering, and architecture. Fixing their actual health problem isn't the difficulty, it's getting them to understand the underlying source of their problem and what they need to do about it. It sometimes seems the holistic principle is so simple that they can't grasp it. In real healthcare, 2 plus 2 does not equal 4. In fact, it equals five, meaning that the whole is greater than the sum of the parts. That concept can be extremely difficult to comprehend for someone with a lot of analytical education.

I remember one very educated fellow, an older optometrist. He did most of the talking when we met, not only telling me what he needed help with, but also how to treat him.

"Circulation is everything," he said.

I did my best to explain that circulation is important but far down the list of importance, and how the nervous system is the true controlling force of all body functions, including circulation. He went away unhappy, unconvinced even when I showed him where his body structure was out of balance and causing his health problems.

Years later, I saw his death notice. A story accompanied it detailing his demise caused by the side effects of medication. I guess it really is true— you can lead a horse to water, but you can't make it drink!

Genetics is a common excuse many people use to doom themselves or at least avoid taking action. Research clearly shows that genetics play a much smaller part in healthcare than most people think. Consider this: even if you truly are predestined to an illness due to genetics, shouldn't that motivate you to do everything possible to delay its progression or minimize its effect on your overall well-being?

Age is another common detractor. "Never give up" is the mantra here. Slow down and modify, yes—but never give up. Strive for your life to be like a candle, which doesn't slowly get dimmer until extinguishing. It stays the same brightness until the very last moment. Keep that flame inside burning strong by staying healthy.

I have dozens of stories about patients who have followed the holistic healthcare lifestyle I advocate throughout this book. I've seen my patients thrive and prosper because of it. I wholeheartedly applaud them and truly believe they deserve gold medals from Medicare and any other establishment that has obscenely profited when people deliberately maintain their health.

One particular gentleman, my oldest patient, Gene, at 103 years, was a perfect example. He was able to stay quite active until his final few months. Among other holistic practices, he regularly visited chiropractors at least monthly for his "tune-ups."

His last few months were in a nursing home. His caregivers there accused him of some sort of senility or dementia due to his frequent bragging about how chiropractic treatment so often helped him. With tears in his eyes, he told me that they laughed at him. It still makes me wonder who really had the mental incapacity over there!

Do you see now how this holistic/vitalistic strategy is so much more logical and effective than waiting until something shows up abnormal on a medical test? By then, the damage is already done. If your medical doctor gives you the proverbial "clean bill of health" without at least asking or suggesting the basic prevention concepts presented in this book, you've really been cheated. But since we need those guys, too, there's not much choice but accepting their shortcomings. That's the main reason I wrote this book: to make you a wiser healthcare consumer.

Back in Chapter 7, "Talking To Your Doctor," I pointed out some things to say, graciously, to deal with the sometimes over-whelming arrogance you may encounter with any professional. There is even a wallet-sized "cheat sheet" to help you remember what to say.

A similar dialogue applies here in regard to prevention advice. For example, if everything checks out okay medically, be thankful, but then go about your personal prevention strategies. If one or more of the medical tests show borderline abnormalities and preventative medications are prescribed, you should say,

"Thank you, Doctor, but I want to try a trial period of changing my lifestyle with holistic methods." Be prepared for controversy, but stand your ground, and insist on cooperation. Get retested in a few months. If your actions haven't been successful, you can always turn to the medications or other medical/allopathic, higher-risk procedures.

So, if there were any thing close to a magic bullet for preventing health problems, it would be this: Carefully consider your mindset. Is your way of thinking aligned with "worldly health-care," the allopathic/mechanistic/ medical way of doing things? The truest, most effective strategy for prevention of illness is to embrace the holistic/vitalistic/natural viewpoint. At the very least, it should be the first priority, the first way tried before turning to the more invasive, higher risk insanity of healthcare that dominates our system.

> *The greatest danger for most of us is not that our aim is too high and we miss it, but that it is too low and we reach it.*
> —*Michelangelo*

The medical/allopathic healthcare machine prides itself and holds up its research to empower itself. They no doubt have more research than exists on my side of the fence, the holistic/ vitalistic approach, but I've learned to be very skeptical about the research. For example, some research clearly shows benefit to the cardiovascular system with regular, light consumption of alcohol. When this information came out, hoorays were heard around the world, with many doctors even recommending an alcoholic drink daily for preventive measures. But today, as I'm writing this, my local newspaper's headline reads: "New Research

Shows Brain Shrinkage With Any Alcohol Consumption!" This is a perfect example of the mistake in making assumptions with a little information versus relying on common sense or basic principles especially in regard to healthcare. Not to mention much of the research on health is directed, if not influenced by, economic factors, such as pharmaceutical companies doing drug studies.

A lot of senior citizens take daily aspirin because there is research that doing so can prevent heart attacks, but I'd bet there will soon be research showing that daily aspirin also causes some harm, perhaps to a person's brain cells like alcohol does. We already know, for example, that even one small aspirin causes stomach bleeding. Also, take a look at the frequent red splotches on the arms of many seniors who take daily aspirin; it makes me suspicious that there is some long term damage occurring in these "aspirin-holic" people. Nobody knows for sure yet, but from a holistic aspect, taking short cuts to better health like this always has long-term ramifications. Swallowers beware!

The biggest challenge you'll face will be overcoming the unbelievable dominance of the old, insane belief system. Remember that not everyone, in fact very few people, are as enlightened about real health as you are now.

> I've observed that when people get focused and motivated to make some lifestyle changes for their health, really doing it and giving their bodies some time to get better, the results can be astounding.
> One lady I specifically remember was Helen. She was a 68-year-old retiree who first came to see me with a real wreck of a body. She essentially hurt

everywhere. On the entrance form that every patient first fills out when coming to my office, there is a list of various complaints (about 40) under a heading "How Can I Help You?" She had nearly every one circled!

When I questioned her about her past health-care, she started pointing out surgical scars from nearly head to toe (hip replacement, two back surgeries, neck surgery, carpal tunnel surgery, gall bladder removal, shoulder replacement, hysterec-tomy, and more). She then pulled out a list of medications that took nearly an entire page. I've acquired a reputation for being able to help some quite complicated cases, but I must admit there are times when I'm tempted to say "I'm sorry, but no" when I encounter these. It's only right to refer patients who need other help than I can offer, but some cases like hers have already tried everything else. They've been through the mill.

So, I took a deep breath and proceeded, not promising anything, explaining as much as possible, looking and probing at what could be attempted. Finally I asked, "What's the one thing you want better out of all these problems?"

She gave the answer that opened the door. She wanted to continue to live independently, to con-tinue to drive herself, wash and feed herself, and not be a burden to others. Although that may sound like a huge challenge, it's the goal that can and needs to be focused on. If her request would have been to make all the pains go away, or to get rid of the medications, I'd have turned her away. At-tempting that would have been just a repeat of what she'd already been: a victim of focusing on symptoms.

I'm happy to report she responded well after we laid out a plan that implemented one or two simple changes. In her case, it was a need to start with some spinal alignments (adjustments) and some eating habit alterations. Later, she got on a regular routine of stretching. This then allowed her to resume some physical activities. We then saw some of her excess body fat lessening, her overall attitude brightening, and her energy level growing. It was like watching a flower blossom. Not surprisingly, her pains did decrease significantly as result of all this. She found a medical doctor who agreed to cooperate and was able to decrease and eliminate many of her medications.

Today, Helen is 84, traveling, volunteering, and enjoying lots of activities with grandchildren.

Another consideration when planning your prevention strategy is this: don't get overwhelmed. If you're like the average person reading this book, you most likely have identified many shortcomings in the way you've been going about your family's healthcare, and you want to change. Congratulations! But I'd highly advise picking out one or two lifestyle changes at the most and focus on just that to start. Go back a few paragraphs and review the prevention checklist. Identify the one bulleted item that really riles you, the one that really "rings your bell." You'll feel that deep inside. It might even be a feeling of denial, guilt, or anger. That's the one! Now focus yourself on improving just that to start.

Take the high road. The more you observe and learn about, the more you'll welcome a vitalistic/holistic lifestyle. When you see the pharmaceutical ads, laugh at them! You'll still be offered medical care when you consult with your MD. Question it! Perhaps you'll feel intimidated when you discuss health with your neighbors, friends, and coworkers. Enlighten them! You'll still encounter medically slanted reporting by the media. See beyond it! You'll still be tempted to buy processed food when it's on sale. Resist it! And you'll still be tempted to reach for some medication when you feel the effects of your body doing what it needs to right itself. Avoid it!

You want to be as healthy as possible? You are the only one who can take charge of your health! *Just do it!*

Chapter 9
Growing Older and
Really Enjoying It
Lessons from my observations of
thousands of "primetime" patients

W hat does this young man know about it, you might ask?
I warned in earlier chapters that I didn't write this book
to make more friends. In fact, I fear that this current chapter
may likely cause some current friends to abandon me, but I'm
determined to tell the truth as I see it, so here goes: retirement is
a joke! It's a joke at least in the conventional image that most
people have and that the media promotes, of an image in which
a person works between 20 to 40 years and then finally can relax,
finally do what he or she has always wanted to do, perhaps travel,
perhaps intensify hobbies, sleep later, and just collect a check
every month. You know, kind of like the bliss they show in the
TV ads for drugs!

Now don't misunderstand me—that kind of life can be
reached, but it's quite superficial. Deep down, sometimes well
hidden, those who obtain that state of earthly nirvana usually are

soon disappointed. This wonderland of retirement may come true occasionally, but if you really look around, most retirees are depressed, in pain, struggling financially or pretending to, cranky and frustrated with either the weather, politics or the economy, or all, and on several prescription medications. When a sense of purpose and responsibility is lacking in one's life, when one's desire to accomplish things amounts to not much more than leisure, than there is going to be trouble.

I'm not writing this to be mean; you'll see I'm attempting to help as you read on. Seniors make up a significant number of my favorite patients and I fully realize I'll be a senior citizen one day. I am writing this criticism of the typical retiree because something's wrong! I refuse to believe that the last stretch of a person's life has to be as miserable as I see many living it. There is no doubt that some have no other choice due to disability, or perhaps simply rotten luck. I want to help those of you who may be stuck in that conventional retirement trap and prevent it for those of you who are nearing it.

In order to help you, I have to tell you some things that you may not like. Now, if you're completely content in your current retirement situation, congratulations! But for the rest of you who suspect you've been misled and are wondering where the golden years are, I have several suggestions. By the way, I'd bet anything

An elderly lady named Shirley once told me, "I have three boyfriends: Ben Gay, Burr Sitis, and Arthur Itis."

that your children and grandchildren want you to do these things. Maybe you should do this for them.

The first advice I want to give you is this: ***Don't ever stop working!*** That's right! You can never stop. Now before you start writing me some hate mail, let me explain that when I say you should keep working, I don't mean you have to keep doing the same job nor do you have to work as much if you don't have to. It's perfectly okay to retire from one job, but then start another, even if for no other reason than to experience some variety; and it's okay to take a little break in between. Also, you don't have to work full time if you don't need or desire to—part-time or a few hours a week is okay. And, who said

> ## You don't grow old. You turn old when you stop growing!
> *—Marie Tyson, age 87*

anything about it having to be a paid job. If you have the means, how about volunteering? The possibilities are endless. Examples include: helping at a food pantry, babysitting, teaching your talent in a class at the local rec department, and even ringing a bell for The Salvation Army. My point is that everybody has the potential to contribute to the good of society, everybody has a need to fulfill a purpose in his or her life, and everybody has to feel a responsibility every day for the rest of one's life.

Without these necessary foundations, which I believe are God-given, a human being's physical body readily begins to deteriorate prematurely, the mental state turns very negative, and the spiritual self yearns for fulfillment. Don't let this happen to you!

You don't have to be one of the victims of retirement. If you're already retired and not content and not feeling good, get to work! It's the easiest and quickest way I know to help you. I'm sorry to have to be the one to wake you up to the fact that many of the people around you deplore the negative, cynical, complaining type comments some of you make because you have too much time on your hands. I know it's hard to believe, as some of you sit there steaming in anger at me, but I write this truth because I care about you.

> **Time may be a great healer, but it's also a lousy beautician.**
> — *Mark Twain*

Also, don't ever stop learning. Always be looking for ways to discover something new, have a new experience, or even look at something familiar from a different perspective. Sorry, just watching TV and reading the newspaper won't do it, especially if it's the news.

If you're exposed to more than one hour of the news each day, I believe you're overdoing it. Those repetitive negative news items are hurting you. You can't do much about them anyway. Show me someone who watches the morning news, then reads the paper, then watches the noon news, then the evening news, then perhaps even the late night news, and I'll show you a person

---

> Don't ever stop working, learning, and laughing.
> Between working, learning, and laughing a lot,
> you won't have time to feel poorly!

---

who is not well. Sadly, there are a lot of you around who do that or are close to it. Like most other things, the media has its value, but be very selective about what you're allowing to go into your mind. Garbage in equals garbage out. The media is getting better and better at knowing what keeps most people tuned in, but it's not necessarily good for us.

I admire those seniors who participate in the short excursions offered at places like their community's Senior Center. Those day trips are reasonably priced, fun, and educational. A great way to socialize, too!

I'll add the importance of spiritual growth here as well. That should never end either. If you think you've got your existence and eternity all figured out and you're patiently waiting for your name to be called, congratulations! Now get up and get going at helping others get it.

> ### I don't know how I had time to work!
> —*my father Julian,*
> *a few months after his*
> *retirement*

> I can't help but add my own testimony here concerning my own salvation and faith. Read these next lines carefully, because they may likely be the most important ones in this book.
>
> There once was a man named Jesus, born about 2,000 years ago. He turned water into wine, fed thousands with a few pieces of bread and fish, walked on water, and healed many ill people, some of whom were blind, insane, paralyzed, and lame. He even raised some who were dead. He had an important message for all of us, quite simple, yet very misunderstood: if we believe that Jesus is the

son of God and live like we believe it, our eternity will be an afterlife with Him in Heaven (John 3:15) "that whoever believes in Him should not perish, but have eternal life."

Many people over the centuries have claimed to have the answers concerning eternity and the afterlife, but I have yet to see or hear of any who performed the miracles Jesus did. That is one of several reasons I choose to follow Him. Some will argue that there's no proof of His miracles, but there is more proof for Him than of many of the things we feel certain of today. The proof lies in the multiple, written, eyewitness testimonies of His early followers—you'll find them all there in the Bible.

Take a look for yourself, and pray for more faith and health. Both are really gifts from God. The best news is ... you've still got time!

Oh, yeah, and don't stop laughing! Most importantly, learn how to laugh at yourself. There are times to get serious, but keep those moments to a minimum. Do you read the comics every day? You should. There's a funny side to almost everything.

All the things I wrote about in earlier chapters—the need to consume better foods, the need to be physically active every day, the need to fill your mind with positive, uplifting information, and the need to keep your body structure balanced—must also be done in the later years of life. Some of the choices, such as those involving physical activity, become a bit limited; but otherwise, the concepts of real health and wellness remain the same.

It's easy to fall back on the common excuses: "My mother or father had this problem" (hereditary); "I have arthritis" (labeling); "It's too late for me to change" (stubbornness); "I can't afford to do it differently" (hoarding); and "I'm too old" (self-pity). Look at other seniors around you. If you look closely enough, you'll discover that the majority are suffering as a result of one or more of those negative thought patterns. You'll also see a few who are not.

Little changes go a long way and are never too late for better health.

Careful observation of those few exceptional people reveals that they've got more than luck, they've likely made some better choices. You can make better choices too! I don't believe that it's ever too late. True, it would have been better if you'd have started earlier, but I've observed that a few simple changes can produce very rewarding results, like gaining more strength and energy, having sounder sleep, living with a more positive, optimistic attitude, experiencing fewer pains, and even enjoying better movement. I want to share the how-tos of these simple changes with you.

There once was a chiropractor who thought he knew a lot about health and wellness, so he decided to write a book. He spent most of his savings getting it published. He ended up getting a lot of people ticked off, especially seniors. He also got a callus on the tip of his index finger, because he never learned how to type!

Let me start by suggesting you first consider your body structure, the alignment of your bones and joints. This may surprise you, because most people think older folks can't do anything about stiffness or lack of flexibility, that it's too late. Let me assure you that amazing improvements can be made even if you have degenerative joints, old injuries, and even joint replacements. I'm not talking about miraculous recoveries that will make you young again. I do believe, though, that lining up your body structure, even if it's a little bit, will produce the most dramatic improvement in your well-being.

In addition, the holistic approach, as practiced by chiropractors like myself, seeks to address the underlying source of your health issues instead of covering or masking them. If you are fearful of utilizing practitioners like me, a doctor of chiropractic, don't be. All DCs have excellent training in caring for seniors. The treatment for seniors is, of course, more gentle. We know how to work around spinal surgeries, hip, knee, and shoulder replacements, pacemakers, colostomy bags, and even osteoporosis.

On one of the few occasions when I was able to get an MD to come to my office, hoping to open some communication and break down some barriers, I put up an X-ray of an 80-year-old senior I was treating. The spine was quite arthritic. I did my best to point out the obvious structural misalignments. The poor doctor practically fainted with the thought of me adjusting this lady's back bones and arthritic joints. I tried to explain that these type cases are commonly seen and safely helped by chiropractors. Sadly, he never did see past the arthritis. He never

referred any patients to me and I never heard from
him again. I often wonder if a better approach
would have been to first point out which of us is the
safer doctor, that what I do has less risk than what
he does, and perhaps even by comparing our
malpractice insurance rates.

When you go to a chiropractor, the doctor will likely personally
take your history and consultation. An examination will be made
involving a lot of hands-on analysis of your joints, especially of
your spine. X-rays will show additional details, such as
misalignments, arthritic deterioration, old injuries, and osteoporosis. If problems appear outside the scope of chiropractic
treatment, the chiropractor will refer you to another professional.
Options will be provided to you based on the nature of your
health issues and your goals. Very likely, your health insurance
(ahem, sickness insurance) will cover some or all of your
treatment. If not, the cost will usually be $30 to $40 per

A pipe burst in a doctor's house, so he called the
plumber.
    The plumber arrived, unpacked the tools, did some
plumber-type things and handed the doctor a bill for
$600.
    The doctor exclaimed, "This is ridiculous! I don't even
make that much as a doctor!'"
    The plumber answered quietly, "Neither did I when I
was a doctor."

treatment and you will likely need several. In most cases, the risks involved are minimal or insignificant, especially when compared to traditional medical treatment of prescription medications, injections, or surgeries.

Talking or writing about money and the costs of healthcare is always awkward for me. I've always intentionally tried to stay out of those matters and let my staff handle those details, so the money issues would not influence the advice I'd give to patients. I still think that's a good way to go about it for any doctor. But some things need to be asked and said here.

For example, I truly believe that chiropractic treatment is one of the best values in healthcare available. It gives you the most benefit for the money spent. Some of you seniors have been good savers and been blessed financially. What are you doing with your money? Saving it for the nursing home? Saving it for your children's inheritance, so they can squander it on elaborate vacations, boats, or other unwise purchases? If that's your wish, so be it. That's your business. But does it make sense to you that perhaps spending at least some of it on your own well-being would be money well spent? I wrote in earlier chapters that investing in yourself is the best investment you can make. I believe your children would be happy if you spend at least some of your money on yourself, so you can feel better, be more active, and enjoy more things. I know this is a sensitive subject, but I promised earlier in this book and again in this chapter that I would tell it like I see it.

An elderly gentleman came to my office for help with his back and shoulder/arm pain. He took three or four treatments and got a little progress. I tried to encourage him to have a few more treatments as I knew I could help him more, but he said he couldn't afford the $3.25 Medicare co-payment.

I never mind making a financial concession to help my patients when necessary, but I'm also no fool. I couldn't help notice he drove a very nice car to the office, traveled a lot, and lived in the best neighborhood. I wished him well.

He came back several months later after his problem worsened, stayed for a few treatments, and then discontinued prematurely again with the same financial explanation.

Years later, through a coincidental mutual family member, I learned that he had passed away with hundreds of thousands of dollars in his checking account!

Common sources of structural disturbances in seniors are postural ones, especially spinal misalignments. For example, many neck, shoulder, and upper back disturbances are the result of seniors falling asleep while sitting. Can you picture it? Their head bobs as they alternately dose and wake. Done repetitively, this produces an effect similar to that of a whiplash. Lying back in a recliner can minimize the head movement, but the reclining posture can cause disturbances in the low back. It's best to lie down flat if you're feeling sleepy. If you spend any significant time in a recliner, tuck a small cushion or pillow behind your lower back, at your belt line, as this minimizes the negative effects of the fetal posture that recliners produce.

With regard to sleeping posture, it's best to lie flat, either on your back or side, with one pillow. Consider investing in a supportive pillow. These pillows are usually shaped with an indentation in the middle. My favorite is a pillow with a water insert. The weight of your head displaces the water, which then fills the gaps to give you customized support. Another advantage is that you can increase or decrease the amount of water to suit your preferred firmness.

Another good idea for seniors is to place a small supportive cushion between the knees when side sleeping. This minimizes pressure on the low back and hips. (Check our website www.WholeHealthHealing.com for information about water pillows and other supportive cushions.) Avoid getting in a habit of favoring one sleeping position. Lying on the couch or bed with your head propped up to read or watch TV is out of the question.

Your mattress should be firm but with a pillow-top padding. I don't believe the fancy mattresses advertised with air compressors or memory foam are worth the money. Make sure your mattress is flipped not only over, but head to toe at least every six months. Get help with this.

There is no set rule on how long a mattress will last, but generally, if your mattress is more than eight years old, I'd get suspicious. You can check its worthiness by stripping it bare and looking across the surface. If it dips more than an inch in the center, it needs replacing. Also, use your hand to press firmly in the middle and then one foot in along the border. There should only be a slight difference. If your joints or muscles are extra tender, consider adding an inch or two of foam padding to the top.

Stretching and Exercise

Seniors need to keep physically active everyday. All the concepts I describe in Chapter 2, "Exercises that Really Work," are equally important in the later years of life, maybe just slower and done more gently. Make physical activity a priority! Mornings are still the best time to exercise, because even though you may have more time on your hands, your day will seem to fly by, and exercise easily gets put aside.

Ideally, plan on at least 15 minutes of stretching and at least 30 minutes of physical activity each day. The stretching is extra important and needs to be done first due to the stiffness that comes with aging. If you're a creature of habit and prefer to stick with a regular routine, more power to you, but most need a variety to ward off boredom. Boredom is the greatest detriment to exercise and the most common cause of discontinuing. I'd suggest a combination of swimming, walking, bicycling, dancing, and golf. Sounds like fun, doesn't it? Back in Chapter 2, "Exercises that Really Work," I point out the importance of exercise being fun. It's all the more important for seniors. Who said the fun ever stops? If you desire to add some resistance exercises with weights or machines, go ahead, but keep it light as your risk of injury increases with age.

Engage in some physical activity and stretch every single day.

I'm sure some of you are thinking "What if I fall?" "What if I break my hip?" "I can't because I have arthritis." "I'm too tired." "I'm too old." No doubt there are risks in every activity, but the benefits in regard to stretching and exercise far

Get outside whenever possible.

outweigh any risks. I'll go a step further and say that you're at an even higher risk without regular physical activity. Inactivity in itself is a source of accelerated osteoporosis, arthritis, muscle weakness, and low energy. Even if you are confined to a wheelchair there are options, like the "Sit and be Fit" program shown on public television every day. You can easily combine your physical activity with socializing by attending one of the many group sessions at your local fitness center, rec program, or senior center. Whenever possible, choose outdoor activities to take advantage of the health benefits of fresh air and daylight.

Strive for direct skin exposure of daylight for at least 10 minutes daily, even if it's just to your face, hands or arms. I've observed this to be very important, not only for prevention of osteoporosis, but many other aspects of your well-being.

There is risk with over-exposure, but with caution, the benefits far outweigh the risks.

Eat Well. You Deserve It!

The senior years are no time to throw healthy food choices out the window. If you're choosing to be less active, it's all the more important to eat smaller portions and make wiser food selections. And it's never too late to make improvements to your eating habits if you're new to these healthier concepts.

There exists the tendency with aging to eat one large meal per day for convenience, cost, or just not being that hungry. But the benefits of eating several small, wholesome meals, ideally one every two to four hours of daylight, are just as important at any age. This grazing-type eating habit results in much better blood sugar balance.

Publicly sponsored senior meal programs serve a vital need, but I highly suggest eating just a small portion of the serving on site, take the remainder home, and then supplement those with some raw fruits and vegetables.

I love encouraging people to grow at least a little of their own food. "Me? Garden at my age?" you might ask. Tell me what's so difficult about tending to a potted tomato or a short row of lettuce and onions? Don't be overly concerned if a few weeds show up. Your garden doesn't have to look like the ones on television. I know it's cheaper and easier to buy the stuff, but there's something magical and very rewarding to working a bit of soil, sowing a few seeds, watering, watching the growth, and then harvesting some produce. It's about more than just the nutrients. Don't worry about what you'll do with the excess; any food pantry would love to take it off your hands. I'm sure that by now you know the joy that comes with giving.

Don't let the benefit of eating a lot of variety as described in Chapter 3, "Enjoying Eating," slip away with age. It's easy to get set in your ways, or just plain stubborn with your favorites. The more variety you have, the less chance exists of any vitamin/mineral deficiencies.

Should seniors take vitamin and mineral supplements? You'll hear many different arguments on that subject. Based on my observations of many senior patients, the answer is over-whelmingly "Yes!" I'd highly recommend taking a high-quality, organic multivitamin/mineral supplement every day, together with a calcium and an Omega 3 capsule. (See my advice on the preferred type of calcium in Chapter 6, "Help For Your Ail-ments.") Keep in mind, though, that nothing tops proper eating. Be wary of too-good-to-be-true specials on vitamin supplements like 3-for-1 offers or freebies; they tend to be poor quality. Insist on pharmaceutical-grade products; they are high quality. And

A fellow walks in to a doctor's office and the reception-ist asked him what he had.

He said, "Shingles."

She took down his name, address, and medical insur-ance number, then told him to have a seat.

A few minutes later, a nurse's aide came out and asked him what he had. He said, "Shingles."

She took down his weight, height, and a complete medical history, and told him to wait in the examining room.

Ten minutes later, a nurse came in and asked him what he had.

He said, "Shingles."

So she gave him a blood test, a blood pressure test, and an electrocardiogram, told him to take off all his clothes and wait for the doctor.

Fifteen minutes later, the doctor came in and asked him what he had.

He said, "Shingles."

The doctor asked, "Where?"

The man said, "Outside in the truck. Where do you want them?"'

skip the synthetic varieties that are commonly advertised; they don't absorb well into your system.

With regard to liquids, nothing beats plain water. Don't be fooled by juices; they contain too much sugar even if they are naturally sweetened. Artificially sweetened varieties hold their own kinds of ill effects. Limit coffee and tea to no more than 2 cups daily. Alcohol? Have no more than one serving daily.

Don't be afraid to splurge on occasions such as holidays and parties. I know you gotta live a little. Simply add more fiber later to compensate.

Downsizing and De-cluttering

Your junk is making you sick. I'm not kidding! I told you I'd be honest with you, and this particular advice is brutal for some of you. The majority of you have too much stuff and it's contributing to your health problems. I have observed, for example, that clutter can be a very hidden source of depression in seniors. You're overwhelmed by the overfilled closet, basement, attic, drawers, and/or garage. In part, this is due to the prevalence of materialism in our society.

Try clearing out even one small area and you'll see what I mean—your entire outlook on life brightens. It's very difficult to start to even think about what to do with all that stuff you've been blessed with all your life. Begin by setting a goal to haul out at least a grocery-size bag each week. For some of you, it will take a full year or more to truly clean up your act.

When is it time to sell your home and move to an apartment or condo? Quite simply, it's when you are no longer able or willing to keep up with the maintenance. When you move, do so with an attitude of staying active socially and physically, as much as possible.

I'm always fascinated by my senior patients who look and act 10, 20, or even 30 years younger than their actual age. I call them "super seniors." Just lucky, some would say. Sure, genetics plays a part, but choices play a bigger part.

One such patient was John, an 85-year-old man. He was as strong as an ox, always laughing, and eager to learn something new. He also shared with me many tragedies that had happened in his life. His pride was his garden and he gave away more produce than he used himself.

When his family finally convinced him to sell everything and get an apartment, he went down hill fast. I've seen this happen all too often to be coincidence. Downsizing property is usually a good thing with aging but can be too much too fast. It needs to be accompanied with careful planning to find substitutes for the lost activities and responsibilities. I know what choices I'm going to make as I age. How about you?

A patient said to the doctor, "Whenever I drink coffee, I have this sharp excruciating pain."

The doctor said, "Try to remember to remove the spoon from the cup before drinking."

Either give away the stuff you don't need, sell it, or dispose of it. If you've got some valuable things there, a great little job for you is to learn how to use E-Bay on the computer. You'll never have to leave your home because UPS will pick the items up for you and the check comes in the mail.

The best option is to rent a Dumpster® and have it dropped off in your driveway. Brutal I know, but listen, your kids are going to do it anyway when you're gone. Do it now and save them the trouble! And set a new personal rule—if something new comes into your house, something else has to go out. If you're not able to do any de-cluttering on your own, there are services that will do it all for you. Check the phone book.

So there you are. Some of you might already be feeling a stir in your soul as a result of what you read here. I encourage you to act. Pick out one item in this chapter that rings your bell and focus on it.

I want both you and me to be "super-seniors."

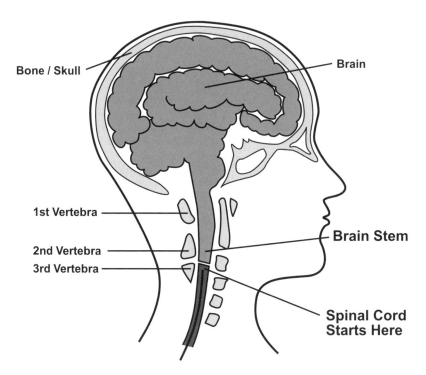

Bone / Skull

Brain

1st Vertebra

Brain Stem

2nd Vertebra
3rd Vertebra

Spinal Cord
Starts Here

This diagram shows the relationship of the brain/brain stem and vertebrae of the upper neck. Notice how the brain stem extends down to the third vertebra in the neck. This upper neck area is extremely vulnerable to misalignment, especially in babies and children. Abnormal pressure on the brain stem can cause many autonomic disturbances to breathing, digestion, mental, and physical development, and even learning and concentration. It is imperative that all babies and children be examined by a chiropractor for this reason.

Chapter 10
Raising Healthier Children
Passing a Healthier Torch

Please believe me—I'm not bragging, but I do think my children are healthier than most. Much healthier. I bring this up because the information I give you here is not only from what I've been taught, trained, and observed with my patients, but mostly from what I've experienced raising my own three children: at the time of this writing, Andy is 12, Emily is 10, and Mike is 7. I want your children to be healthier, too!

I treat many kids in my practice. I observe other children at my kids' school, at playgrounds, at events with friends and families, at the mall, at the grocery store, and so on. And I'm worried about what I see. I see a lot of obesity, a lot of flab, poor posture, and difficulty concentrating. I see either too much energy or too low energy. I see them struggling with minimal exertion. I see them eating a lot of poor-quality food, fast food, soft drinks, and not enough protein. I see a lot of them taking prescription medications. And most worrisome, I don't see the sparkle that should be in every young person's eyes most of the time.

My family's medical bills have been at or near zero year after year. The kids have never needed any prescription medication. They are far from perfect, but most times you'll find them strong, solid, straight, and well-balanced in energy, and having strong immunity. Have they been ill? Oh yes! We've spent plenty of time cleaning up bodily fluids, watching fevers, losing sleep thanks to their loud coughing, and worrying when they lose their appetites. The difference between my family and most others is that we have enlightenment about what real health really is. If you don't know about real health yet, go back and read Chapter 1, "What is *Real* Health?" Here's a brief reminder: it has little to do with how a person is feeling. It's a state of total mental, physical, social, and spiritual well-being. Without that knowledge, the upcoming information will confuse if not alarm you.

Briefly stated, for review purposes, most medical care involves covering symptoms. Holistic care, like my family follows, involves having more respect for the innate, God-given intelligence of the human body. We look at true health from the perspective that your body will do exactly what it needs to do to right itself. This holds true the majority of the time with rare exceptions; and that, although medical care is also a godsend at times, it's easily and frequently abused by both patients and medical doctors. The safer, more economical holistic methods need to come first in non-emergency situations.

If you're employed by or thoroughly engulfed in the medical industry, you're probably starting to freak out right about now. You've got a lot to learn. Let me add that all three of my children were born at home, two of them were breech births, and they have had no immunizations either. So there! Oh, yeah, one last thing ... Boo!

Take fever, for example. My kids have had plenty of those. Fever is another gift from God. The human body has many ways of fighting foreign invaders like bacteria and viruses. Raising its core temperature, as in the case of a fever, is one of them. Many of the undesirable bugs can't thrive in a body that is warmer than it normally should be. Fever is rarely comfortable. With elevated temperature comes body pains, tiredness, lack of appetite, chills, sweating, headache and general uneasiness. Nobody likes having a fever and I wouldn't wish it on anyone, but most times it's a blessing from the perspective of your body doing exactly what it needs to do. Leave fever alone whenever possible.

> Only parents should have the right to decide what's best for their children. Consider having more respect for the God-given, innate intelligence in the bodies of these wonderful little blessings.

The more you try to fight a fever, the longer it will last and the longer you'll be ill. There are all kinds of scary reports of children getting brain damage or other disabilities from fevers, that's very rare and many of the reports are unfounded. In the few cases where damage has occurred, the source of the damage is more likely from something else, like the side effects of the drugs given to feverish children, or from dehydration. There is more risk from the side effects of the medications given for fevers than there is from the fever itself. If you do choose to monitor it with a thermometer, most references say not to be alarmed with anything less than 104 degrees Fahrenheit. You'll rarely see any fevers above 102 degrees. Encourage a child with fever to remain inactive, either lying or sitting. Encourage lots of fluid intake preferably pure water, soup, juice, or white soda. If they're sweating pull the blankets down. If they're cold, cover them up. Many times that cold then hot then back to cold feeling is common and is a good sign. Feed them quality food if they'll eat. Give them immunity-boosting nutrition like garlic, olive leaf extract (an herb), lysine (an amino acid), or vitamin C. Don't automatically reach for the meds thinking that's what a good parent does, I know you mean well but most times it's not necessary.

I'm a big fan of garlic. It's a wonderful natural herb that benefits the body in many ways including breaking down the cell membranes of viruses, so your body can more easily fight them. Use more garlic in your cooking. Take garlic capsules if you wish. But I've observed it's most effective if taken orally in its raw state. My wife and I slice a clove into a swallowable size and down it like a vitamin bi-weekly, more so if we're sick. If you try this, don't chew the garlic slice or you'll taste it for days.

Kids have a hard time swallowing garlic pieces or capsules even if these are small. Nor do kids like the taste if they chew the garlic. The trick to get them to take it is to slice up a clove or two, put it in your pickle or olive jar, and wait about a week. This will denature the taste to a point where they won't mind chewing it and may even crave it. If you're worried about the odor, we've carefully watched for that and haven't found it to be a problem unless you take it for more than three days in a row. Besides, you'll repel more people by sneezing and coughing than you will by smelling like garlic.

It's a similar story with discharges like vomiting, diarrhea, nasal mucous, and coughing/sneezing. As disgusting, messy, irritating, and unpleasant as those things are, once again, the body is doing just what it needs to in order to right itself. It's flushing, blowing, or draining out the undesirable bad stuff. Sometimes it does so quite violently! I say let her rip!

Maybe even help the immune system along with a vaporizer at night, lots of warm liquids throughout the day, and rest. Be aware that some liquids are likely to help and some are likely to hamper. For example: milk, orange juice, and sweet liquids usually increase heavy mucous formation and clogging. Grapefruit juice, lemon juice, herbal tees, and low-sugar cranberry juice are likely to cut mucous and ease its exit.

You don't catch germs. They catch you when your resistance is low.

Most of the uncomfortable bother associated with mucous, such as the headaches, cough, sinus pressure, and stuffy nose comes from mucous that's not flowing out properly. Watch for signs of dehydration (see table on page 294), inability to hold down any fluids, and discoloration in the discharge; these would be reasons to seek medical attention.

Antibiotics are a godsend when used properly, but their abuse is legendary. I'm so pleased to see that the abusive use of antibiotics is becoming common knowledge.

Some problems with antibiotics include:

- ♦ They are frequently prescribed for viral conditions, even though they have no benefit.
- ♦ All colds and flus are viruses. Antibiotics only kill some bacteria, not viruses at all.

Symptoms associated with dehydration

(Adapted from C. Duggan, M. Santosham, R. Glass, "The management of acute diarrhea in children; oral rehydration, maintenance and nutritional therapy," *MMWE* 1992; 41; and World Health Organization, " The treatment of diarrhea; a manual for physicians and other senior health workers," Geneva, Switzerland, 1995.)

SYMPTOM	MINIMAL OR NO DEHYDRATION (< 3% LOSS OF BODY WEIGHT)	MILD TO MODERATE DEHYDRATION (3-9% LOSS OF BODY WEIGHT)	SEVERE DEHYDRATION (>9% LOSS OF BODY WEIGHT)
Mental status	Well; alert	Normal, fatigued or restless; irritable	Apathetic, lethargic, unconscious
Thirst	Drinks normally; might refuse liquids	Thirsty; eager to drink	Drinks poorly; unable to drink
Heart rate	Normal	Normal to increased	Irregular heart beat
Quality of pulse	Normal	Normal to decreased	Weak, thread, or impalpable
Breathing	Normal	Normal; fast	Deep
Eyes	Normal	Slightly sunken	Deeply sunken
Tears	Present	Decreased	Absent
Mouth and tongue	Moist	Dry	Parched
Skin fold (pinched gently and pulled up)	Instant recoil	Recoil in < 2 seconds	Recoil in > 2 seconds
Capillary refill	Normal	Prolonged	Prolonged; minimal
Extremities	Warm	Cool	Cold, mottled, cyanotic (blue-colored)
Urine output	Normal to decreased	Decreased	Minimal

- The un-killed bacteria mutate and become resistant to the antibiotic.

- Antibiotics kill some beneficial bacteria also, such as those in the digestive tract.

- Destruction of the beneficial bacteria leads to proliferation of parasites like yeast.

I bite my tongue when the medical establishment lays claim to discovering they've been over-prescribing; all of us holistic practitioners have been screaming that for decades! If you're not already aware, antibiotics have no effect on viruses. Most common illnesses like colds and flus involve viruses. When an antibiotic is taken for these conditions, a patient may likely feel better, but it's now been shown that they would have likely felt better soon, even without the antibiotic. Worse yet, the human body contains billions of normal, natural bacteria that suffer as a result of taking an antibiotic. It's sometimes hard to imagine that bacteria can be good, but the truth is that most are beneficial and they are in your mouth, urinary tract, digestive system, on your skin, and even in your eyes. That's called your natural flora. It's a very important part of a human's wellness. Messing with the normal flora balance contributes to all kinds of complications including more infections, asthma, and allergies.

> Not too long ago, manufacturers got the bright idea to add antibiotics right into the plastic of children's toys, pacifiers, jumper seats, and so on. Sounds brilliant, doesn't it? But all kinds of negative ramifications for children were soon seen. That bright idea was soon shelved. Surprise, surprise!

So let's focus more on strengthening children's immune systems or, better yet, their overall wellness. Not only when they're sick but even before they're sick. It's not that hard, especially in the case of children, partly because they haven't yet formed many of the bad habits and irrational belief systems of us bigger folks. The younger you start them, the easier it is for both of you.

The path to more children's wellness and, specifically, stronger immunity, is not that different from the information given in previous chapters for adults.

Let's Talk Eating!

Just the other day, I was doing the weekly grocery shopping and I decided to do some spying on other shoppers. As I pushed my cart along, pretending to be desperately looking for the items on my list, I began taking note of what other shoppers had in their carts. I focused mainly on shoppers who either had kids tagging along, or on those typical frazzled-looking 20- to 40-year-olds, who I assumed had children.

An obvious pattern to the items in their shopping carts began to emerge—lots of poor-quality, high-carbohydrate foods. I saw a preponderance of sugar-coated breakfast foods like toaster pops, frozen French toast, pancakes, cereals, pastries, and jellies. I saw lots of sugar-laden juices. I saw a lot of "white foods" like white bread, white rice, and white pastas. I saw very few high-quality proteins like meat, eggs, or fish. I saw minimal fresh fruits and vegetables.

When I finished my own shopping, I looked down into the basket and saw a few of the undesirable items mentioned above; but mostly fresh vegetables and fruits like lettuce, broccoli, carrots, onions, apples, oranges, pineapple, and bananas. I also saw several high-quality protein items like beef, tuna, salmon, cheese, almonds, walnuts. (I didn't buy eggs because I raise my own chickens). The bread items I had were whole wheat, whole grain, dark-in-color items.

Some people would quickly argue that, sure, I can afford those things being a doctor. But this particular grocery store was in an upscale suburb with lots of huge homes on big lots. I'd bet most of the people I was observing would be classified as upper middle class at the least. My point is that these other shoppers surely should have been able to afford a little better quality food choices.

So I next paid close attention to the cash register totals being rung up all around me as I stood in the check-out lane. The shopping carts that had about the same fill as mine, the many that contained all those less desirable foods, were ringing up only slightly lower than mine on average. If buying healthier, better quality food cost a bit more, it's not much more. And the benefits of eating better save money in the long run

> **If you're parenting an uncooperative, troubled child, consider looking at his or her eating habits before discipline, counseling, and medication.**

through less illness, less medication, fewer doctor visits, as well as calmer, more cooperative, and more productive children. The ultimate long-term benefits are immeasurable and staggering in estimation. Top off your better grocery shopping habits by adding some organic produce. At the very least, try to purchase organic varieties when buying produce on the list of most chemically treated fruits and vegetables (see chart on page 66).

I treat many teachers in my practice. I began asking several of them if they noticed a difference when their students don't eat well. They were all astonished that finally somebody was taking notice of the difference. Unanimously, they related incredible stories about how closely attention span, cooperativeness, focus, demeanor, memory, and reasoning related to whether or not a student has had something decent to eat. Several said they can easily point out which students are eating properly and which ones are not, particularly in the morning, just by observing their behavior.

As I've indicated throughout this book, I'm very much of a realist. I know many of you reading this are thinking, "my child will never eat this or that." Or, "I can't control what my child eats when I'm not around." Having three children of my own, I know it's not easy to implement and maintain the better choices. But I've learned a few tricks I want to share with you.

First, consider that no child ever starves to death if you get tough, lay down some rules, and eliminate some of the undesirable foods in your home. One of the best pieces of advice I've heard about raising children is this: be their parent first and then their friend. Tough love is good, although a bit painful for both parties at times. Start by explaining your intentions first and don't expect an applause from your kids. You'll likely be happily surprised though when after the initial complaints subside, and they catch on to your seriousness about better eating, they'll become the cheerleaders. Be prepared for future comments like, "Mom, are you sure you should eat that?"

Next, start very slowly replacing poor-quality food items with better ones. For example, if your cupboard regularly contains potato chips or similar snacks, replace them with nuts and unsweetened dried fruits. Allow the undesirables at parties or other special occasions; you can't fight it at these venues. Replace about one of your regular poor-quality items a week. Start insisting that a vegetable item be eaten with lunch and dinner, and that it be finished before a second helping of the main item or dessert. Also, insist on a quality protein, especially for breakfast.

If you have to get so tough that they go away hungry for a few meals, bravo to you! Welcome to the world of real parenting! I promise you it will pay off eventually.

At my practice, I also treat a lot of families. Yes, believe it or not, there are many entire families who come in and get chiropractic treatment for prevention or whatever ails them. They do it regularly, about twice monthly, mother, father, and all the kids; I call them "super-families." These are the healthiest groups of people I know of. One such family, with four kids under 10, seemed exceptionally healthy. On questioning the mother, I learned that besides crediting their regular chiropractic adjustments, they watched little television, spent a lot of their free time outdoors, and ate lots of fresh fruits and vegetables. "There is one last thing," said the smiling mom. "We don't do sugar!"

If your kids are already in a habit of regular consumption of juices, or worse yet, soft drinks, changing this may be your greatest challenge. They will likely undergo withdrawal symptoms. I'm not kidding! Be prepared for mood swings, violence,

Don't be fooled by juices or soft drinks that indicate "no sugar added" or "naturally flavored." The fact is—unless it's freshly squeezed or organic, pure juice—you're drinking poison, particularly if consumed on a regular basis. The diet, artificially sweetened varieties of beverages are no better.

and accusations of abuse. Those poisons are running their little bodies and minds, and righting the situation won't be easy. You must persist and transition them to pure water. I'll stand my ground here and say that not doing so is the real abuse. Start by explaining first, then very gradually start eliminating that trash. I'll allow soft drinks and juices for my kids only at special events, but in limited amounts. Giving a kid a full can of soda is the equivalent of one of us drinking three or four.

The only juice I approve of is the kind you make at home with a juicing machine that contains lots of pulp. The fiber in the pulp is what makes all the difference. Kids love it, crave it, and have fun making different combinations. Insist that at least one vegetable be added per cup such as a carrot, celery stalk, or chunk of cucumber. The taste of the fresh fruit easily covers the vegetable taste. As with most things, you get what you pay for with buying a juicing machine. The cheaper ones leave you with a lot of waste and little juice.

Never consume juice unless it contains a lot of the pulp.
—*fitness icon Jack LaLanne*

I gotta have more of that fresh juice!
—*my son Andy*

What's in Your Medicine Cabinet?

I hate to imagine! I'll tell what *should* be in there: adhesive bandages, aloe vera lotion, colloidal silver (a natural antibiotic), Echinacea tea bags, cod liver oil, chewable children's organic multivitamins, Pepto Bismol®, and children's Tylenol®, or Motrin®. Perhaps even keep all your vitamin/mineral supplements there.

Subtle changes in your household can go a long way. If you're truly serious about instilling true wellness values to your children, consider changing the name of your "medicine cabinet" to your "wellness cabinet." If you are keeping either current or old prescription medications in there, I'd highly recommend adding a lock. Children can easily climb up on sinks and access these things. Don't be fooled by supposedly childproof caps on the medications; they only work for the youngest of children!

I really practice what I preach and it's fun to watch the effect on my kids. The other day I was watching TV with the kids and during one of the many ads for prescriptions drugs, my ten-year-old turned to me and said, "Dad, they're trying to make us take pills again!" On another occasion, one of my kids said, "Who would want to take those pills if you're gonna get all those bad feelings (side effects) from it?" What do you think about when you see those ads? Can you see beyond the images of the beautiful, happy people they show? They're banking on the many of you who can't!

This subject of the "should or should not" of utilizing medical treatment and medications is so controversial that I must again clear the air by restating my position. I have and will continue to state that much of what medicine has to offer can be very necessary, save lives, and even be miraculous at times, but the abuse of it is stunning. If you or your child needs medical care, you should get it! But, when you begin to be enlightened to the tremendous ability of the human body to heal itself, to the wonderful, God-given, innate intelligence we all possess, you then realize that much of what the world of medicine has to offer has little to do with what real health really is.

Unless there is an emergency or the most serious of circumstances, medications, surgeries, and other medical procedures should be left as the last resort. Enhancing the body's healing ability through nutrition, structural balance, lifestyle changes, and more has for too long been placed second to the allopathic/medical approach.

Taking the holistic approach to your children's well-being can be easy when you have this enlightenment, combined with their generally higher natural healing ability. If you take this higher road, be prepared for some struggles that will come with that decision. For example, I always encourage my patients to be open with their medical practitioners about what they're doing, both with their own utilization of holistic methods and that of their children. But don't expect acceptance! In fact, expect resistance from medical practitioners when it comes to holistic care for our children. Remember, they likely mean well, but their training is, not surprisingly, medical care. You may very likely have more understanding about holistic approaches than they do.

> On numerous occasions, I've tried to provide MDs with information about the holistic approach to health that I advocate. In one instance, I gave a

pediatrician a very well-written book about natural approaches to helping children with ear infections. The approach that many pediatricians take is to prescribe antibiotics over and over again, even though their own research proves it practically useless, and worse yet, may be harmful to the long–term wellness of the child. Even ear tubes are questionable. Now you would think I'd get a thank you, an acknowledgment, a note, maybe even a shoulder shrug or grunt. No way! Years later, I sheepishly asked his wife if he got the book. "Yes," she answered, "but the book was never read."

Don't be afraid to seek another medical doctor if you encounter anything more than hesitation, concern, or disagreement from his or her end. Insist on reasonableness and cooperation. In non-emergency situations, a trial period of holistic care before medication or surgery is certainly reasonable. In Chapter 7, "Talking to Your Doctor," I illustrated several approaches to obtaining an MD who is on your team, versus being your opponent. And be wary of those who try to give you holistic advice; they've probably only attended a weekend seminar or two on the subject at the most.

Kids Have Structure, too!

In Chapter 5, "Structure-Based Healthcare," I start out writing that body structure and how it relates to wellness are frequently overlooked. For children, it's more than overlooked; I'd even call it grossly ignored. Many people accept that nutritional and lifestyle changes can help kids be healthier relatively easily. However, getting parents to take their kid to a chiropractor like myself, even for a musculoskeletal complaint like back pain, can be difficult. Then, getting parents to take their kid to a chiropractor for non-musculoskeletal complaints, like difficulty breathing, poor digestion, or low immunity issues can be like asking them to jump off a bridge.

I'm sympathetic, though, and understand that parents mean well and are concerned mainly for their children's well-being, but many are misinformed about all the options when it comes to health. Without the knowledge and enlightenment of how common structural disturbances are in children, what causes them, how they impact a child's health, and how we address them, I certainly see how parents would be hesitant if not resistant. I can relate to this very well because I am the first in my family to embrace and utilize holistic methods.

When I first heard of the concepts I'm trying to share with you, my initial reaction was somewhere between anger and skepticism, until I learned more. If and when you do embrace

and utilize holistic methods, especially structural-balance care like chiropractic for your children, the benefits can be dramatic! I can assure you, you'll rarely be disappointed.

Birth trauma (image modified from *Obstetrics and Gynecology*, Mosby, 1958:336.)

One of my first patients was a six-month-old girl brought to me by her parents. They told me I was their last resort. Looking into their bloodshot eyes, I struggled to listen between the child's screams while they described the severe colic.

Near-constant crying day and night is a common symptom of babies with colic and this child was no exception. Carefully checking the child's spinal structure, I discovered a large misalignment, one we chiropractors say "you could hang your hat on." It was the atlas vertebrae, the first spinal bone below the skull, also known as first cervical.

After explaining the significance of that structural disturbance, how it frequently occurs in babies as a result of birth trauma, and how it can cause pressure or irritation to the child's spinal chord, they agreed to the treatment. I carefully positioned the child and made a gentle, controlled, but quick thrust on the disturbed area.

I told the parents to bring the child back to me for follow-up in four days, but the very next morning, there they were, standing at my office door, baby in arm, when I arrived.

Being a young, minimally experienced doctor, my heart sank as negative thoughts filled my mind like, "What did I do wrong now?" But as I walked closer, I noticed their smiles and the quietness of the baby.

"Whatever you did," they said with joy, "do it again, because for the first time, the baby slept all night and seems content!"

All babies should get a chiropractic evaluation as soon as possible after birth, periodically as they mature, and then as needed in response to stress and trauma.

As dramatic and miraculous stories like that seem, they are more the rule than the exception with chiropractic care for babies and children. From the beginning days of chiropractic's discovery, babies and children have been helped with a variety of health issues. All chiropractors receive training in pediatric issues. The treatment is safe, especially considering the alternative options of drugs and surgeries. Their young spines and nervous systems are not much different than those of adults, other than being smaller and more responsive. Pointing this out to hesitant parents helps them to understand the concept.

What causes these structural disturbances in youngsters? Pretty much the same sources as those in adults: stress and trauma. For children and babies, birth trauma, over-aggressive handling, and falling hundreds of times as they learn to walk are common sources.

If that's not enough, then consider the traumas of horseplay, falling down steps, falling off bikes, sports injuries, poor postural habits, and carrying backpacks loaded with books. It's a wonder they don't have even more serious disturbances of their structure. In Chapter 5, "Structure-Based Healthcare," I illustrated how these structural disturbances, particularly of the spine bones, can impinge or irritate the vital nerve flow causing a sort of short circuit to one's internal communication system. This restriction of vital force can lead to a plethora of health disruptions.

As I stepped into one of my office's treatment rooms, there sat a 17-year-old boy named Larry and his father. With Larry exhibiting sheepish body language, his father anxiously described their mutual frustration with one of the most embarrassing problems a young man can have—bedwetting. This problem is devastating for any child, catastrophic for those at or near young adulthood like him.

"We've tried everything! The pediatrician kept assuring us he'd grow out of it. Can you help him?" pleaded the loving father.

Analyzing the young man's structure, I detected the usual source of this type of problem—misalignment of the sacrum, a.k.a. tailbone.

Explaining the connection of the nerves branching from the tailbone region and how they control bladder function, but making no promises with this chronic condition (he'd wet the bed nightly all his life), they both boldly wanted me to try.

I'd love to tell you that Larry made a miraculously fast recovery, but instead, he made a miraculously slow recovery. It took a full year involving dozens of treatments. The only thing that kept us from giving up was the random, sporadic, yet progressive improvement (1 dry night the first month, 3 dry nights the second month, and so on) that indicated we were on to something. This father and son had more confidence in me than I had in myself.

We all had tears when finally, his body was healed and Larry could enjoy a life free of the embarrassment. One could argue that perhaps he finally did grow out of it, but, no, we chiropractors have seen enough of these cases get better with chiropractic treatment to know that the progress is more than coincidental.

Chapter 6, "Help for Your Ailments," has more details on several other infant and child health issues, such as repetitive infections, scoliosis, headaches, allergies, and others.

The structure-based approach to helping children, and adults also, is not a cure-all. There are many other issues to consider such as nutrition and lifestyle, but chiropractic is a simple, safe, economical, and effective natural way to allow your body to return to a more normal state.

After 20-plus years of practicing chiropractic, I still am astounded by the potential benefits. Should every baby and child get chiropractic treatment? No, but I do believe that all of them should get examined by a chiropractor. This first examination should take place as soon as possible after birth (yes, I mean within the first few days!) and then periodically throughout the year. And why not? How would this type preventive procedure be any different than, say, dental check-ups or oil changes?

I warned earlier that you ought not expect support or even understanding from your M.D. if you share the news of your child getting holistic care, although there are exceptions. Be prepared for even harsher criticism when your medical doctor hears of your child getting chiropractic treatment specifically! It's hard enough for many of them to accept the need or benefit of chiropractic for adults. So go easy on these sadly misinformed professionals. But do insist on reasonable cooperation.

Does it cost anything to take your children to a chiropractor? This depends on how you look at it. Considering the potential benefits that are routinely observed, chiropractic care doesn't cost money, it saves! I've examined and treated my three children's structures since the day each was born, and I'm convinced that it's one of the major reasons for their exceptional health.

In addition, many insurances cover the services. If you must pay out of pocket, consider that the alternatives of medications, therapy, or surgery are a far greater cost. Value also lies in the preventative benefits of chiropractic treatment, and that benefit is the same if not more as commonly seen with adults getting chiropractic treatment—mainly in stronger immunity. Your pocketbook will appreciate that babies and children, on average, respond faster and more thoroughly than adults. It makes sense since children, although they can sometimes be quite ill or sustain quite serious traumas, haven't had the years of accumulated trauma that we adults have likely attained.

Additionally important, chiropractic treatment for babies and children has an excellent safety record. As with any type healthcare, there are always some risks, but with chiropractic treatment, the risks are insignificant. The safety record of chiropractic really stands out when compared to the riskier alternatives in typical medical care. With the enlightenment gained through this book, you'll be able to see through the covert agendas (usually economic) of the "healthcare terrorists" I discussed in Chapter 1, "Health." These adversaries are still active, spreading false information with the intention of alarming and controlling consumers. As the healthcare marketplace becomes more competitive, their tactics will increase and become more aggressive.

If I haven't shocked you enough by now, maybe this true story will. I treat children with brain-function disorders like autism, PDD, and ADHD. They all benefit in some way or another, with their parents reporting that the kids get calmer, concentrate better, become more physically coordinated, and sometimes even need less medication.

I'll never forget one outstanding case—a six-year-old boy who was diagnosed with PDD (Pervasive Development Disorder). His mother brought him in and was so suspicious and skeptical I could have cut the negative vibes with a knife! She eventually consented to allowing me to treat the boy and relaxed when I explained how it worked.

The boy had the typical spinal misalignment pattern that we chiropractors see in most of these cases. Still, I didn't promise much nor was I very optimistic, mostly because of the mother's attitude. Lo and behold, after just one adjustment, the child was like a different person. I wrote the details of this up in a type of research document called a case study and presented it to other doctors at a conference. You can view it in the Appendix.

The mother, you might wonder? She's been referring patients ever since.

What can you expect when you take your child to a doctor of chiropractic? Most practitioners prefer to take their own consultation/history and perform an examination. The exam will involve a lot of touching and looking because the focus is on finding and changing and/or correcting body structure. Chiropractors are well trained on when and how to refer to other professionals. Some common questions might be: "How did the birth take place, vaginal delivery or C-section? Were forceps utilized? Was the child breastfed and for how long? Has the child sustained any significant trauma like falls or serious horseplay?

How are the child's eating habits? What previous treatment has the child received? Do you notice any unusual postural habits?"

Treatment, if warranted, will likely consist of a gentle, well-controlled chiropractic adjustment. If children have any fears, these usually quickly disappear when they experience the ease of treatment. If the child receives a hands-on type of treatment, as is commonly done, sometimes a slight popping or cracking sound is heard. On occasion, the child may experience a mild soreness or redness in the area of treatment, especially with the first one. Beyond this, most children are then eager to climb up on the treatment table.

The doctor will likely suggest a treatment plan that may involve a few days or a few weeks, depending on the severity and

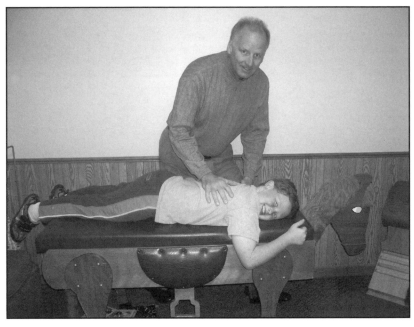

The author, Dr. Tom Potisk, and son MIke

nature of the problem. Lifestyle or nutritional changes and exercises may also be part of the recovery plan. X-rays may be necessary. Feel welcome to ask openly about any aspect of chiropractic. Some chiropractors specialize in the treatment of children, and may even receive advanced certification, but all DCs receive ample pediatric training as part of their chiropractic curriculum.

If you choose to utilize regular chiropractic treatment as prevention, its greatest benefits are seen when treatment is consistent, perhaps once a month minimally. Why? Because as I explained earlier, structural disturbances (subluxations) occur as a result of trauma, stress, and toxins. What child isn't constantly exposed to those?

Those noises that often accompany chiropractic adjustments are technically called cavitations. That means there is a slight, harmless pressure change in the joints that are moved. It's quite similar to the phenomenon involved when a suction cup is pulled from a piece of glass. Beware that critics, adversaries, and uninformed people often use this sound phenomenon to scare and discourage those who utilize chiropractic treatment. They'll say

> Children say and do many comical things. When they get chiropractic treatment, they are no less funny. Many times I've heard them comment that the noise their spines make when they get adjusted "...sounds like popcorn!" One young girl said "I'm here to get my rice crispies! You know, snap, crackle, and pop!"

that the joints are wearing out or becoming arthritic from the repetitive treatment, but these accusations are completely unfounded. If this was even partially true, then the spines of chiropractors and their families would all be worn out, because we practice what we preach.

Some common lifestyle sources of structural disturbances in children involve their postural habits. Often, children get into habits of lying and sitting in unusual, asymmetric positions.

For example, lying on the couch with the head propped up on the arm rest, either on the side or on the backs, will cause neck, shoulder, and upper back disturbances when done repetitively. Impact sports like football do contribute to structural disturbances. At the very least, encourage your kids to carefully follow preventative measures like stretching and warm-ups.

School backpacks, when overloaded and carried awkwardly, can also be a source of structural problems. Several preventive measures can be followed:

- Pack so that heavier items are kept closer to the body.
- Carry the backpack with both straps over the shoulders.
- Encourage the use of backpacks that have extendable handles and wheels.

Kids are increasingly using cell phones. Holding the phone between the ear and shoulder repetitively leads to structural disturbances of the neck and upper back. For those kids with marathon phone sessions, encourage use of a headset.

Computers and hand-held electronic games, when used in repetitively poor posture, lead to significant structural problems. Guide your children in the proper ergonomic use of these:

- Keeping the screen at eye level
- Keep forearms parallel to the floor when at the keyboard
- Sit all the way back in the chair.

I highly suggest limiting the time they are allowed to use these devices. A two-hour per day maximum is the limit I've set for my kids. Also, I require them to perform some exercise before they use the computer or TV. My kids do 30 push-ups, 30 sit-ups, 30 squat thrusts, and 100 jumping jacks before any computer or TV use. They may not like it, but I'm proud to be their parent, not their friend, under such circumstances.

The rising level of inactivity in children really concerns me. I certainly don't want to see more hyperactive children, but I do believe children need lots of physical activity every day. The benefits are immeasurable and result in better sleep, blood sugar balance, emotional well-being, and of course, weight control. Parents have a responsibility to enforce this. I've strived to encourage physical activity in my children by acquiring toys that involve physical motion. Bikes, scooters, skate boards, skis, sleds, balls, hoops, rollerblades, ice skates, Frisbies, pogo sticks, and a trampoline can be seen all around my yard. Don't give me any nonsense about you're not being able to afford these things; they can easily be found very reasonably at garage sales, thrift stores, and used sporting good stores. If you add up the cost of all the stuff I have listed above, you'll find that it still totals less than the cost of many electronic game consoles.

Don't forget the power behind your setting of a good example. Do they see you, the parent, eating better food choices? Do they see you, the parent, staying physically active on a daily basis? Do they see you take the stairs instead of the escalator or elevator? Do they see you walking or biking to work when feasible? Do they see you practicing holistic healthcare, especially being aware of the importance of balanced body structure?

And lastly I ask, when a child is feeling a little low, and some fool someday offers them a recreational drug like alcohol, marijuana, cocaine, or crack, who do you think is more likely to say "no"? A child raised in a holistic-minded household or one raised in the common, traditional, and worldly "take a medication to cover the symptom"-minded household?

Goal: Raise a drug-free, healthy family!

Emily and Mike Potisk— strong, healthy. drug-free kids.

Afterword

I struggled with a suitable ending for this book until I opened today's issue of my local newspaper. What I saw made it easy.

Within the first few pages, I noticed several articles that justify the need for this book. One article tells of a common medication, once thought to help with breathing and wheezing, that has now been found to be of no help and even has several serious side effects. The next page tells about several medical doctors who work as professors at the local university medical school. Their quoted salaries of $675,000 to $900,000 per year are only part of the outrage; they've been caught with just a little side job. They've been teaching privately practicing medical professionals, over expensive meals at exclusive restaurants, about drugs and how to use them for health problems they were not designed for. The pharmaceutical company that makes the drug pays the professors several thousand dollars for the two- to four-hour meetings.

But wait! On the front page is a big, bold headline: *ORTHOPEDIC DOCTOR MADE 19 MILLION.* Thanks for the help with the ending of this book, guys.

In case you haven't noticed, *there's a crisis and it's getting worse*. I'm not kidding when I tell you that you and your family are in grave danger if you continue to follow the current healthcare system.

If you're overwhelmed by all of this, you're not alone. Most of the population follows the easier path, the "worldly way" of healthcare. The results shown in these few articles are the tip of the iceberg.

The solution? How can you protect yourself? The answer is: take more personal responsibility and make better healthcare choices. Look at the Frequently Asked Questions at the end of this Afterword to get some more ideas and answers.

So how do you start being more personally responsible for your health? Pick one thing from this book that gets your attention and act on it. Perhaps you need to get more physically active. Perhaps you've been neglecting your body structure. Or, perhaps you need to confront your doctor about the medications you're taking. I've done my best to put all the answers I know of in this book.

I've heard and read the debate on whether healthcare is a right or a privilege. There are good arguments for both, but I notice what's always missing—that first and foremost, health, real health, is primarily a personal responsibility.

Put control of your health in the hands of somebody else, (the exception would be when you need emergency and crisis care) and you'll be a potential victim of rampant greed and corruption. You'll get symptom-oriented, mechanistic-type treatment, aimed at covering symptoms instead of creating real health, and, at best, early detection instead of true prevention.

Rely on your food to come from the cheapest, easiest sources, and you'll get corporate-grown, nutrient-deficient, highly processed and preserved—but pretty—produce.

Rely strictly on your "health" insurance (sickness insurance) and you'll get what the administrators determine will improve the stock price. Spend most of your free time in front of the TV, and you'll get an average of 20 drug commercials injected into your and your children's minds each day, programming you to reach for a prescription whenever you don't feel good.

So again I ask, as I did at the beginning of the book, *"Where's your outrage?"*

Health, real health, is not a luxury—it's a necessity. It's a necessity that has to be fought for. I can't do this by myself. I need your help and your protection. I need you to understand and be enlightened by what real health is. I need you to want real health and demand it. You're going to have to demand that your doctor cooperate with your holistic approach to health. You're going to have to demand that your grocery store has an organic food section. You're going to have to demand that your children exercise, eat better, and limit their computer, video games, and television time. Don't forget to set a good example with your own actions. The battle is worth it because we owe it to ourselves and our children.

Some people believe this can't be done, that the system can't be changed. Help me prove them wrong. My family and I are doing these things, many of my patients are doing these things, and more of you can also. I believe most people want the better options I've explained in this book, but never knew about these holistic concepts or how to go about using them. Can you help me reach more people? Please!

May God bless you and your family with good real health.

Some Frequently Asked Questions

Q Do I need to do the things you propose, like going to a chiropractor, taking nutritional supplements, and so on, for the rest of my life?

A Yes and no. it depends on your goal. You can use these holistic concepts temporarily to recover from an injury or an illness. But if you desire optimum health and prevention, you must keep them up, making them a regular part of your routine and lifestyle. In my observations of thousands of patients, the choice to keep up these holistic procedures will save you time and money over the long run and enhance the quality of your life.

Q Why do you leave out many other holistic issues like antioxidants, electromagnetic radiation, enzymes, and chelation?

A This book would be 1000 or more pages long if I had tried to cover everything. Most of us are creatures of simplicity. Therefore, I've provided the concepts and treatments that are the easiest to implement and will give a person the maximum benefit in the shortest, most economical way. I apologize if I neglected anything that you feel has helped you— perhaps I'll cover it in the next book.

Q How much research has been done on this information you provide?

A I fully admit that hard-core research on most holistic care is lacking, but there is more than most critics will face up to. Also, there is tremendous clinical evidence, which I've enjoyed experiencing as I've practiced for over two decades. Also, keep in mind that even good medical sources admit that only somewhere between 15 to 30 percent of common medical procedures are backed by hard-core research. Sadly, much of that research is increasingly shown to be tainted, performed by people on the payroll of the drug or other manufacturers.

Q Can you guarantee that these things will work, that they are safe?

A No, the human body is far too complex to assure that it will always respond in an expected way. If any doctor ever gives you a guarantee, don't walk out of the facility—run! But I do feel confident that the methods discussed in this book should be attempted, at least on a trial period, and that the benefits far outweigh the risks. Always utilize traditional medical care in emergencies, crises, or life-threatening situations.

Q How long will it take for me to get better?

A In some cases, noticeable improvements will be dramatically quick, in others it may take weeks or months. Each case is unique. Generally, one should allow at least six weeks as a trial period to notice some significant improvement; full recovery may take much longer. It's really a matter of sticking to the principle that the human body has amazing self-healing abilities when there is no interference to that ability. In most cases, it's a matter of time and repetition of doing the right things, and allowing the body to return to its optimum balance. It's pretty unlikely you'll waste your time or money by eating better, getting more physically active, following a regular stretching routine, or getting chiropractic adjustments. Even if your specific health problem still needs medical care, your body will be improved by doing those things. At the very least you'll be practicing real prevention.

Q My father lived to be 94 and he never did any of the things you propose. Why should I?

A Sometimes it doesn't seem fair. I know some people like that, too. But those cases are much more the exception than the rule. Consider also that those same people, had they practiced a healthier lifestyle, might have lived even longer and enjoyed it more. I'm not taking any chances and, in my opinion, you shouldn't either!

Q Do you think all medical care should be avoided?

A Not at all. Medical professionals refer patients to me and I refer patients to them. This book is not intended to widen the divide, but to unite for the patient's benefit. I had to point out the shortcomings of the current health system because it's dominated by the medical/allopathic/mechanistic practitioners. They've done a remarkable job of marketing their profession so the majority of the public believes that what it offers is the only option for health.

What medical professionals have is excellent for emergencies, crises, and life-threatening situations, but they fall remarkably short when it comes to real health, both in what it is and how patients should get it. When patients understand and take more personal responsibility for their health, there is less need for the emergencies and crisis care. Other members of my profession and I have taken the information provided in this book and more to them and have not gotten very far at all. I believe the solution to shaking up—if not breaking up—the current health racket, is to empower you, the patient, to make better healthcare choices.

Q I went to a chiropractor for my back pain but it didn't help, so why would I consider taking my family as you suggest?

A Chiropractic has little or nothing to do with back pain. It's all about freeing and aligning body structure, particularly the spine, to allow the proper flow of nerve signals through the nervous system. The nervous system has a direct influence on nearly all other body systems, organs, and functions. Chiropractic is the single-most important consideration for real health, yet it is the least understood and least utilized. It's safe, economical, and effective. It's not a cure-all, but I've seen patients report improvement with all kinds of problems and conditions. Chiropractic does not aim to treat any specific condition, but to remove or reduce nerve system interference so the body can right itself and self-heal.

Wishing you wonderful health and a long life!
—*Tom Potisk*

Resources

1. Types of Calcium Supplements
2. Autism Case Study
3. Traditional and Modern Uses for Common Herbs
4. Know Your Vitamins and Minerals
5. References
6. Recommended Websites
7. Recommended Reading

1. Types of Calcium Supplements
Advantages and Disadvantages

Types	Advantages	Disadvantages
Microcrystalline Hydroxyapatite Concentrate (MCHC) (25% calcium)	◆ Very well absorbed ◆ Complete bone food ◆ Can reduce bone loss ◆ Absorbed by some malabsorbers	◆ None
Citrate (24% calcium)	◆ Very well absorbed ◆ Reduces risk of kidney stones ◆ Absorbed by those with poor digestion	◆ Not a complete bone food
Aspartate (20% calcium)	◆ Well absorbed	◆ Not a complete bone food
Amino Acid Chelate (10-20% calcium)	◆ Well absorbed	◆ Not a complete bone food ◆ Often incorrectly made as a soy blend
Ascorbate (10% calcium)	◆ Well absorbed ◆ Non-acidic vitamin C	◆ Not a complete bone food
Lactate (15% calcium)	◆ Well absorbed	◆ Not a complete bone food ◆ May contain milk and/or yeast by-products ◆ Made from fermentation of molasses, whey, starch or sugar with calcium carbonate
Carbonate (40% calcium)	◆ Cheapest source of calcium	◆ Not a complete bone food ◆ May not be absorbed well by those with poor stomach digestion ◆ Antacid effect. Interferes with digestion, causes gas
Bone Meal (39% calcium)	◆ Contains multiple minerals needed for bone	◆ May contain high lead, arsenic, cadmium, and so on ◆ Organic constituents substantially destroyed, leading to reduced effectiveness

2. Autism Case Study

A case study and research paper presented by the author by invitation to the World Federation of Chiropractic Convention, Paris, France, 1991.

Patient:
A five-year-old male with Autism/Pervasive Development Disorder (PDD) who responded remarkably and quickly with chiropractic treatment (CM-19) at my office.

What is Autism/PDD?
A developmental/neurological disorder usually evident by age 3 that affects a child's ability to communicate, understand language, play and relate to others (1). Incidence varies by source from 1 in 2000 (1) to 1 in 312 (7). The cause is theorized as being genetic (2), environmental (2), or a side effect of vaccination (3)(7).

History:
A five-year-old Caucasian male with mild autism/ PDD as diagnosed by medical profession at age 3. There was no history of traumatic incident. No medication usage. Fully vaccinated. See chart below for initial symptoms.

Exam/X-Ray:
Fixation, tenderness and nervoscope readings on right side of C1 and sacrum. Full spine weight-bearing X-rays reveal no pathologies/ deformities. Gonstead listing of C1-ASR and Sacrum PR derived from exam and X-ray findings (4)(5).

Treatment Method/Duration:
Chiropractic manual adjustments administered using Gonstead cervical chair and Gonstead pelvic bench to vertebral subluxations at C1

and sacrum (4)(5). Seven total adjustments were given over a two-week period.

Results:
Re-examination revealed a gradual decrease in tenderness and fixation of C1 and sacrum motor units was noted as treatment progressed. The patient's mother rated the symptoms based on her observations. She reported an overall improvement of 98 percent at the end of two weeks of treatment. A follow-up evaluation 3.5 years later revealed progress was maintained without any further intervention. The mother commented:

> "I was amazed at how quickly some of these areas improved. The chiropractic intervention you provided helped him immeasurably. Our pediatricians were skeptical that chiropractic might help. They were amazed to see the improvement in his toileting and motor skills. Today he is an eight-year old in a regular third-grade classroom, getting excellent grades and enjoying life more fully than anyone predicted he would have when he was first diagnosed at age three."

Conclusion:
This child's progress far exceeded the standard medical prognosis (6). Perhaps vertebral subluxation is a causative or contributing factor to autism/ PDD. Perhaps autism/ PDD can be prevented with routine post-natal chiropractic exam/ treatment. Further investigation, clinical trials and double-blind studies are planned.

Mother's Rating of symptons 1 (bad) - 10 (excellent)	Overall Autism / PDD	Balance	Strength	Coordination	Accident Prone	Muscle Tone / Development	Restlessness	Sleep	Appetite	Concentration	Attention Span	Eye Contact	Verbal Communication	Fine Motor Skills	Bowel Control	Balance Control	Immunity	Alertness	Total Score	Average Score	% of Improvment
Prior To Chiropractic	4	4	4	4	2	3	4	5	6	5	5	4	4	4	3	3	3	3	70	3.9	—
After 2 Weeks of Treatment	8	8	7	6	7	7	9	9	9	8	9	7	7	6	9	9	7	7	139	7.7	98%
3 1/2 Year Follow-up	9	8	9	7	8	8	9	9	10	10	10	8	9	7	9	9	9	9	157	8.7	102%

Mother's ratings prior to chiropractic treatment, after 2 weeks of treatment and at 3.5-year follow-up.

REFERENCES:

1. National Information Center for Children and Youth with Disabilities, USA, 1999.
2. Dr. Bristol-Power, National Institute of Child Health and Human Development, USA, 1999.
3. *Milwaukee Journal*, Medical Briefing Sections, 4/24/01.
4. *Textbook of Clinical Chiropractic*, Plaugher, 1993.
5. *Textbook of Clinical Chiropractic Pediatrics*, Anrig, Plaugher, 1996.
6. *Current Issues in Autism*, Schopler, Mesibov, 1995.
7. *Shots in the Dark*, Barbra Loe Fischer, 1999.

3. Traditional and Modern Uses for Common Herbs

The information presented here is for educational purposes only and should not be used for the diagnosis or treatment of disease. The following is a brief listing of herbs and the traditional or modern uses typically ascribed to them.

Alfalfa – Extremely high nutritional value, high in chlorophyll, vitamins such as vitamin K, minerals, trace elements, and protein (25%). Used in arthritis, bleeding disorders, and menopause.

Aloe Vera – Herb acts as a powerful laxative. Juice or jell acts as a general healer/cleanser and topical aid to wound healing and burns.

Bayberry – Astringent to stop bleeding from lungs, uterus and colon, poultice for slowly healing sores, and as a gargle for sore throat and gums.

Black Walnut – Used for poison ivy and skin eruptions and rashes. Useful for intestinal parasites and worms.

Black Cohosh – Female tonic acting as an antispasmodic for all nervous conditions, menstrual cramps, and pains. Reduces joint inflammation.

Buchu – For urinary and kidney disorders such as bladder weakness infection and inflammation. Diuretic and urinary antiseptic.

Burdock – Blood purifier used for arthritis, rheumatism, sciatica, and skin problems. High in iron.

Calendula / Marigold – Infections, fevers and colds. First aid for wounds to speed healing and soothes pain and irritation.

Cascara Sarada – Laxative and bowel tonifier. Less habit-forming than other laxatives. Stimulates secretion of entire digestive system.

Catnip – For diarrhea, flatulence, or colic in children. Mild sedative for nervous and emotional tensions.

Cayenne – Stimulant and strengthener of the digestive and circulatory system. For digestion, circulation, and to potentiate the effectiveness of other herbs.

Chamomile – Calming to the digestive and nervous systems. Used for insomnia, stomachaches, and for colic and teething in children.

Chaparral – Blood purifier for arthritis, tumors, and skin problems. Contains a powerful natural antioxidant.

Chickweed – Mild diuretic and laxative. Used for obesity, bleeding, and externally for skin problems and hemorrhoids.

Comfrey – Healing properties help in ulcers, fractures, lung problems, and arthritis. Helps soothe mucous membranes, relieve and improve digestion.

Damiana – Mild aphrodisiac. Helps balance female hormones, improve appetite, and relieve nervous depression in men and women.

Dandelion – Blood builder and liver cleanser. High in calcium and iron. Mild laxative and diuretic. Roasted root used as coffee substitute. For hepatitis and high blood pressure.

Devil's Claw – Anti-inflammatory used in joint inflammations and arthritis.

Dong Quai – Aids female reproductive system. Menstrual and hormone regulator. Useful for hot flashes and PMS.

Echinacea – Cleanser for the blood and lymphatic system. Stimulates immune function in colds, flu, sore throats, and allergies.

Eyebright – Detoxifier for inflammations and congestion. Used for allergies, colds, and hay fever. Strengthens eyes and improves eye problems of all types. Can be used as an eyewash.

Fennel – Normalizes appetite. Used for colic, flatulence, morning sickness, and with laxatives to prevent cramping.

Fenugreek – Soothes mucous membranes, lubricates intestinal tract, and removes sinus and bronchial congestion. Used in fevers and headaches.

Feverfew – For arthritis in the active inflammatory stage, vertigo, tinnitus, and migraine headaches.

Garlic – Herb that has anti-viral and anti-bacterial properties, is a blood thinner, and general detoxifier. *Potential Problems*: Acts as an herbal anticoagulant and may increase risk of bleeding. Garlic can also increase the activity of anti-platelet products. Should not be taken in conjunction with anti-coagulant medications or the protease inhibitor Saquinavir.

Ginger – Stimulant that aids digestion and appetite, flatulence, colds, and flu. Helps with nausea with sea, air, and morning sickness. *Potential Problems:* May increase the absorption of all herbs and medicines. It is classified as an herbal anticoagulant and may enhance bleeding. Monitor use of ginger if taking anti-coagulant drugs.

Gingko Biloba – Improves peripheral, cerebral, and coronary blood flow. Recent research shows extract to improve memory and thinking, and to protect nerve cells through its anti-oxidant properties. *Potential Problems:* Inhibits

PAF receptors and primary blood clotting. Use with caution if taking aspirin, heparin, or warfarin, since these medications affect secondary blood clotting, fibrin production, and coagulation. Ginko use may increase bleeding if used with these medications. It also has potential interactions with monoamine oxidase (MAO) inhibitors and may potentate activity and increase side effects of these classes of drugs.

Ginseng – Popular tonic available in Chinese, Korean, American, and Siberian varieties. Mental, physical, and nervous stimulant. Helps to adapt to stress. Reputed to assist longevity and sexual tonic. *Potential Problems:* Concurrent use of ginseng with caffeinated beverages increases the likelihood of side effects such as anxiety, insomnia, or hypertension. It has a mild effect on platelets and may increase bleeding if taken with warfarin and other anticoagulants. This herb may also potentate the action of steroids and should be avoided with their use. Ginseng should not be taken with MAO inhibitors or lasix, since it decreases these drugs' therapeutic effect.

Goldenseal – Natural antibiotic and antiseptic properties. Useful in colds, flu, and infection. Stimulates digestion and appetite. For mucous membrane and skin health. Use topically as an eyewash.

Goto Kola – Nerve tonic used in senility, epilepsy, loss of memory and mental and physical exhaustion or sluggishness.

Hawthorne – Heart tonic to strengthen the heart muscle, improves circulation. Regulates both high and low blood pressure.

Hops – Calming and sedative effects for insomnia, anxiety, muscle tension, and spasms. Often combined with skullcap.

Juniper Berries –Stimulating diuretic and antiseptic used for bladder and kidney conditions such as edema, uric acid build-up, and chronic bladder infections.

Licorice – Expectorant for congestion. Soothes coughs, sore throats, and laryngitis. Possesses estrogenic activity. Helps in blood sugar problems and the deglycyrrhizinated form has benefited ulcers. *Potential Problems:* Licorice inhibits fluid loss and increases potassium loss, so should not be used with diuretic drugs. It should not be taken with anti-hypertensive drugs, since licorice inhibits the drugs' activities. Since licorice decreases effectiveness and increases side effects related to potassium and sodium, it should not be taken concurrently with digitalis. It can also potentate corticosteroid drugs and should be used with caution with these.

Lobelia – Antispasmodic and powerful bronchial dilator for asthma and bronchitis. Popular ingredient in stop-smoking pills.

Marshmallow – Mucilaginous properties make it excellent for soothing mucous membrane irritation in the urinary tract, gastrointestinal and respiratory system. High in minerals and calcium.

Milk Thistle – Antioxidant and liver protector. Used in hepatitis and liver damage due to alcohol, drugs, and chemical toxins. Actually regenerates the liver.

Mullein – Expectorant used for congestion, sinus and bronchial asthma and earaches.

Nettle – For food and environmental allergies. Popular hair tonic for baldness and dandruff. Rich in iron, silica, and potassium.

Oregon Grape Root – Stimulates bile secretion and acts to tonify the liver and remove toxins from the blood. Therefore, it is useful in psoriasis, eczema, herpes, acne, hepatitis, and rheumatoid arthritis.

Parsley – Excellent diuretic. Used for bladder infections, gallstones, kidney problems, arthritis pain, and to stimulate digestion.

Passion Flower – Antispasmodic and nerve sedative. Used for nerve conditions such as headache, worry, anxiety, and PMS.

Pau D'Arco – Also known as "taheebo" or "lapacho." Popular for Candida yeast infection and other fungal, bacterial and viral infections. Immune system booster and blood purifier. *Potential Problems:* This herb should be used cautiously with anticoagulants because they may potentate the effects of these drugs.

Pennyroyal – Improves blood flow and muscle tone in uterine problems. Also for cramps and late, spotty menses.

Red Clover – Blood purifier and cleanser. Calms nerves. Combined with chaparral to treat cancer and break up tumors.

Red Raspberry – Useful during the whole of pregnancy due to ability to strengthen reproductive system, relieve nausea, prevent premature labor and miscarriage, and improve milk production.

Sarsaparilla – Contains steroidal compounds and possible hormone precursors. Used as a blood purifier in rheumatism, and physical weakness. Extracts popular for muscle building.

Saw Palmetto – Helps break down mucus and fat. General tissue and endurance builder. Shown to benefit prostate problems.

Senna – Powerful laxative for chronic constipation.

Skullcap – Nutritive herb for the nervous system. Aids nerve health, spasms, twitches, and insomnia.

Slippery Elm – Has mucilage properties that help to soothe ulcers and gastrointestinal inflammations, sore throats, and burns.

St. John's Wort – Used in pain and depression. Recently popular as extract against viral infections, such as herpes and Epstein-Barr. *Potential Problems:* Potential interaction problems. May increase anxiety, nervousness, or panic disorder if taken with theophylline. Use cautiously in conjunction with SSRIs, as it has been reported to cause serotonin syndrome, with symptoms such as sweating, agitation and tremor. It also increases cyclic P450 (CYP3A4) activity, any drug metabolized by the cyclic P450, such as digoxin, will be affected. It may also lower blood levels of protease inhibitors in healthy individuals.

Uva Ursi – Relatively safe diuretic used for urinary tract problems, kidney stones, and water retention.

Valerian – Strong tranquilizer and nervous system sedative for pain, headaches, excessive nervousness, and insomnia.

Yarrow – Opens pores to increase sweating in colds and flu. Helps sore throat.

Ailments and Beneficial Herbs

Acne – Burdock, Chaparral, Dandelion

Allergy / Hay fever – Echinacea, Marsh Mallow

Anemia – Alfalfa, Dandelion

Arteriosclerosis – Hawthorne, Garlic

Arthritis – Black Cohosh, Chaparral, Feverfew

Baldness – Chaparral, Nettle

Bladder and Urinary Disorders – Burdock, Cranberry, Goldenseal, Juniper, Marshmallow

Blood Pressure (high) – Cayenne, Garlic, Hawthorn, Passion Flower

Blood Pressure (low) – Dandelion, Parsley

Bronchitis – Comfrey, Lobelia, Cayenne

Colds / Infections – Echinacea, Eyebright, Garlic, Goldenseal

Constipation – Senna, Cascara Sagrada

Diabetes – Goldenseal, Juniper, Dandelion

Diuretic – Cranberry, Juniper, Uva Ursi, Parsley

Female Hormone Imbalance – Alfalfa, Dong Quai, Sarsaparilla

Female Tonic – Blue Cohosh, Black Cohosh, Dong Quai, Red Raspberry

Gall Bladder – Barberry, Cascara Sagrada, Dandelion

Headache – Feverfew, Hops

Immune Deficiency – Echinacea, Pau D'Arco

Insomnia / Anxiety – Chamomile, Hops, Skullcap, Valerian

Indigestion – Comfrey, Dandelion, Ginger, Peppermint

Liver Problems – Dandelion, Chaparral, Oregon Grape Root, Milk Thistle

Lung Congestion / Cough – Licorice, Lobelia

Memory – Gotu Kola, Gingko Biloba

Menopause – Alfalfa, Dong Quai, Licorice

Menstrual Problems – Black Cohosh, Blue Cohosh, Dong Quai

PMS – Dandelion, Dong Quai, Sarsaparilla

Prostate Problems – Burdock, Comfrey, Chaparral, Red Clover

Stimulant / Tonic – Ginseng, Cayenne, Ginger

Ulcers – Comfrey, Aloe Vera Gel, Marshmallow, Slippery Elm

Sources: Adapted from Chiropractic Economics*, March 22, 2004;*
Natural Resources Health Foods listing

For Notes and Observations:

4. Know Your Vitamins and Minerals

VITAMINS

Vitamin A

Body parts affected: Bones, eyes, hair, skin, soft tissue, teeth
Body functions facilitated: Immunity booster, body tissue reparation & maintenance, visual purple production (necessary for night vision)
Deficiency symptoms: Allergies, loss of appetite, blemishes, dry hair, fatigue, itching, loss of smell, night blindness, rough or dry skin, sinus trouble, soft tooth enamel, susceptibility to infections
Use for: Acne, alcoholism, allergies, arthritis, asthma, athlete's foot, bronchitis, colds, cystitis, diabetes, eczema, heart disease, hepatitis, migraine headaches, psoriasis, sinusitis, stress, tooth and gum disorders
Complementary vitamins and minerals: B-complex, choline, C, D, E, F, calcium, phosphorus, zinc
Sources: Green and yellow fruits and vegetables, milk, milk products, fish liver oil
Characteristics: Fat-soluble (absorbs and accumulates in fat cells); take with meals

Vitamin B Complex

Body parts affected: Eyes, gastrointestinal tract, hair, liver, mouth, nerves, skin
Body functions facilitated: Energy, metabolism of carbohydrates, fats, proteins, muscle tone, maintenance of the gastrointestinal tract
Deficiency symptoms: Acne, anemia, constipation, high cholesterol, digestive disturbances, fatigue, hair (dull, dry, falling out), insomnia, rough or dry skin
Use for: Alcoholic psychoses, allergies, anemia, baldness, barbiturate overdose, cystitis, heart abnormalities, hypoglycemia, hypersensitive children, Ménière's Syndrome, menstrual difficulties, migraine headaches, obesity, postoperative nausea, stress
Complementary vitamins and minerals: C, E, calcium, phosphorus
Sources: Brewer's yeast, liver, whole grains
Characteristics: Water-soluble (absorbs in non-fat cellular body tissues and fluids)

Vitamin B1—Thiamin

Body parts affected: Brain, ears, eyes, hair, heart, nervous system
Body functions facilitated: Appetite, blood building, carbohydrate metabolism, circulation, digestion (hydrochloric acid production), energy, growth, learning capacity, muscle tone maintenance (heart, stomach, intestines)
Deficiency symptoms: Appetite loss, digestive disturbances, fatigue, irritability, nervousness, numbness of hands and feet, pain and noise sensitivity, pain around heart, shortness of breath
Use for: Alcoholism, anemia, congestive heart failure, constipation, diarrhea, diabetes, indigestion, nausea, mental illness, pain (alleviates), rapid heart rate, stress
Complementary vitamins and minerals: B complex, B2, folic acid, niacin, C, E, manganese, sulfur

Sources: Blackstrap molasses, brewer's yeast, brown rice, fish, mean, nuts, organ meats, poultry, wheat germ
Characteristics: Water-soluble (absorbs in non-fat cellular body tissues and fluids)

Vitamin B2—Riboflavin

Body parts affected: Eyes, hair, nails, skin, soft body tissue
Body functions facilitated: Antibody and red blood cell formation, cell respiration, metabolism (carbohydrate, fat, protein)
Deficiency symptoms: Cataracts, cracks and sores at corners of mouth, dizziness, itching or burning eyes, poor digestion, retarded growth, red or sore tongue
Use for: Alcoholism, anemia, congestive heart failure, constipation, diarrhea, diabetes, indigestion, nausea, mental illness, pain (alleviates), rapid heart rate, stress
Complementary vitamins and minerals: B complex, B6, niacin, C, phosphorus
Sources: Blackstrap molasses, nuts, organ meats, whole grains
Characteristics: Water-soluble (absorbs in non-fat cellular body tissues and fluids)

Vitamin B6—Pyridoxine

Body parts affected: Blood, muscles, nerves, skin
Body functions facilitated: Antibody formation, digestion (hydrochloric acid production), fat and protein utilization (weight control), maintenance of sodium/magnesium balance (nerves)
Deficiency symptoms: Acne, anemia, arthritis, convulsions in babies, depression, dizziness, hair loss, irritability, learning disabilities, weakness
Use for: Atherosclerosis, baldness, high cholesterol, cystitis, facial oiliness, hypoglycemia, mental retardation, muscular disorders, nervous disorders, nausea in pregnancy, obesity, post-operative nausea, stress, sun sensitivity
Complementary vitamins and minerals: B complex, B1, B2, pantothenic acid, C, magnesium, potassium, linoleic acid, sodium
Sources: Blackstrap molasses, nuts, organ meats, whole grains
Characteristics: Water-soluble (absorbs in non-fat cellular body tissues and fluids)

Vitamin B12—Cobalimin

Body parts affected: Blood, nerves
Body functions facilitated: Appetite, blood cell formation, cell longevity, nervous system, metabolism (carbohydrate, fat, protein)
Deficiency symptoms: General weakness, nervousness, pernicious anemia, walking and speaking difficulties
Use for: Alcoholism, allergies, anemia, arthritis, bronchial asthma, bursitis, epilepsy, fatigue, hypoglycemia, insomnia, obesity, shingles, stress
Complementary vitamins and minerals: B complex, B6, choline, inositol, C, potassium , sodium
Sources: Cheese, fish, milk, milk products, organ meats, cottage cheese
Characteristics: Water-soluble (absorbs in non-fat cellular body tissues and fluids)

Biotin / B Complex

Body parts affected: Hair, muscles, skin
Body functions facilitated: Cell growth, fatty acid production, metabolism (carbohydrate, fat, protein), Vitamin B utilization
Deficiency symptoms: Depression, dry skin, fatigue, grayish skin color, insomnia, muscular pain, poor appetite
Use for: Baldness, dermatitis, eczema, leg cramps
Complementary vitamins and minerals: B complex, B12, folic acid, pantothenic acid, C, sulfur
Sources: Legumes, whole grains, organ meats
Characteristics: Water-soluble (absorbs in non-fat cellular body tissues and fluids)

Choline / B Complex

Body parts affected: Hair, kidneys, liver, thymus gland
Body functions facilitated: Lecithin formation, liver and gall bladder regulation, metabolism (fats, cholesterol), nerve transmission
Deficiency symptoms: Bleeding stomach ulcers, growth problems, heart trouble, high blood pressure, impaired liver and kidney function, intolerance to fats
Use for: Alcoholism, atherosclerosis, baldness, high cholesterol, constipation, dizziness, ear noises, hardening of the arteries, headaches, heart trouble, high blood pressure, hypoglycemia, insomnia
Complementary vitamins and minerals: A, B complex, B12, folic acid, inositol, linoleic acid
Sources: Brewer's yeast, fish, lecithin, legumes, organ meats, soy beans, wheat germ,
Characteristics: Water-soluble (absorbs in non-fat cellular body tissues and fluids)

Folic Acid (Folacin, B Complex)

Body parts affected: Blood, glands, liver
Body functions facilitated: Appetite, body growth and reproduction, hydrochloric acid production, protein metabolism, red blood cell formation
Deficiency symptoms: Anemia, digestive disturbances, graying hair, growth problems
Use for: Alcoholism, anemia, atherosclerosis, baldness, diarrhea, fatigue, menstrual problems, mental illness, stomach ulcers, stress
Complementary vitamins and minerals: B complex, B12, biotin, pantothenic acid, C
Sources: Green leafy vegetables, milk, milk products, organ meats, oysters, salmon, whole grains
Characteristics: Water-soluble (absorbs in non-fat cellular body tissues and fluids)

Inositol (B Complex)

Body parts affected: Brain, hair, heart, kidneys, liver, muscles
Body functions facilitated: Retardation of arterial hardening, cholesterol reduction, hair growth, lecithin formation, metabolism (fat and cholesterol)
Deficiency symptoms: Cholesterol (high), constipation, eczema, eye abnormalities, hair loss

Use for: Atherosclerosis, baldness, cholesterol (high), constipation, heart disease, obesity
Complementary vitamins and minerals: B complex, B6, choline, linoleic acid
Sources: Blackstrap molasses, citrus fruits, brewer's yeast, lecithin, meat, milk, nuts, vegetables, whole grains
Characteristics: Water-soluble (absorbs in non-fat cellular body tissues and fluids)

Niacin (Niacinamide / B Complex)

Body parts affected: Brain, liver, nerves, skin, soft tissue, tongue
Body functions facilitated: Circulation, cholesterol level reduction, growth, hydrochloric acid production, metabolism (carbohydrate, fat, protein), sex hormone production
Deficiency symptoms: Appetite loss, chancre sores, depression, fatigue, halitosis, headaches, indigestion, insomnia, muscular weakness, nausea, nervous disorders, skin eruptions
Use for: Acne, baldness, diarrhea, halitosis, high blood pressure, leg cramps, migraine headaches, poor circulation, stress, tooth decay
Complementary vitamins and minerals: B complex, B1, B2, C, phosphorus
Sources: Brewer's yeast, seafood, lean meats, milk, milk products, poultry, desiccated liver
Characteristics: Water-soluble (absorbs in non-fat cellular body tissues and fluids)

Pantothenic Acid (B Complex)

Body parts affected: Adrenal glands, digestive tract, nerves, skin
Body functions facilitated: Antibody formation, energy (conversion of proteins, fats, carbohydrates), growth stimulation, vitamin utilization
Deficiency symptoms: Diarrhea, duodenal ulcers, eczema, hair loss, hypoglycemia, intestinal disorders, kidney trouble, muscle cramps, premature aging, respiratory infections, restlessness, nerve problems, sore feet, vomiting
Use for: Allergies, arthritis, baldness, cystitis, digestive disorders, hypoglycemia, tooth decay, stress
Complementary vitamins and minerals: B complex, B6, B 12, biotin, folic acid, C
Sources: Brewer's yeast, legumes, organ meats, salmon, wheat germ, whole grains
Characteristics: Water-soluble (absorbs in non-fat cellular body tissues and fluids)

PABA (Para-aminobenzoic Acid)

Body parts affected: Glands, hair, intestines, skin
Body functions facilitated: Blood cell formation, color restoration of graying hair, intestinal bacteria activity, protein metabolism
Deficiency symptoms: Constipation, depression, digestive disorders, fatigue, gray hair, headaches, irritability
Use for: Baldness, graying hair, overactive thyroid gland, parasitic diseases, rheumatic fever, stress, infertility. *External* — burns, dark skin spots, dry skin, sunburn, wrinkles
Complementary vitamins and minerals: B complex, folic acid, C

Sources: Blackstrap molasses, brewer's yeast, liver, organ meats, wheat germ
Characteristics: Water-soluble (absorbs in non-fat cellular body tissues and fluids)

Vitamin C (Ascorbic acid)

Body parts affected: Adrenal glands, blood capillary walls, connective tissues (skin, ligaments, bones), gums, heart, teeth
Body functions facilitated: Bone and tooth formation, collagen production, digestion, iodine conservation, healing (burns and wounds), red blood cell formation (hemorrhaging prevention), shock and infection resistance (colds), vitamin protection (oxidation)
Deficiency symptoms: Anemia, bleeding gums, capillary wall ruptures, bruising (easily), dental cavities, low infection resistance (colds), nosebleeds, poor digestion
Use for: Alcoholism, allergies, atherosclerosis, arthritis, baldness, cholesterol (high), colds, cystitis, hypoglycemia, heart disease, hepatitis, insect bites, obesity, prickly heat, sinusitis, stress, tooth decay
Complementary vitamins and minerals: All vitamins and minerals, bioflavonoids, calcium, magnesium
Sources: Citrus fruits, cantaloupe, green peppers
Characteristics: Water-soluble (absorbs in non-fat cellular body tissues and fluids)

Vitamin D

Body parts affected: Blood vessels, heart, lungs, nerves, pituitary gland, skin
Body functions facilitated: Calcium and phosphorus metabolism (bone formation), heart action, nervous system maintenance, normal blood clotting, skin respiration
Deficiency symptoms: Burning sensation in mouth and throat, diarrhea, insomnia, myopia, nervousness, poor metabolism, softening of bones and teeth
Use for: Acne, alcoholism, allergies, arthritis, cystitis, eczema, psoriasis, stress
Complementary vitamins and minerals: A, choline, C, F, calcium, phosphorus
Sources: Egg yolks, organ meats, bone meal, sunlight
Characteristics: Fat-soluble (absorbs and accumulates in fat cells; take with meals)

Vitamin E (Tocopherol)

Body parts affected: Blood vessels, heart, lungs, nerves, pituitary gland, skin
Body functions facilitated: Aging retardation, anti-clotting factor, blood cholesterol reduction, blood flow to heart, capillary wall strengthening, fertility, male potency, lung protection (anti-pollution), muscle and nerve maintenance
Deficiency symptoms: Dry, dull or falling hair, enlarged prostate gland, gastrointestinal disease, heart disease, impotency, miscarriages, muscular wasting, sterility
Use for: Allergies, arthritis, artherosclerosis, baldness, cholesterol (high), crossed eyes, cystitis, diabetes, heart diseases, menstrual problems, menopause, migraine headaches, myopia, obesity, phlebitis, sinusitis, stress, thrombosis, varicose veins. *External —* burns, scars, warts, wrinkles, wounds.

Complementary vitamins and minerals: A, B complex, B1, inositol, C, F, manganese, selenium, phosphorus
Sources: Dark green vegetables, eggs, liver, organ meats, wheat germ, vegetable oils, desiccated liver
Characteristics: Fat-soluble (absorbs and accumulates in fat cells; take with meals)

Vitamin F (Fatty Acids)

Body parts affected: Skin, hormones, blood, cellular function, hormones
Body functions facilitated: Growth, behavior, cell membranes, hormones, immune system, regulation of cholesterol levels, skin health
Deficiency symptoms: Hair loss, eczema, behavioral disturbances, slow healing, high blood pressure, cholesterol, blood clotting
Use for: Skin, blood, bruising, learning disabilities, arthritis, memory, healing, over-weight
Complementary vitamins and minerals: Vitamin D
Sources: Evening primrose oil, grape seed oil, flaxseed oil, and oils of grains, nuts and seeds, such as soybean, walnuts, sesame, and sunflower; avocado, salmon, trout, mackerel and tuna.Omega-6 EFA is found in raw nuts, seeds, legumes, grape seed oil and flaxseed oil. Omega-3 EFA is found in fish, canola oil, and walnut oil.
Characteristics: Fat-soluble (absorbs and accumulates in fat cells; take with meals)

MINERALS

Calcium

Body parts affected: Blood, bones, heart, skin, soft tissue, teeth
Body functions facilitated: Bone/tooth formation, blood clotting, heart rhythm, nerve transmission, muscle growth and contraction
Deficiency symptoms: Heart palpitations, insomnia, muscle cramps, nervousness, arm and leg numbness, tooth decay
Use for: Arthritis, aging symptoms (backache, bone pain, linger tremors), foot/leg cramps, insomnia, menstrual cramps, menopause problems, nervousness, overweight, premenstrual tension, rheumatism
Complementary vitamins and minerals: A, C, D, F, Iron, magnesium, manganese, phosphorus
Sources: Milk, cheese, molasses, yogurt, bone meal, dolomite, almonds

Chromium

Body parts affected: Blood, circulatory system
Body functions facilitated: Blood sugar levels, glucose metabolism (energy)
Deficiency symptoms: Altherosclerosis, glucose intolerance in diabetics
Use for: Diabetes, hypoglycemia
Sources: Brewer's yeast, clams, corn oil, whole grain cereals

Copper

Body parts affected: Blood, bones, circulatory system, hair, skin
Body functions facilitated: Bone formation, hair and skin color, healing processes of body, hemoglobin and red blood cell formation
Deficiency symptoms: General weakness, impaired respiration, skin sores
Use for: Anemia, baldness
Complementary vitamins and minerals: Cobalt, iron, zinc
Sources: Legumes, nuts, organ meats, seafood, raisins, molasses, bone meal.

Iodine

Body parts affected: Hair, nails, skin, teeth, thyroid gland
Body functions facilitated: Energy production, metabolism (excess fat), physical and mental development
Deficiency symptoms: Cold hands and feet, dry hair, irritability, nervousness, obesity
Use for: Altherosclerosis, hair problems, goiter, hyperthyroidism
Sources: Seafood, kelp tablets, salt (iodized)

Iron

Body parts affected: Blood, bones, nails, skin, teeth
Body functions facilitated: Hemoglobin production, stress, disease resistance
Deficiency symptoms: Breathing difficulties, brittle nails, iron deficiency, anemia (pale skin, fatigue), constipation
Use for: Alcoholism, anemia, colitis, menstrual problems
Complementary vitamins and minerals: B12, folic acid, C, calcium, cobalt, copper, phosphorus
Sources: Blackstrap molasses, eggs, fish, organ meats, poultry, wheat germ, desiccated liver

Magnesium

Body parts affected: Arteries, bones, heart, muscles, nerves, teeth
Body functions facilitated: Acid/alkaline balance, blood sugar metabolism (energy), metabolism (calcium and vitamin C)
Deficiency symptoms: Confusion, disorientation, easily aroused anger, nervousness, rapid pulse, tremors
Use for: Alcoholism, cholesterol (high), depression, heart conditions, kidney stones, nervousness, prostate troubles, sensitivity to noise, stomach acidity, tooth decay, overweight
Complementary vitamins and minerals: B6, C, D, calcium, phosphorus
Sources: Bran, honey, green vegetables, nuts, seafood, spinach, bone meal, kelp tablets

Manganese

Body parts affected: Brain, mammary glands, muscles, nerves
Body functions facilitated: Enzyme activation, reproduction and growth, sex hormone production, tissue respiration, vitamin B1 metabolism, vitamin E utilization
Deficiency symptoms: Ataxia (muscle coordination), dizziness, ear noises, loss of hearing
Use for: Allergies, asthma, diabetes, fatigue
Sources: Bananas, bran, celery, cereals, egg yolks, green leafy vegetables, legumes, liver, nuts, pineapple, whole grains

Phosphorus

Body parts affected: Bones, brain, nerves, teeth
Body functions facilitated: Bone/tooth formation, cell growth and repair, energy production, heart muscle contraction, kidney function, metabolism (calcium, sugar), nerve and muscle activity, vitamin utilization
Deficiency symptoms: Appetite loss, fatigue, irregular breathing, nervous disorders, overweight, weight loss
Use for: Arthritis, stunted growth in children, stress, tooth and gum disorders
Complementary vitamins and minerals: A, D, F, calcium, iron, manganese
Sources: Eggs, fish, grains, glandular meats, meat, poultry, yellow cheese

Potassium

Body parts affected: Blood, heart, kidneys, muscles, nerves, skin
Body functions facilitated: Heartbeat, rapid growth, muscle contraction, nerve tranquilization
Deficiency symptoms: Acne, continuous thirst, dry skin, constipation, general weakness, insomnia, muscle damage, nervousness, slow irregular heartbeat, weak reflexes
Use for: Acne, alcoholism, allergies, burns, colic in infants, diabetes, high blood pressure, heart disease (angina pectoris, congestive heart failure, myocardial infarction)
Complementary vitamins and minerals: Vitamin B6, sodium
Sources: Dates, figs, peaches, tomato juice, blackstrap molasses, peanuts, raisins, seafood, apricots (dried)

Sodium

Body parts affected: Blood, lymph system, muscles, nerves
Body functions facilitated: Normal cellular fluid level, proper muscle contraction
Deficiency symptoms: Appetite loss, intestinal gas, muscle shrinkage, vomiting, weight loss
Use for: Dehydration, fever, heat stroke
Complementary vitamins and minerals: Vitamin D, potassium
Sources: Salt, milk, cheese, seafood

Sulfur

Body parts affected: Hair, nails, nerves, skin
Body functions facilitated: Collagen synthesis, body tissue formation
Deficiency symptoms: Appetite loss, intestinal gas, muscle shrinkage, vomiting, weight loss
Use for: Arthritis. *External*— skin disorders (eczema, dermatitis, psoriasis)
Complementary vitamins and minerals: B complex, B1, biotin, pantothenic acid
Sources: Bran, cheese, clams, eggs, nuts, fish, wheat germ

Zinc

Body parts affected: Blood, lymph system, muscles, nerves
Body functions facilitated: Burn and wound healing, carbohydrate digestion, prostate gland function, reproductive organ growth and development, sex organ growth and maturity, vitamin B1, phosphorus and protein metabolism
Deficiency symptoms: Delayed sexual maturity, fatigue, loss of taste, poor appetite, prolonged wound healing, retarded growth, sterility
Use for: Alcoholism, atherosclerosis, baldness, cirrhosis, diabetes, internal and external wound and injury healing, high cholesterol (eliminates deposits), infertility.
Complementary vitamins and minerals: A (high intake), calcium, copper, phosphorus
Sources: Brewer's yeast, liver, seafood, soybeans, spinach, sunflower seeds, mushrooms

5. References

Baldwin, Tammy, "Americans pay more for healthcare but are far from the healthiest," *Milwaukee Journal/Sentinel*, in "The Cure for What Ails Us," Nov. 19, 2006.

Anrig, Claudia, "Children benefit from chiropractic treatment," in *Clinical Chiropractic Pediatrics*, 1996.

Eddy, David M., MD, PhD. "Only 13% of all medical interventions are supported by scientific evidence," in *British Medical Journal*, 1991 (Oct 5) 303:798-799.

"Enhanced phagocytic cell respiratory burst induced by spinal manipulation." *J Manipulative Physiol Ther* 1991; 14:399.

"Fewer than 30 percent of conventional medicine procedures have been thoroughly tested." *Office of Technology Assessment of the US Congress*, 2003.

Fisher, Barbara Loe, *A Shot in the Dark*, "Immunization risks you need to know about," 1999.

Gray's Anatomy: "Nervous system controls and coordinates all body systems." 30th edition (1985).

Gray's Anatomy: "Nervous system first identifiable structure in fetal development." 30th edition (1985).

Groopman, Jerome. *How Doctors Think,* "Marketing, Money, and Medical Decisions," Houghton-Mifflin, 2007, p. 203.

"High patient satisfaction with chiropractic care" (Factors associated with patient satisfaction with chiropractic care: survey and review of the literature.) *J of Manipulative Physiol Ther* 2006:29: 455-462.

"Immunological correlate of reduced spinal mobility." *Proceedings of the 1991 International Conference on Spinal Manipulation.* FCER: 118.

Mendelsohn, Robert, MD. *How to Raise a Healthy Child in Spite of Your Doctor*, NTC/Contemporary Publishing Company, 1986.

"Most chemically-treated produce." *Am J Ind Med* 1993:24(6): 753-766.

National Center of Complimentary and Alternative Medicine. "Alternative medicine use growing." 2007.

National Institute of Health, "High incidences of reactions and complications of medication and surgery than alternative health methods," 2006.

National Institute of Health, "More patients utilizing alternative medicine," 2007.

"Osteopathic success in the treatment of influenza and pneumonia." *J Am Osteopathic Association*, 1991; 18:565. *Save The Children* report, "US infant mortality lower than other countries, November, 2006.

"Quality of organic versus conventional produce." *J Alt Coml Med* 2001: 7(2):161-173, *J Agric Food Chem* 2003;51(19):5671-5676.

Wayne, Howard, MD. *Do You Really Need Bypass Surgery? A Second Opinion* (2006)

World Health Organization. "American health is declining. Higher incidence of chronic illness" 2007.

6. Recommended Websites

American Association For Health Freedom,
  www.healthfreedom.net

American Holistic Health Association, www.ahha.com

American Chiropractic Association, www.amerchiro.org

American College of Nutrition, www.amcollnutr.org

American Herbal Products Association, www.ahpa.org

Citizens For Health, www.citizens.org

International Chiropractors Association, www.chiropractic.org

Organic Trade Association, www.ota.com

Organic Consumers, www.organicconsumers.org

Square-Foot Gardening, www.squarefootgardening.com

www.alternative-therapies.com

www.holistic.com

wwww.JerryZelmPresentations.com

ww.mercola.com

www.nutriondynamics.com

www.sugarshock.com

7. Recommended Reading

Anderson, Bob. *Stretching*

Atkins, Robert, MD. *Dr. Atkin's Vita-Nutrient Solution*

Atkins, Robert, MD. *New Diet Revolution*

Angell, Marcia, MD. *The Truth About Drug Companies, How They Deceive Us*

Balch, James F., MD. *Prescription for Natural Cures*

Balch, Phyllis A. *Prescription for Nutritional Healing*

Cooley, Bob. *The Genius of Flexibility*

Carter, James P., MD. *Racketeering In Medicine: The Suppression of Alternatives*

Chopra, Deepak, MD. *Grow Younger, Live Longer*

Christensen, Clayton M. *The Innovator's Prescription*

Cohen, Jay S., MD. *Overdose: The case against drug companies*

Coulter, H. *A Shot in the Dark*

Cunnien, Susan S. *A Profession of One's Own; Organized Medicine's Opposition to Chiropractic*

Fueling, Timothy J. *Chiropractic Works: Adjusting to a Higher Quality of Life*

Fischer, Barbara Loe. *The Consumer's Guide to Childhood Vaccines*

Gaby, Alan, MD. *The Natural Pharmacy*

Gott, Peter H., MD. *No Flour, No Sugar Cookbook*

Haldeman, Scott, DC. *Principles and Practices of Chiropractic*

Haneline, Michael T. *Evidence-Based Chiropractic Practice*

Herlinger, Regina. *Who Killed Healthcare?*

Haley, Daniel. *Politics in Healing*

Jensen, Bernard, MD. *Foods That Heal*

Krohn, Jacqueline, MD. *Natural Detoxification*

Lydall, Wendy. *Raising a Vaccine-Free Child*

McKeith, Gillian. *Food Bible*

Mendelsohn, Robert S., *Confessions of a Medical Heretic*

Mendelsohn, Robert S., *How to Raise a Healthy Child in Spite of Your Doctor*

Mendelsohn, Robert S. *Immunizations: The Terrible Risks Your Children Face*

Mitchell, Deborah. *What Your Doctor May Not Tell You About Immunizations*

Moynihan, Ray. *Selling Sickness*

Ni, Maoshing, MD. *Secrets of Self-Healing*

Nichols, Trent W., MD. *Optimal Digestive Health*

Null, Gary. *Encyclopedia of Natural Healing*

Null, Gary. *Get Healthy Now*

Palmer, D. D., DC. *Chiropractic: A Science, an Art, and a Philosophy*

Plaugher, Greg, DC. *Textbook of Clinical Chiropractic*

Reinagel, Julius. *The Inflammation-Free Diet Plan*

Roizen, Michael, MD. *You on a Diet*

Rondberg, Terry A., DC. *Chiropractic First: The fastest growing healthcare choice*

Rowe, Barbara. *Anti-Inflammatory Foods For Health*

Schlosser, Eric. *Fast Food Nation*

Sears, Barry, MD. *A Week in the Zone*

Sklar, Jill. *Eating For Acid Reflux*

St. Amand, Paul, MD. *What Your Doctor May Not Tell You About Fibromyalgia*

Sweere, Joe J. *Golden Rules for Vibrant Health in Body, Mind and Spirit*

The Merck Manual of Medical Information

The Physician's Desk Reference for Herbal Medicines

Venuto, Tom. *The Body Fat Solution*

Wardell, Walter I. *Chiropractic: History and Evolution of a New Profession*

Weil, Andrew, MD. *Spontaneous Healing*

Weil, Andrew, MD. *Health and Healing*

White, C. Rocky, MD. *Healthcare Meltdown*

Wiehe, Robert, MD. *Alternative Medicine for Treatment of Cancer*

Wilk, Chester, DC. *Medicine, Monopolies, and Malice*

Zelm, Gerald, DC. *What Your Doctor Never Told You*

Index

Index

Index

cholesterol and, 181
as common sense, xvi–xvii
depression and, 187
digestive problems and, 191
fibromyalgia and, 196
foot support and, 202
gout and, 197–198
health insurance and, 6
for hypertension, 172
hypertension and, 171–172
as investment in health, 9–12
knees, 207
as a lifestyle choice, 13–14
menstrual problems and, 210–211
osteoporosis and, 216
patient anecdote, 52–53
personality types, 52–53
role in wellness program, 29–34
sleeping problems and, 205
stretching, 37–44
weight loss and, 214
Extension exercises, 49
EZFlex®, 231

F

Fast food, 72–74, 77, 191
Fasting, 78–79, 194
Fat
    dietary, 162
    measuring body fat, 85, 214–215
Feet
    gout, 197–198
    heel spurs, 201–202
    posture and, 112–115
Fem-Premenstrual®, 211
Fever
    covering up symptoms, 16–18
    symptoms and meaning of, 4
    treatment for, 291–296
Fibromyalgia
    detoxing and, 194–195
    holistic healthcare and, 192–193
    patient anecdote, 8
    patient Q&A, 192–197
Fibroplex®, 197
Fish/fish oils, 81, 211, 301
5-hydroxytryptophan, 196–197
Flatback posture, 94–95, 108–111
Flax, 81, 211
Flu. See Influenza
Food allergies. See Allergies
Food and Drug Administration (FDA), 61
Food choices. See also Diet; Weight manage-

ment
    aging and, 282–285
    author's favorite recipes, 87–89
    chancre sores and, 176–177
    for children, 296–301
    cholesterol and, 180–181
    eating in moderation, 74–78
    growing your own, 69–73
    immune response and, 174
    improving nutrition through, 65–69
    inflammation and, 80–81
    trace minerals and, 84–85
    for well-being, 13–14
Food poisoning, 16–18
Foot Levelers®, 202
Football, 46
Franklin, Benjamin, xix
Free weights exercises, 53
Frequently Asked Questions (FAQs), 320–324
Full body diagnostic scanning, xvi–xvii

G

Gall bladder, 335
Gandhi, Mahatma, xiv
Gardening, 31, 69–73, 283
"Garbage can diagnosis," 193
Garlic, 172, 293, 331
Gastro-esophageal-reflux-disorder (GERD), 189–191
Genetically modified foods, 71
Genetics
    aging and, 286
    back pain and, 169
    body structure and, 93, 96
    healthcare and, 261
    high blood pressure and, 173
    myths, 9
    obesity and, 63–64, 212
    posture and, 93, 96
    preventive care and, 261
Germs, 16–18
The Gerson Miracle (Kroschel), 70
Get-fit-quick machines, 32
Glucosamine, 165, 206
Gluten, 80
Glycemic Index, foods, 82–83
God, belief in. See Creation/Creator
Golf, 31–33, 46
Gonstead, Clarence, 150–151
Gonstead Method, 150–151
Good Manufacturing Practices (GMP), 83
Gout, 197–198
Government-run health insurance, 6–7

Orthotics
correcting posture with, 112–114
for heel spurs, 202
knee and ankle problems, 206
patient anecdote, 112–113
to prevent sports injuries, 46
Osteopathic manipulation, 120–125, 195
Osteoporosis, 215–216, 236, 239
Over-the-Counter (OTC) drugs, 22, 301. *See also* Prescription drugs

P

Pain management, 17–18
Pain reliever medications, 22
Palmer, Bartholomew Joshua, 10, 97
Palmer, David Daniel, 138–141
Palmer College of Chiropractic, xviii
Palpation, 103, 151
Parents
children's eating habits, 297–299
children's exercise and, 314–315
children's health and, 291
patient anecdote, 304–305, 309–310
responsibility for health, 304, 306
as a role model, 21, 53–54, 315
tough love, 298–299
Patient anecdotes
addiction to pain medications, 17–18
automobile accidents, 125
back surgeries and stretching, 44
chiropractic adjustment, 152–153, 156
chiropractic principles, 154–155
controversy with traditional medicine, 143–144
focusing on symptoms, 264–266
healthcare costs, 8, 279
hearing loss, 140–141
hiccups, 119–120
ignoring a diagnosis, 112–113, 260–261
ignoring lifestyle choices, 3–4
living a long life, 260–261
medical advice, 236, 239
referral to a chiropractor, 242
shoes and spinal misalignment, 114–115
weight and back pain, 15
Pauling, Linus, 183
PDD (pervasive development disorder), 309–310
Pediatric chiropractic. *See* Children
Pepto Bismol®, 301
Personal responsibility
enlightenment and acceptance of, 10–12
fixing the system involves, 6–7

health as a, xviii–xxi, 23, 318–319
Pharmaceutical industry
doctor relationships with, 317–318
market research, 5
smoke and mirrors of, xviii–xxi
vitamin and mineral supplements, 83
weight loss drugs, 61–62
Physical activity. *See* Exercise
Physical relaxation exercise, 35–36
Physical therapy, 120–125
Physical well-being
aging and, 269–275
checklist for, 13–14
covering up symptoms and, 16–18
downsizing and de-cluttering, 285–287
health as a state of, 2–5
as an investment, 7–12
lifestyle choices and, 174–175
the mechanistic person and, 20
nervous system and, 195
patient anecdote, 52–53
personality contributes to, 52–53
preventive care and, 253–256
sleeping problems and, 205
the vitalistic person and, 19–20
Pillows, cervical-support, 99, 204, 279–280
Plantar fasciitis (heel spurs), 201–202
PMS. *See* Menstrual problems
Pneumonia. *See* Breathing
"Policeman's heel," 201
Popping noises. *See* Cavitation; Grinding/cracking/clicking
Posture. *See also* Head-forward posture
aging and, 279–280
back pain and, 168–169
chest pain and, 177–178
compensatory changes, 105–107
computer workstations and, 96, 100
eating habits and, 190
evaluating deformities, 93–96
headaches and, 200
immune response and, 174
issues with children, 306, 313–314
osteoporosis and, 215–216
positional habits, 98–100
well-being and, 13–14, 91–93
Posture improvement
correcting misalignments, 102–104
as goal of exercise, 29–34
stretching exercises for, 37–44
what you can do about, 120–125
Potassium, 172, 345
Potisk, Andy, 54, 289, 300
Potisk, Emily, 54, 289, 315

About the Author

One of America's top natural health-care practitioners, Dr. Thomas Potisk is considered a leader in his field. He was elected Chiropractor of the Year by his peers in 2006. A graduate of Palmer College of Chiropractic, "Dr. Tom" opened his practice in 1985. Since then, he has added hundreds of hours of postgraduate training and is certified in nutritional counseling and wellness.

He enjoys sharing lessons on building and maintaining *real* health from his professional training and daily clinical encounters by publishing articles, books, and speaking internationally. His extensive world travels to remote places, sometimes on volunteer medical missions, add to his unique perspective.

Gardening, outdoor recreation, family life, and Christian studies are among his other passions. He and his family, all of whom enjoy superior health, live on a small farm in Wisconsin.

To contact Dr. Tom, invite him as a speaker for your event, or provide feedback about Whole Health Healing, please visit www.WholeHealthHealing.com.